Colin Rule

Online Dispute Resolution for Business

B2B, E-Commerce, Consumer, Employment, Insurance, and Other Commercial Conflicts

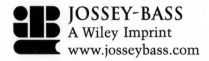

JOSSEY-BASS
A Wiley Imprint
www.josseybass.com

Published by Jossey-Bass
A Wiley Imprint
989 Market Street, San Francisco, CA 94103-1741 www.josseybass.com

Jossey-Bass books and products are available through most bookstores. To contact Jossey-Bass directly call our Customer Care Department within the U.S. at 800-956-7739, outside the U.S. at 317-572-3993 or fax 317-572-4002.

Jossey-Bass also publishes its books in a variety of electronic formats. Some content that appears in print may not be available in electronic books.

Readers should be aware that Internet websites offered as citations and/or sources for further information may have changed or disappeared between when this was written and when it is read.

Library of Congress Cataloging-in-Publication Data

Rule, Colin.
    Online dispute resolution for business : B2B, e-commerce, consumer, employment, insurance, and other commercial conflicts/[Colin Rule].
        p. cm.
    Includes bibliographical references and index.
    ISBN 0-7879-5731-3
    1. Arbitration and award—Automation. 2. Dispute resolution (Law)—Automation.
3. Internet—Law and legislation. I. Title.

K2400 .R847 2002
347'.09'0285—dc21   2002072982

Printed in the United States of America

FIRST EDITION
HB Printing 10 9 8 7 6 5 4 3 2 1

~~~ Contents

Be Rich Enough to Resolve Disputes? • How Can Neutrals Be
Convinced of the Utility of ODR? • When Should a Dispute
Go to ODR? • How Should Companies Advertise the Avail-
ability of ODR Services? • Won't New Technology Eliminate
Online Disputes? • How Can Online Resolutions Be
Enforced? • How Much Should ODR Services Cost?

—⁓— Preface

The writing of this book has taken place over a very turbulent year. In 1999 when I started working at Mediate.com the Internet was the place to be. Friends were jealous when I told them I had secured a position at a small start-up. In 2002, however, things are quite different. Now when I tell people I work for an Internet start-up they look concerned and ask me how I'm doing.

The Internet is a social phenomenon, and it is hard for people to understand the scope of the impact it is having on global society. There is a tendency to clump all Internet-related projects into a single category. Technology and innovation inevitably have their ups and downs, especially as they are completely dependent on vicissitudes of the economy. The shake-out of 2000 and 2001 has sealed the fate of a large number of Internet companies. Now, in a contracted economy, interest in innovation has waned.

Yet the promise of online dispute resolution (ODR)[1] remains as strong as ever. The momentum behind the expansion of ODR, much like the momentum behind the spread of global computer networks, has a tidal inevitability to it. Scholars, governments, non-profits, international organizations, and corporations have all concluded that ODR is an essential part of solutions to the problems raised by the Internet. Eventually, ODR will become an indistinguishable part of the way people around the world resolve their disputes. Whether or not the technology of today is sophisticated enough to fulfill the promise of ODR is not the key issue, because technology will continue to evolve. It may take longer than we previously assumed at the height of the Internet revolution, but the emergence of ODR is all but certain.

One of the challenges of writing a book that deals with technology is trying not to look silly after two or three years when the technology has changed so much that the observations of the book seem quaint and antiquated. I recall my first computer programming class in the early 1980s when my teacher would wax poetic about his halcyon days of punch cards and paper tape. Yeah, yeah, I thought to myself, just let me get at the cutting-edge stuff. Now when I reminisce about my old green-screen 48k Apple II+ younger programmers roll their eyes. The cycle continues.

This is not a technology book in the purest sense. I am not going to go through the technological specifics of any one online dispute resolution platform in great detail, or even discuss the code under the hood of ODR programs. What this book does is explain the benefits of ODR in a wide variety of business applications and describe state-of-the-art ODR practice. I believe these lessons will be relevant even when the technology has advanced to the point where our current tools and techniques seem primitive.

The field of ODR is new but it has deep roots. The thought and practice underlying ODR is based on decades of work in the alternative dispute resolution (ADR) field. Any discussion of ODR divorced from the body of ADR literature is bound to be shallow and ungrounded. One of the tenets of my work in ODR has been working to build online practice from the foundation of offline dispute resolution research, practice, and experience. This is a very new area of the dispute resolution field, and theory specifically focused on ODR has yet to emerge. It is a wonderful opportunity to be able to contribute to the development of ODR at this early a stage in its growth.

I must acknowledge up front the only other book published in the field of ODR at the time of my writing, Ethan Katsh and Janet Rifkin's *Online Dispute Resolution*. Ethan and Janet are the leading minds in this space, and their book does many things so well I am not going to try to replicate them here. Where possible, I try to apply their concepts to my observations, but it is essential for anyone seriously interested in ODR, and particularly the theory behind it, to examine their work in addition to this one.

Many people made important contributions to this book. John Helie and Jim Melamed, my co-founders at Online Resolution (OR), helped me think through the challenges of ODR and design OR's initial technology. Their decades of experience in dispute resolution and their pioneering role in applying the power of the Internet, both in OR and at Mediate.com, brought a depth of thought to our efforts that I could not have provided on my own.

Michael Lang and Anne-Marie Hammond also played a crucial early role in visualizing this book and giving it form. Michael's expertise in dispute resolution training and Anne-Marie's knowledge of the insurance world also helped to shape our efforts in the early days of Online Resolution. The research project they conducted at Royal Roads University remains the most comprehensive study of user experiences with ODR ever undertaken. Their writing skills also helped to hone the way we described ODR to our users and communicated how useful ODR could be to them. Their ideas resonate throughout this book.

Finally, Online Resolution's staff were the ones who really figured out how ODR would work when the rubber hit the road. Karen D'Amore, Troy Morgan, Wes Helms, Bill Toll, David Steele, Dana Haviland, and Resourceful Internet Solutions' Carol Knapp and Byron Knapp were the ones who turned the airy ideas into actual tools and worked with users to make them go. Whatever lessons I've learned about effective ODR practice come from all of their hard work.

COLIN RULE
Cambridge, Massachusetts
July, 2002

For Clifton and Ian

—w— Introduction

*Computers were first born as arithmetic engines, but my
own view, and the view of some other people as well, is that
they're much more interesting and powerful as communication devices because they mediate human-to-human
communication.*

*Bob Taylor, creator of ARPAnet,
the precursor to the Internet*

Disputes are a fact of life in business. Whether between buyers and
sellers, manufacturers and suppliers, supervisors and employees, or
business and government, conflict is inevitable when the interests of
different parties collide.

There's no way to prevent conflict from arising. In fact, businesspeople often benefit from conflict, as it can result in energy,
motivation, productivity, and creativity. The challenge lies in managing conflict so that it doesn't impede progress, or worse, destroy the
capacity to achieve business goals.

This book is for managers, employees, union representatives, and
others who are looking for a better way to handle conflict in their businesses and organizations. If you're in human resources, customer
service, information technology, or the legal department, dealing with
conflict is a big part of your job. Whether the conflict is inside a company (a workplace dispute, or a conflict between business divisions)

or outside (a dispute with a supplier, or with a regulatory agency) businesspeople need to proactively engage disputes before they escalate if an organization is to stay on track and deliver its plan.

Organizations have traditionally dealt with disputes in a variety of ways, usually with little strategy or coordination. For workplace disputes, the matter is usually passed to the human resources department, if it's dealt with at all. For buyer-seller disputes problems are often ignored until they get more severe, and then relationships are ended or lost to competitors. Insurance cases are put into a complex claims process where overburdened claims representatives attempt to resolve them. If any problem escalates beyond the point where it can be ignored, a lawsuit is often initiated. Once the decision is made to go to court, however, costs and tempers can easily spin out of control.

In the United States, courts are swamped with filings, cases routinely experience multi-year delays, and judges are overburdened. The systemic problems in the courts show few signs of improvement, as tens of millions of new cases are filed each year, driving the total yearly cost of litigation in the United States to more than $200 billion. In many other parts of the world the problem is much worse, with longer delays, confusing legal requirements, and rampant judicial corruption.

THE GROWTH OF ALTERNATIVE DISPUTE RESOLUTION

More and more executives, managers, and general counsels are coming to recognize the inefficiencies inherent in resolving disputes through the courts. In response, a new field has grown rapidly over the last few decades: alternative dispute resolution. Fueled by research in negotiation and a desire to create a more efficient way to work out differences, a growing pool of professional dispute resolvers has created an alternative to the court system that enables disputing parties to resolve their disagreements much more rapidly and effectively.

Using mechanisms like mediation, arbitration, and expert evaluation, parties can resolve their disagreements in weeks instead of years. Discussions are confidential, parties can decide how much control over the process they want to retain, and participants are usually much more satisfied with the outcome than they would have been had they decided to go to court. The parties can select the person they want to serve as their neutral facilitator, usually choosing someone knowledgeable about the subject matter of the dispute, saving the parties endless hours of educating a judge. In complex, transboundary matters, dispute resolution allows the parties to resolve their matter without having to pay for endless legal analysis about which country's law applies to each component of the dispute.

THE GROWTH OF
INFORMATION TECHNOLOGY

At the same time that alternative dispute resolution is growing, businesses worldwide are rapidly integrating information technology into the ways they do business. The computer revolution that has taken place over the last twenty years, along with the emergence of the Internet as an always-on global marketplace, has transformed the face of business. Now project teams work over the Internet on round-the-clock cycles, and projects are outsourced to business units around the world without a second thought. Deals can be consummated with partners sight-unseen, with online marketplaces acting as the connectors between buyers and sellers. Companies that could only support a regional presence in the past are now confronted with the possibility of doing business all over the world. Whereas before the whole company could probably meet in a conference room to discuss open issues, now companies can almost never convene their whole office in a single room.

These two factors, dispute resolution and information technology, have combined into an important new tool, a new system, a new way of doing business that is more efficient, more cost effective, and much more flexible than traditional approaches. The tool is called online dispute resolution (ODR), and it combines the efficiency of alternative dispute resolution with the power of the Internet to save businesses money, time, and frustration.

ONLINE DISPUTE RESOLUTION MEETS
THE NEEDS OF MODERN BUSINESS

Online dispute resolution is not tied to geography, so disputants can reach resolution even if they are located on different continents. ODR can move to resolve matters before they escalate so that disputants can quickly resolve the matter and get back to business. ODR is not tied to particular bodies of law, so there is no need for each side to retain expensive legal counsel to learn the legal structure of the other side's country. ODR can be priced much more reasonably than legal options, and even less than the cost of a single plane ticket. ODR can also leverage expertise from skilled neutrals around the world, ensuring that the participants will get a fair hearing from someone who has knowledge and experience in the matter at hand. ODR enables businesses, governments, and consumers to achieve the best resolution possible in the shortest amount of time.

These advantages apply to all kinds of disputes. Intellectual property disputes, insurance claims, and business-to-business (B2B) and business-to-customer (B2C) e-commerce matters are all good fits with the power of ODR. Some disputes are over more abstract issues unrelated to money, like privacy or workplace conflict. For example, the Internet Corporation for Assigned Names and Numbers (ICANN) faced monumental problems when it decided to build a global process to handle domain name disputes. What courts should govern the matter? What laws should apply? No one country has the jurisdiction over domain names; it is a truly international system. ICANN solved the problem by creating a global domain name dispute resolution process, the UDRP, administered by a variety of ODR providers. Since 1999, this process has resolved thousands of disputes all over the world. Similar ODR systems will soon be created for a wide variety of areas, such as insurance, commerce, privacy, government, workplace, and finance.

THE NEW CHALLENGE: ONLINE-ONLY DISPUTES

Many businesses are facing types of disputes they've never had to deal with before:

- Transactions take place all over the world, sometimes between buyers and sellers that have never met face-to-face. Inevitably, 1 to 3 percent of these transactions will go awry. When you're in the same town you can drive over and work the dispute out with the other side, or maybe take the matter to court if it gets complicated. How do you resolve a dispute with someone tens of thousands of miles away, who may not even speak the same language?

- Internal work teams these days frequently interact entirely online, perhaps involving telecommuters or overseas partners. Projects are passed around the globe on twenty-four-hour work cycles. Just like in the real world, workplace disputes can arise between the members of the group. But where is the workplace? How can those disputes get resolved before they escalate?

- Companies put up a website and it can instantly be accessed all around the world. The website may gather information from users in dozens of countries, all of which have different laws regarding confidentiality and privacy. How can a company meet its obligations to respond effectively to user complaints when its users are on five continents?

In all these circumstances the monetary value under dispute may be less than the cost of convening the disputants in the same room, maybe less than the cost of a teleconference. It may even be that the value of the dispute is impossible to determine.

The online-only dispute is a new type of dispute. It can develop between businesses and customers, suppliers, regulators, and insurers. It can emerge between strangers or between partners. Almost any business that does business online will increasingly become entangled in these kinds of disputes. How should your business respond?

Courts Do Not Work for Online Disputes

The court system may have its shortcomings, as pointed out before, but the rapid growth in online-only disputes has cast these shortcomings in even starker relief. Legal systems are tied to geography almost by definition. In the United States, lawyers are only admitted to the bar on a state-by-state basis, facing penalties if they even offer legal advice to clients in other states. Enforcement of court decisions involves jails and police officers whose jurisdiction is similarly restricted to a limited geographical area.

It is obvious that transaction partners who meet on the Web can take little comfort from the redress options provided in the face-to-face world. You can't merely recreate offline judicial mechanisms online and expect them to work, with e-judges making e-rulings enforced by e-police running e-jails. The model doesn't work, on a fundamental level, when participants in the system can change their identity as easily as they change their email address. It might work to hunt down the odd international criminal who shuts down the stock exchange with a virus, but there's no way law enforcement is going to be able to get every fraudulent seller on eBay, especially when they may be on the other side of the planet.

The delays of face-to-face processes also hamper their applicability to online transactions. Over the Web, consumers and businesses expect that any service they need should be available online, twenty-four hours a day. Courts, in contrast, have long been designed to involve delays, ornate filing requirements, and strict procedural rules, to deter potential users from being cavalier in their decision to file new cases. If two businesses engage in a transboundary transaction that goes awry they have no interest in waiting months for an offline dispute resolution body to initiate a process to resolve the dispute. They want to get the matter resolved as quickly as possible so that they can get back to business.

Simply put, offline courts do not work for online disputes. Courts can operate as an effective safety net for those cases that involve criminal wrongdoing, or where the parties are unwilling to use a non-public forum, or when they put the highest priority on due process and precedent. But for a huge number of cases that crop up online, where the value under dispute is less than likely legal bills, or where both parties truly participated in the transaction in good faith, online dispute resolution is the best solution.

THE GROWING CONSENSUS BEHIND ODR

In response to these conclusions, the consensus behind online dispute resolution is growing rapidly. International organizations (the Organisation for Economic Co-operation and Development, the Hague Conference on Private International Law, the United Nations), consumer groups (the Trans-Atlantic Consumer Dialogue, the Better Business Bureau), governmental bodies (the U.S. Federal Trade Commission and Department of Commerce, the European Union), professional associations (the Association for Conflict Resolution, the American Bar Association, and the American Arbitration Association) and business organizations (the Global Business Dialogue on e-Commerce, the International Chamber of Commerce) have all issued recommendations calling for high-quality online dispute resolution. While there is some debate about how to ensure that online dispute resolution services are fair to consumers, or how best to oversee online dispute resolution service providers, there is no debate over whether or not online dispute resolution is the best option for providing redress on the Internet.

Online dispute resolution is the future. Businesses that integrate it into the way they do business will reap rewards in the form of greater efficiency, cost savings, more satisfied employees, protection from liability, and more loyal customers. Those businesses that ignore it will continue to be drawn into expensive and inefficient legal proceedings that breed ill will and sap competitive strength.

THE GOAL OF THIS BOOK

Online Dispute Resolution for Business is designed to inform the senior management, general counsels, and risk managers of large companies and start-ups alike about the benefits of using Internet-based dispute resolution to resolve disputes before they escalate. It is intended to provide businesspeople with the information necessary to begin integrating ODR into the way their organization operates.

There is no way that a single volume could contain all the lessons organizations will learn in the process of implementing an effective ODR system. The goal of this book is to provide enough information to get businesspeople thinking about how ODR could benefit their organization, to give a snapshot of the current global environment for ODR, and to provide some pointers and suggestions to help get the process started.

THE PLAN OF THE BOOK

This book explains what ODR is, shows its application in some major industries, and describes how to build effective ODR services into the way your business does business.

This book's organization separates background information on ODR from details of its application in a variety of industries. Everyone should read Part I to get information about what ODR is and what advantages it offers. Then readers can pick and choose in Part II which industry areas they are interested in. Part III presents information useful to businesspeople building their own ODR systems, or even evaluating third-party ODR providers. It details the technology underlying ODR systems and offers specific implementation suggestions.

Part I presents the background information newcomers to ODR need in order to understand what it is and how it works. Chapter One begins with the development of ADR and its successful application in business. It also describes the development of ODR and the current landscape for ODR. Chapter Two then explains how ODR works, examining the different techniques for resolving disputes. Chapter Three lays out ODR's advantages and disadvantages for parties, neutrals, and corporations.

Part II analyzes the application of ODR in a variety of business contexts. Each chapter (Four through Twelve) explores a particular application area for ODR: B2C and B2B e-commerce, insurance, workplace, government, privacy, and transboundary disputes, as well as others. Readers can refer to the section that most interests them and feel free to skip sections that may not be applicable to their situation. Each chapter is intended to be free-standing, so none of the information in any one particular chapter is required to understand the other chapters in Part II.

Part III explores how ODR is actually done. This is the section of most importance to those building or designing an ODR platform from the ground up. The first three chapters examine the key considerations in putting together an ODR program: people, process, and technology. Chapter Thirteen examines the human side of ODR, deconstructing online dispute resolution services from the perspective of both the disputant and the neutral. Chapter Fourteen gets into the details of the technology, both from a design and practice perspective. Chapter Fifteen details the process challenges in putting together an ODR service, as well as describing the different standards for ODR practice that have come out of organizations, task forces, and conferences over the last year, as any ODR platform designer should be cognizant of the standards that might govern their system in the future. Chapter Sixteen then answers some frequently asked questions about ODR, including pricing, which disputes should go to ODR, and enforcement.

PART I

What Is ODR?

CHAPTER ONE

Overview

—ᴥ— In medieval times, travel to faraway destinations was a difficult thing for the average person to muster. Most people spent their lives in the same geographic area, learning of the rest of the world second hand from the stories of travelers and traders who had seen the world's wonders with their own eyes. This exposure to the diversity of the world through trade was a popular diversion, and as a result many cities throughout Europe held huge annual fairs, attracting traders from the Middle East, Russia, and Africa, as well as other European countries. These fairs gave average people a chance to wander through a microcosm of the world's diversity where the marvels of the globe were put on display for all to see.

European law a thousand years ago was not as developed as it is today, as there were no detailed books filled with precedent-setting cases or clearly defined areas of legal jurisdiction. Public and private institutions were difficult to distinguish from each other, as the king often ruled over his territory more like a landlord than as a publicly supported leader. So when a dispute arose among the traders attending these annual fairs there was quite a bit of confusion. What law should be applied to resolve the matter? Most of these traders traveled to different annual fairs in different towns every couple of weeks, and none of the traders were from the particular city where the fair happened to be when the dispute arose. In fact, none of the traders probably knew or cared what the local law was in that particular city anyway. The parties to the dispute could be from different religions and different countries, subject to different laws and different rulers. How could such conflicts be resolved?

What evolved to address these types of cases were special institutions called fair courts.[1] Each fair created its own dispute resolution body to resolve commercial matters that arose between the participating traders. The local ruler (lord, king, or whomever) would often select a judge to manage the court, but the juries were always made up of other merchants participating in that particular fair. Over time, these fair courts created their own special commercial law called the Law Merchant. This body of law was transnational, administered by the merchants themselves, speedy (as the traders were soon moving on to the next fair), and based upon fairness as a guiding principle.

These international fairs were marvels in medieval times. It must have been overwhelming for attendees to view exotic animals, to taste new foods, and to see works of art from other parts of the world. These fairs were the closest the medieval world got to the power of the Internet. And the challenges faced in dealing with the disputes among traders back then mirror the challenges faced in dealing with Internet disputes today. The Internet is like an always-on, immense international fair, filled with billions of stalls displaying the wonders of the world. And the mechanisms we have put in place to deal with the face-to-face disputes that arise in our cities and towns are about as relevant to disputes on the Internet as the laws of a particular city were to the traders at the fairs in medieval times. The traders needed to resolve disputes that the default system was not able to capably address, so they created an alternative system. It is becoming increasingly obvious that we will need to do the same for the Internet.

The Law Merchant was not eliminated by the spread of more structured legal systems based on precedent, geography, and national sovereignty. It evolved into what we currently call international arbitration and commercial arbitration. These techniques, along with mediation, expert evaluation, and structured negotiation, exist to resolve disputes outside of formal legal proceedings. Much like the fair courts, modern disputants agree on the rules they want to govern the resolution of the dispute and then work out a resolution without having to depend on judges, courtrooms, or legal precedents. They design a system, using basic resolution techniques, that meets the needs of their particular dispute, and then they work the matter out.

The overall term for these resolution techniques is *ADR,* or alternative dispute resolution. Dispute resolution has always defined itself as an alternative to the courts. Dispute resolution is usually explained to people as an alternative to the default means of resolving a conflict, which is traditional litigation. As a result the development of ADR has happened "in the shadow of the law," as Robert Mnookin has put it,[2] more of a footnote to the legal process or a second-tier option than an equivalent institution.

Online dispute resolution (ODR) grows directly out of the history of offline ADR. The lessons learned in ADR over the years about the importance of impartiality, how to effectively move parties toward resolution, about the importance of listening and transparency, and the challenges of managing power imbalances all are central to effective ODR practice. In its earliest incarnations, ODR procedures were simply unchanged ADR procedures conducted online.

Over time, however, the unique challenges and capabilities of ODR practice have made plain some new possibilities for dispute resolution. The ability to build technology into the dispute resolution process gives both the disputants and the neutrals new powers. The lack of face-to-face interaction changes the dynamics of dispute resolution processes as well. Most important, for the first time dispute resolution isn't really an alternative—the courts don't work in many online situations, so dispute resolution is often the default.

While ODR does present new challenges and opportunities, the best way to approach it is from the standpoint of proven dispute resolution practice. As Peter Martin has observed, "surviving and successful applications of technology to dispute resolution will, I suspect, need to be informed by the best scholarship on adjudicative and nonadjudicative methods for settling disagreements."[3] Thus the best place to begin any discussion of online dispute resolution is with the roots of face-to-face dispute resolution.

A BRIEF HISTORY OF ADR

Alternative dispute resolution has a long history. In the lobby of the Chartered Institute of Arbitrators in London there are framed arbitration awards from the fourteenth and fifteenth centuries. In them, arbitrators (essentially private judges) appointed by the king handled matters typical of the time period: land disputes between neighboring lords, or decisions about whose peasants could farm which fields. The language and structure of those awards could have been lifted directly out of a modern arbitration award. The general types of issues, and the manner chosen for resolving them, is largely the same today as it was hundreds if not thousands of years ago. Some scholars have argued that the roots of English arbitration can be traced back to the Roman Code of Justinian, written in the sixth century.

Mediation and consultative dispute resolution methods, which help parties negotiate an agreement as opposed to rendering a binding decision, also have long histories. Societies without formal judicial systems have long relied on conciliation and facilitated decision making to resolve disputes. Anthropological studies from the first half of the twentieth century describe the dispute resolution processes of different communities around the world, and the age-old lessons and structures of those programs closely mirror the structure of modern mediation processes.

Many other societies, including the United States, have relied on private dispute resolution mechanisms throughout history when more formal judicial resources were not trustworthy or not available. The original seventeenth-century charters of William Penn and the Virginia Company gave proprietors the power to establish local courts to render decisions, subject only to the caveat that more important matters could be transferred back to the royal courts in England. Statutes enacted in Pennsylvania in 1705 and 1810 both allowed for the arbitration of pending court matters.

At the beginning of the twentieth century, international arbitration was seen as the likely foundation of a new world order. In his championing of the League of Nations, U.S. President Woodrow Wilson spoke often of "open agreements openly arrived at" as the basis for a world society that transcended the anarchy of international relations.[4] Many major ADR organizations were founded during this period, including the International Court of Arbitration at the International Chamber of Commerce (1923) and the American Arbitration Association (1926).

THE DEVELOPMENT OF THE ADR FIELD

The first major institutional use of dispute resolution to resolve conflicts in the United States was in the labor-management area. Repeated strife between corporations and their employees was a major problem in the United States, and litigation was not an effective way to deal with the disputes in most circumstances. A body of practice surrounding dispute resolution in labor-management contexts began to grow, and institutions were created to handle these disputes, such as the Federal Mediation and Conciliation Service (founded in 1918 as the U.S. Conciliation Service and renamed in 1947).

Labor management dispute resolution remained on the cutting edge until the 1960s and 1970s, when dispute resolution techniques began to be applied in other areas. There was recognition in the 1970s that litigation was not the best resolution strategy for every type of dispute. Frank Sander, a professor at Harvard Law School, envisioned the creation of a "multi-door courthouse," where disputants could be directed to the dispute resolution mechanism most appropriate to their type of conflict.[5] Law schools began to study negotiation theory and to create innovative dispute resolution programs to apply that theory. Community mediation centers began popping up around the country, and dispute resolution techniques began to be applied in environmental disputes, family disputes, and commercial matters.

Academics took the lead in developing the theory underlying ADR, and influential books were penned during this era that presented the ideas of dispute resolution in an easy to understand way. *Getting to Yes* by Roger Fisher and William Ury is easily the most popular of these books, but others (such as *Social Conflict* by Dean Pruitt and Jeffrey Rubin, *The Mediation Process* by Chris Moore, and *The Art and Science of Negotiation* by Howard Raiffa) helped to make dispute resolution into a defined discipline.

Foundations funded the growth of the dispute resolution field, and organizations such as the National Institute for Dispute Resolution (NIDR), the Society for Professionals in Dispute Resolution (SPIDR), and the National Association for Mediation in Education (NAME) all played a role in sponsoring dispute resolution research, creating professional communities for dispute resolvers, and helping people access quality dispute resolution training.

The 1990s saw an expansion and professionalization of the field. Conferences focusing on ADR, such as the National Conference on Peacemaking and Conflict Resolution, were routinely drawing thousands of attendees. The American Bar Association (ABA) acknowledged the growth of the sector with their creation of an ADR section in 1993. The section remains the fastest-growing section in the ABA, with more than 6,300 members at last count, many of whom are not lawyers. The merger in 2001 of three of the largest ADR organizations (SPIDR, the Academy of Family Mediators, and the Conflict Resolution in Education Network) into a single organization, the Association for Conflict Resolution (ACR), also signals a new maturity and focus for the ADR field.

Increasingly, individuals were defining themselves to be dispute resolution professionals instead of members of some other field who had dispute resolution training. A growing number of students were devoting themselves full-time to dispute resolution. Academic programs sprouted up around the country to offer graduate degrees in dispute resolution, and trainers began crossing the country offering forty-hour mediation trainings that could lead to certification as a mediator with some credentialing organizations (such as the Academy of Family Mediators or SPIDR).

Martindale-Hubble, the definitive directory of legal professionals, launched their Dispute Resolution Directory in the 1990s, listing mediators and arbitrators willing to work with parties to resolve their disputes. Mediate.com also launched in 1995, offering the Locate a Mediator database to help connect disputants with mediators in their local area.

The government also signed on to dispute resolution in a big way, passing the Administrative Dispute Resolution Act in 1993. The act called on all agencies of the federal government to appoint dispute resolution specialists, and to explore how operations could be made more effective by using dispute resolution to avoid lawsuits. Dispute resolution was applied to the policy-making process through regulatory negotiation, during which stakeholders were offered an opportunity to give their input on proposed regulatory changes before they were set in stone, in an effort to head off future legal challenges. The Department of Justice also created an Office of Dispute Resolution to handle many of the government's legal matters.

The major dispute resolution service providers have also seen their caseloads jump dramatically over the last decade. The American Arbitration Association, the largest business-to-business dispute resolution service provider in the United States, handled more than 150,000 cases in 1999, while Judicial Arbitration and Mediation Services (JAMS) handled more than 60,000. The Better Business Bureau (BBB), the premier business-to-consumer dispute resolution service provider, handled more than 450,000 cases in 2000.

Today dispute resolution has simply become the way business is done in many industry sectors. Arbitration clauses can be found in almost every template contract available on the shelves of your local office supply store. Many professional mediators and arbitrators have their calendars filled with cases to be addressed in a wide variety of sectors: workplace disputes, insurance claims, construction defects, intellectual property, and public policy disputes, to name only a few.

ADR AND BUSINESS

Paralleling the growth of ADR in society as a whole, use of dispute resolution by businesses has been increasing steadily over the past few decades. As businesses have come to understand the huge costs associated with legal proceedings interest has grown in alternatives.

Over the past thirty years business-focused ADR organizations such as the Center for Public Resources (CPR) and the American Arbitration Association (AAA) have grown in prominence, spreading the word about ADR among the business community. CPR maintains a listing of more than 4,000 operating companies, including more than half of the Fortune 500 list, that have signed the *CPR Corporate Policy Statement on Alternatives to Litigation,* which obligates them to explore the use of ADR in disputes with other signers.

The use of ADR by businesses continues to grow. Broad-sample statistical analysis supports this trend. As John Bickerman and Divonne Smoyer reported in the *Legal Times,*

> An on-going study of the country's 1000 largest corporations being conducted by Cornell University in cooperation with the Foundation for Prevention and Early Resolution of Conflict (PERC), a non-profit organization in New York City, shows that, in the past three years, the vast majority of U.S. corporations have used one or more forms of ADR in resolving a broad range of disputes, including: employment, environmental, sexual harassment, contracts, securities and age discrimination claims. Based on the survey responses of more than 600 corporate counsel, deputy counsel and chief corporate litigators, Cornell researchers believe that this use is likely to grow significantly in the future, due to, at least in part, the rising costs of litigation, an increase of ADR provisions in employment and commercial contracts and court mandates of ADR processes.[6]

The PERC study revealed that businesses are coming to favor ADR, as they perceive it to be a "more satisfactory process" than litigation.[7] Users suggest that mediation "preserves good relationships," and that they find it more cost-effective than litigation.[8] Arbitration is used primarily in industries with long-standing contracts with clauses that require its use, while newer contracts are increasingly suggesting mediation as a viable ADR option. Use of ADR is also more common in commercial and employment disputes.

Another chief finding of the Cornell/PERC study is that use of ADR generally tends to vary by company size and age. The larger, "blue chip" companies favor ADR, and they are several times more likely to use ADR than litigate. These firms tend to be more established and their negative experience with past litigation (for example, class actions, labor disputes, and the like) leads them toward ADR. In contrast, the most litigious corporations tended to be younger, less-established companies. These companies are more likely to reject ADR in favor of litigation.

A different survey of general counsel and outside corporate attorneys conducted by the accounting firm Deloitte & Touche also revealed an increase in the use of ADR—as much as 28 percent—especially in the area of mediation.[9]

One of the largest domestic users of ADR is the government. A 2001 Department of Justice report on the successes of ADR implementations within the federal government indicated ten common benefits ADR provides:

- Complaints are processed more quickly and resolved earlier.

- Litigation and other costs are lower.

- Future complaints are avoided as parties learn to communicate better with each other.

- Parties are more satisfied with the problem-solving process and with the results.

- Relations with contractors and other outside parties are improved.

- The process leads to more creative solutions.

- Internal morale is improved.

- Turnover is lower.

- Parties comply better with their settlement agreements.

- Productivity is improved.[10]

The United States Postal Service, which has one of the most sophisticated and widely used employment ADR programs in the federal government, found that 81 percent of mediated cases are eventually closed without a formal complaint being filed. Satisfaction was also extremely high, with exit surveys completed anonymously by 26,000 participants indicating that 88 percent of employees are highly satisfied or satisfied with the amount of control, respect, and fairness in the ADR process. This figure is very significant because the satisfaction rate for the Postal Service's traditional adversarial workplace process is only 44 percent. Moreover, both employees and supervisors are equally satisfied with ADR. The Postal Service program is projected to save millions of dollars each year, in addition to improving morale and productivity.

The Air Force also found ADR very effective in the government contracts area, where it used ADR in more than 100 cases, of which more than 93 percent have settled. Of particular note is the agency's recent successful use of ADR to resolve a $785 million contract claim with the Boeing company that had been unresolved, prior to the use of ADR, for more than ten years. In another case, the agency settled a $195 million contract claim. Litigating either of these extremely large and complex cases would have been enormously expensive and uncertain in outcome. Litigation could also have damaged relationships with some of the military's most important suppliers. The Secretary of the Air Force has recognized the success of these programs and codified them in formal agency procedures. It is now official Air Force policy to use ADR "to the maximum extent practicable."[11]

The applications of ADR in business are growing rapidly in a wide variety of industry sectors. Dispute resolution techniques are being applied routinely in insurance claims resolution, workplace disputes (such as Equal Employment Opportunity Commission matters), labor management disagreements, construction defect matters, intellectual property, class actions, and environmental conflicts. Businesses like ADR because it is quicker, cheaper, and more effective than traditional litigation. It also allows them to keep matters from escalating and to keep them confidential.

THE DEVELOPMENT OF ODR

My introduction to dispute resolution came while I was an undergraduate at Haverford College, a small liberal arts institution just outside Philadelphia. My first ADR training was with several members of the Friends Suburban Project, a project of the American Friends Service Committee (AFSC). Haverford had a campus mediation program called Communication Outreach that worked in concert with the Dean's Office to resolve disputes between students, faculty, and administration, and the AFSC helped Haverford train new student mediators each year.

In the middle of my sophomore year a controversy broke out between a few students and the Dean's Office over parental notification rules. The matter escalated fairly quickly and generated a lot of acrimony. Communication Outreach played an informal role in trying to facilitate dialogue between the deans and the involved students. I participated in several contentious public meetings and followed the endless letters exchanged on the editorial page of the campus newspaper and the public "comment board" in the student center. These exchanges received a lot of energy and attention from the campus community, and everyone seemed to have a strong opinion on the matter.

Most people on campus were unaware that the dispute was also playing out online. The students directly involved in the dispute were very active on *VAXNotes,* a text-only discussion environment that ran on the college's VAX mainframe. While a face-to-face dialogue was playing out in student council meetings and a written debate was occurring in the newspaper, an emotional exchange regarding the matter was also taking place on *VAXNotes.* Armed with my basic dispute resolution training, and brandishing my computer nerd credentials, I bravely decided that I would try to mediate the online discussion happening over *VAXNotes.*

At its peak, the online discussion was generating hundreds of messages a day. Many of them were very angry, with almost all of that anger directed at the deans. The deans were not participating in the *VAXNotes* discussion, and that led to a very one-sided presentation of the issues. A handful of the discussion participants were siding with the deans, but they were quickly drowned out by the torrent of messages in favor of the aggrieved students. It was very hard for me, as a single participant (a sophomore, no less) with no formal role, to make a dent in this flow of messages. It was also easy for points to be lost, especially subtle ones attempting to reframe the issue in a way that would promote resolution. The most extravagant comments, taking the most extreme positions and making the most outrageous points, always drew the bulk of the participants' attention. I did feel that the discussion made some progress on certain key issues, however, and I sensed that later some of the issues that had been worked out in the *VAXNotes* environment contributed to the eventual resolution that was achieved.

This was my first experience attempting to apply dispute resolution principles through technology, and it was admittedly a frustrating one. However, it made clear to me that there was a place for dispute resolution in online environments, and that with better tools and more developed theory the idea of technology-assisted dispute resolution held great promise as a way to help people reach agreement.

I was unaware of it at the time, but it turns out many other people in North America were coming to a similar realization based on their own experiences with technology, law, and dispute resolution. In retrospect, the seeds of a new professional field were being planted. None of us knew at the time that technology-assisted ADR would eventually evolve into online dispute resolution, or that the academic computer networks we used for sending email would eventually become an "information superhighway" and a core component of the global commercial infrastructure. The expansion of the Internet would raise the importance of these questions, and eventually develop online dispute resolution into an international concern.

If only I could have figured all of this out back then things would have turned out differently. For instance, I would have registered the domain name Business.com, sold it for $6 million or so, and I'd be on vacation down in the Bahamas right now (and someone else would have had to write this book). As they say, hindsight is 20/20.

A BRIEF HISTORY OF ODR

In their book *Online Dispute Resolution*, Ethan Katsh and Janet Rifkin break the development of ODR up into three different stages. The first, which they say lasted until about 1995, consisted of specialized dispute resolution in specific contexts. The second, which they date from 1995–1998, coincided with the growth of the Internet, particularly as a medium for commerce. A sense was also developing that this growing "cyberspace" required institutions much like the offline world. The experiments in ODR during this phase were largely sponsored by academics and non-profit institutions. The third period is the most recent phase, during which commercial entities began to show interest in online dispute resolution. This has coincided with a new interest on the part of government and international institutions in ODR, both from regulatory and standard-setting perspectives.

Katsh and Rifkin did an excellent job analyzing the growth of ODR through the period from 1995 to early 2001, and I'm not going to duplicate their work here. I will instead provide something of a personal history, touching on some of the key events as I have experienced them, as well as presenting some of the developments that have taken place since their book was published. The emergence of the Internet as a commercial phenomenon has resulted in an explosion of interest in online dispute resolution, and the history of ODR is being updated all the time. Because the Internet is so young, ODR is by definition young as well. The history of ODR has just begun to be written.

While there were experiments with ODR in the pre-Internet days, they were small and specialized by definition. Before 1990, online communication happened almost entirely through networks of "bulletin boards," or software packages that allowed computers to dial up a central computer and to participate in discussions, share files, or view pictures. Because these networks were dependent on telephone lines, the traffic was largely confined to specific regional areas, where phone calls were free.[12]

Most of the people that spent time on these boards were avid computer hobbyists or professionals who had access to computers through their work. These bulletin boards were almost entirely text-based, and top modem speeds at the time were almost a hundredth of what they are now, so the user experience was not a particularly pleasing one.

There were some early efforts at dispute resolution back in the days of bulletin boards, but not in an organized way. Dispute resolution is a natural component of human interaction, as many anthropologists observed in the 1940s and 1950s. All societies and human social groups (including both families and nations) need to have effective ways to resolve disputes that arise. Online communities were and are no different.

On some of these bulletin boards "flame wars" would periodically erupt between users who disagreed about something. Occasionally boards would create specific discussion areas were users could unload on each other. The anonymity of online interaction was particularly freeing, and people would really vent in some of these discussion groups. However, conflicts would arise in every discussion area, including the book club, political discussion, and others. A famous dispute arose in the early 1990s over a newsgroup focusing on cats that was invaded by posters who made crude jokes about cats being harmed in a variety of ways. Because the participants were from all over the Web, and because the forum was openly accessible to anyone who wanted to participate, it was difficult to shut out the offenders.

To a very large degree conflict is what makes conversations interesting; opinions diverge, the group examines each perspective, and individuals make up their own minds. Participants were constantly wrestling with disputes that arose between users, and doing the sorts of things that people do face-to-face to resolve disputes between friends, co-workers, and family members. But most bulletin boards had no formal dispute resolution program and no guidelines for how best to perform these services. Also, efforts on the bulletin boards to resolve disputes had no special technology provided for that purpose. Early ODR used the same discussion technology that was available for the broader conversation. Most bulletin boards did have private messages, a precursor to email, so it was possible to make private comments to other specific parties.

In academic circles, hardwired computer networks were already in use, like BitNet, which was an early network that tied together colleges and universities around the country. The military developed ARPAnet, the precursor to the Internet, in the 1970s, along with a secure network for military applications called MilNet. In the early 1990s these specialized computer networks were used primarily for communication between researchers and academics. Slowly the type of interaction found on bulletin boards began to make its way onto these hardwired networks.

USING TECHNOLOGY
FOR DISPUTE ANALYSIS

I attended a session at the 1993 National Conference on Peacemaking and Conflict Resolution on how to integrate technology and ADR. At the time, computer networking inside the office was still considered to be cutting edge, and the discussion didn't even mention the Internet. The focus was on how computers could be used to help disputants clarify their underlying needs to help move toward resolution.

One of the presenters at that session was Ernie Thiessen, the founder of SmartSettle. Using various mathematical algorithms Thiessen had developed a way to help parties find a resolution to their dispute that maximized benefits for both participants. Once the parties had figured out all the key issues in the dispute and ranked them in terms of priority the algorithm could step through various proposals to help the parties reach the most efficient resolution.

The focus of people trying to integrate technology into the ADR process in the early days was to have computers do what computers do best: work with the numbers. The mathematical origins of the ADR field began with economists and game theorists who tried to use numbers to model the payoff structures for various negotiations. Early technology and ADR integrations used these mathematical approaches to build computer programs that could perform similar analyses on active disputes. The point of these efforts was to distribute the pie as efficiently as possible. The algorithms allowed parties to claim value that might have been left on the table without the accurate calculations of the computer.

These efforts began long before the Internet was widely used. Thiessen wrote a paper about technology-assisted decision-making in water resource disputes as early as 1983. His platform, SmartSettle, has since grown into a very sophisticated and intuitive program, and now has even integrated the Internet into its tools. Thiessen has consistently updated his platform for the last decade, and SmartSettle is now the most sophisticated evolution of this analytical strand of technology and dispute resolution.

TECHNOLOGY AS AN ADMINISTRATOR AND ORGANIZER

Software platforms for administering dispute resolution cases were also being sold in the late 1980s and early 1990s. Individual case administration entities, like community mediation centers or arbitration offices, could use these pieces of software on a single computer to coordinate case intake, the assignment of neutrals, and follow up in particular matters. These programs were used only internally in a single office, but they did provide a technologic infrastructure for the later integration of collaborative technology.

In the mid-1980s Jim Melamed, a mediator from Oregon, designed a program called Agree that was intended to help disputants reach agreement through the use of a DOS computer program running on a single, non-networked machine. The program operated much like a workbook, asking questions and storing the responses of the parties. In contrast to the earlier technology efforts, which focused on using algorithms and number crunching to make progress in disputes, programs like Agree focused on the human side of the equation.

The Agree program was an example of technology being applied to the thinking process that parties go through in analyzing their involvement in a dispute. The goal was to use technology to provide a structure to analyze the issues in the dispute, not to use mathematic equations to divide the pie more efficiently. There was a sense that people could work with machines to help clarify their positions before they got into a negotiation, and even during the negotiation. This was a different application of technology, one that foreshadowed the human side of computing.

TECHNOLOGY AND COMMUNICATIONS

There was a growing awareness as well that the most promising application of technology could be as a communications tool. In 1988 John Helie, a mediator in Berkeley, California, was working to expand the local community mediation program. He wanted to get some materials from the Community Boards, a prestigious dispute resolution institution in San Francisco, but he didn't want to drive all the way into the city to get them. So he fired up his modem and asked the Community Boards if he could get the information transmitted that way. Then the idea hit: Why couldn't technology be used to help grow the dispute resolution field more generally? If the materials he was downloading were useful to him they would likely be useful to people around the country and around the world.

In response, Helie founded ConflictNet, an online resource that was a project of the Institute for Global Communications (IGC), which also served as the home of PeaceNet, EcoNet, and LaborNet. Each of these sites served as an online meeting place for activists and professionals in a variety of fields. ConflictNet quickly became a home for dispute resolution information, hosting dozens of discussions on ADR-related topics, offering a library of articles, and offering basic online services (such as email).

There was an awareness about online dispute resolution even back in those pre-Internet days. John Helie's guidelines for online discussion, written in 1990, sound much like the advice given to online dispute resolvers in ODR trainings today. However, because online interaction was not perceived as a medium for commercial transactions, there was no real sense of need for online dispute resolution. Pre-Internet, online communication was primarily intended for information exchange among friends and associates, and the only conflict that could come out of that type of interactivity was personal disputes and relationship problems, neither of which held much promise for commercial success.

Most talk about ODR in the early 1990s focused on virtual communities and discussion lists. Flame wars would erupt and insults would be hurled, and occasionally a dispute resolution expert would be called in to help the online community resolve the matter. As Katsh and Rifkin describe in their book, the most famous early online dispute resolution procedures took place on listservs or in MUDs ("multiuser dungeons," essentially text-based online places where users could interact) and they focused on interpersonal relationships.[13]

THE ARRIVAL OF THE INTERNET

John Helie and Jim Melamed joined forces in the early 1990s because they shared a vision for how technology could be applied to the ADR field, and in 1995 they launched Mediate.com, the first online community for dispute resolution professionals. Mediate.com offered an online article library for information about ADR, a searchable directory of dispute resolution professionals, a list of academic programs and organizations that worked in ADR, and a threaded discussion environment where mediators could discuss practice challenges and share information about upcoming trainings and conferences.

The early uses of the Internet, much like academic computer networks, were primarily focused on information dissemination and communication. The computer programs that performed actual functions were largely relegated to desktops, like word processors and spreadsheets. Early Web pages were static information, much like a pamphlet or a brochure. Whatever interactivity there was with a website usually resembled the interactivity that had been found on dial-up bulletin boards throughout the 1980s. But soon, with the excitement about the Internet and all the potential it held, the Web became much more interactive. Web pages started to respond to users like applications on desktops, and users could suddenly do things that were unthinkable in the days of static Web pages.

Quickly programmers got to work on the idea of getting people to use computer networks to connect their machines so that they could work together. The Internet would be the common network through which this communication could take place. Instead of the technology platforms from the 1980s where parties were operating only on their one machine, the Internet could allow users on different machines—either across town or across the world—to work together to solve problems.

In 1996, John Helie was involved in the first use of the Internet to inform a public policy dialogue. Called RuleNet, the program was hosted by the Nuclear Regulatory Commission (NRC) to gather public input about the issue of fire protection in nuclear power plants. Supported by programmers at the Lawrence Livermore Laboratory, Helie and some officials from the NRC designed a multi-stage process through which facilitators would convene a public discussion in an attempt to build consensus on the issue. In the past, agencies would simply conduct a fact-finding process and then issue a rule or regulation on a particular matter.

Dispute resolution had previously been integrated into the offline rulemaking process with a methodology called regulatory negotiation, where all of the relevant stakeholders would be invited to give their input on a particular regulation under consideration. The RuleNet process was the first time the Internet was used to support such a dialogue. The goal was not to draft the full text for a new regulation, but instead to gather public input from a variety of stakeholders with the goal of adopting a more broadly supported rule at the end of the process. While a fractious exercise, the majority of participants gave the initiative a thumbs-up and recommended similar efforts be conducted in the future. (For more information on RuleNet, see Chapter Nine.)

EARLY ODR EXPERIMENTS

As the Internet began to expand more rapidly the legal issues started to come into focus. Some observers began to speculate on how online interactions could be regulated under the law. The first prosecutions against people engaging in threatening or fraudulent activity online took place in the early 1990s, and soon there was a national discussion about how such online criminal activity could be curtailed. The early focus was on Internet service providers (ISPs). Because every user of the Internet had to get access through an ISP somewhere, the argument went, ISPs were the most appropriate point at which to catch and punish those who engaged in criminal or undesirable behavior over the Internet.

Several projects emerged to handle disputes that arose online. The Virtual Magistrate project, CyberTribunal, and the Online Ombuds Office were all early ODR projects that attempted to use technology to resolve disputes, either through arbitration or mediation. The National Center for Automated Information Research (NCAIR) convened the first ODR conference in May 1996, and the field of ODR was born.

The first decision to be rendered after online proceedings arrived in 1996. It was the first and last decision to come out of the Virtual Magistrate project, which was located at Villanova University and sponsored by NCAIR. The decision regarded an advertisement posted on America Online (AOL) advertising the availability of millions of email addresses that could be used for bulk emailings. After four days of hearings the advertisement was found to violate AOL's Terms of Service Agreement, and in response AOL complied with the decision and took down the ad.

Most of the projects leading up to 1998 were non-profit or academic in nature. None of them had large marketing budgets or technology staffs. One, CyberTribunal in Canada, did receive funding on the condition that the commercial possibilities of the concept be explored. But the lack of interest in projects like the Virtual Magistrate (it only received one case) eventually doomed them to end.

ODR AND THE COMMERCIAL INTERNET

The emergence of ODR as a field closely coincides with the emergence of the Internet as a space for commerce. Soon after goods and services started to be sold over the Internet it became obvious that online transactions need to be supported in the same way that face-to-face transactions are supported. If a consumer buys a mattress at a department store and the mattress is defective, the consumer can return to the store to get it replaced. If the store refuses to replace it, the consumer can take the matter to small claims court. Online there are no such institutions to resolve disputes.

Around 1997 the boom in Internet companies started to expand. Venture capitalists had begun pouring money into Internet start-ups with an eye to capturing a piece of the fundamental transformation that was going on in the global marketplace. Technology-focused research firms like Jupiter Research, Gartner Research, and Forrester Research competed with each other to see who could envision the rosiest scenario for the expansion of e-commerce. Estimates put the expansion of e-commerce to staggering heights, such as $7 trillion by 2005.[14]

This perceived boom was not without real-world examples. Initial public offerings by companies like Netscape and VA Linux made their founders instant billionaires. Stock prices were pushed higher and higher by investors looking for the next sure thing. This led to the easy availability of capital for any business with a dot-com at the end of its name. Business schools around the country were losing students in the middle of their degrees who wanted to instead put their time into building the next hot Internet success story.

This led to a ravenous appetite for new ideas. Websites selling everything from pet products to soup to poetry were brought online as quickly as possible in a mad grasp for "first mover advantage." The core belief of the day was that the first mover was the most likely to succeed, and that revenues meant less than "eyeballs"—a mantra that meant that getting the attention of new users was more important in the short term than making money. Venture investors pumped millions of dollars into companies that did not even intend to break even for the first few years of their lives.

As Rifkin and Katsh put it, this period has been characterized by "significant entrepreneurial activity."[15] The last two years have generated a wellspring of interest in ODR, from the commercial side, the governmental side, and from the ADR field. Many new companies have been founded to provide ODR services, including Cybersettle, ClickNsettle, SquareTrade, eResolution, and Online Resolution, as well as many others. (For more information on these providers, refer to the Appendix.)

This period has also been characterized by governmental and nonprofit activity. In 1998 the OECD issued a document suggesting standards for all providers of online dispute resolution services. This action set in motion a global response from different countries and international organizations examining the issue. Each country and organization wants to make sure that whatever system is eventually put in place will meet the needs of its constituents.

In June 2000 the United States Department of Commerce (DOC) and Federal Trade Commission (FTC) convened a conference in Washington to discuss online dispute resolution in e-commerce. The conference attracted more than three hundred attendees from the dispute resolution field, business, non-profits, and government. This conference marked the beginning of a real ODR movement in the United States.

THE CURRENT STATE OF ODR

Over the past two years developments in the ODR space have come fast and furious. ODR has evolved from a promising idea into a global priority. The purpose of this section is to give a quick overview of the major developments, though the brevity of their treatment may be frustrating. Many of these topics are discussed and analyzed in more detail later in the application section of this book (Chapters Four through Twelve).

In the wake of the FTC/DOC meeting a group of ODR service providers planned for the creation of a professional organization representing ODR in Washington, D.C., to be called the Coalition of Internet Dispute Resolvers (CIDR). The organization aimed to set standards for the field and to enable ODR providers to speak with a common voice in U.S. policy-making. Eventually, however, the organization was absorbed into SPIDR (the Society of Professionals in Dispute Resolution), which has now become the Association for Conflict Resolution (ACR). The sole organization representing professional ODR service providers is now the online section of ACR.[16]

In October 2000 the first conference among ODR service providers convened in Phoenix, Arizona. For the first time all the major providers of ODR services sat down to discuss the agenda for the field and to plan for future growth.

In November 2000 the World Intellectual Property Organization held a conference focusing on ODR in Geneva. In December the OECD, the International Chamber of Commerce, and the Hague Conference on Private International Law jointly convened an ODR conference in The Hague, Netherlands. That conference was attended by more than three hundred experts on e-commerce, privacy, and dispute resolution from around the world.

Many organizations have issued standards calling for e-commerce companies to integrate online dispute resolution into their business practices. The Better Business Bureau, the Global Business Dialogue on e-Commerce (which includes AOL Time Warner, Hewlett-Packard, and DaimlerChrysler), the Electronic Commerce and Consumer Protection Group (including Dell, Microsoft, and Visa), the Trans-Atlantic Consumer Dialogue, and the International Chamber of Commerce (ICC) have all issued recommendations that e-commerce companies make online dispute resolution available to their customers to resolve any disputes that arise. (For more information on ODR Standards, see Chapter Fifteen.)

Analysts have also called for the addition of ODR to e-commerce sites. In November 2000, Jupiter Research, one of the premiere e-commerce focused research groups in the United States, released a key finding that e-commerce sites should "work quickly to formulate clear mediation policies," as online businesses "will begin to see conflicts develop between markets and their new trading partners," and dispute resolution is essential to developing "trust between buyers and sellers."[17]

The Global Business Dialogue on eCommerce (GBDe) also convened meetings that discussed ODR in Miami in 2000 and Tokyo in 2001. The GBDe created a working group to focus on alternative dispute resolution, headed up by the CEOs of DaimlerChrysler in Germany and Hewlett-Packard in the United States.

The primary discussion between the GBDe and consumer groups is the degree to which ODR programs are biased in favor of corporate interests. Corporations have called for self-regulation in the rollout of ODR programs, arguing that the marketplace will be able to generate effective ODR solutions and regulation will move too slowly to match the rapid pace of growth in the Internet economy. Consumer advocates have argued in contrast that the playing field is seriously biased in favor of corporations in many ODR programs, as the corporations often pay the bills for the services, use them repeatedly (as opposed to consumers, who will probably use them only once or twice a year), and often choose the provider. There is also debate about how binding these mechanisms should be. (For more information on this debate, refer to Chapter Five.)

During 2001 several international efforts emerged to build global networks to handle ODR. The Better Business Bureau, the largest consumer-focused dispute resolution organization in the United States, announced a partnership with Eurochambres, the network of European Chambers of Commerce, and FEDMA, the European Direct Marketing Association, to build a transatlantic ODR system for handling business-to-consumer disputes. Since this announcement in early spring 2001 several other countries in Asia and South America have signed on to participate in the network.

The European Union has funded the creation of a European B2C ODR technology platform called ECODIR, which was launched in October 2001. This technology was created during a year-long research project at a university in Belgium, with underlying programming support coming from eResolution, an ODR company in Montreal, Canada.

The International Chamber of Commerce (ICC), the most prestigious international arbitration body in the world, has also announced its plan to serve as a clearinghouse for B2C ODR cases around the world. Under the plan the ICC would accept case submissions from consumers and organizations around the world and then refer the cases to the appropriate ODR service providers. The ICC would maintain strict standards for these ODR service providers, and if a provider did not conform to the ICC's regulations they would stop receiving case referrals.

The American Bar Association (ABA) has also gotten involved with e-commerce, convening a task force to discuss online dispute resolution in e-commerce and to issue a white paper with recommendations for how to maximize ODR's effectiveness. The ABA e-ADR Task Force has convened meetings around the world to gather input on the question, as well as to gather online surveys from ODR providers, neutrals, consumers, and other interested groups. The task force's recommendations are due out in 2002, but the initial indication is that they will argue for the creation of a seal to be placed on the websites of ODR provider organizations attesting to that organization's adherence to standards for ODR practice. The task force has no recommendations for what organization might issue or enforce such a seal as of yet, but the ICC or BBB network might be willing to step into such a role.

Also important is the development of the domain name dispute resolution program from ICANN (the Internet Corporation for Assigned Names and Numbers). ICANN's Uniform Dispute Resolution Program (UDRP) has resolved thousands of domain name disputes in the last three years. These disputes have no particular national law that they are governed by, so ICANN created a global ODR system to resolve any disputes that arise over domain names through a complaint hearing process. While it has been hotly debated as to fairness, the program can rightly be called a success, as so many disputes have been resolved through it. ICANN has recently authorized new extensions for domain names, including .info and .biz, which promise to generate many thousands of new disputes. For more information on ICANN's UDRP, see Chapter Eleven: Building a Global Justice System.

Established ADR organizations, sensing the rising tide of ODR programs, have also launched their own online initiatives. The American Arbitration Association, the largest business-to-business dispute resolution organization in the United States, recently launched its Electronic Commerce Group (eCg) initiative to provide dispute resolution in online marketplaces around the globe. Judicial Arbitration and Mediation Services (JAMS), the second-largest ADR firm in the United States, also has announced e-JAMS, an initiative focusing on dispute resolution in class action suits. JAMS has partnered with Poorman-Douglas, an administrator of class action cases, to build the system.

Academic interest in ODR has remained strong, with many schools around the world starting classes in online dispute resolution and hosting conferences. Academic ODR conferences have been held at Northwestern University (2000) and the University of Geneva (2001), and ADR Cyberweek, the largest online conference devoted to ODR, had more than eight hundred global visitors in February 2002. During Cyberweek 2002 the first International Competition in Online Dispute Resolution (ICODR) was held, involving teams of law students from around the world. The plan is to turn ICODR into a yearly event and to grow the number of participating teams each year.

The North American Free Trade Agreement (NAFTA) 2002 ADR Committee recently decided to conduct a pilot program using online dispute resolution to resolve transboundary disputes between companies in Mexico, the United States, and Canada. The services will be in French, English, and Spanish, and they will be provided by six dispute resolution organizations, two from Mexico, two from the United States, and two from Canada.

Many countries in the developing world, faced with the creation of a new telecommunications infrastructure, are electing to skip the deployment of land-based phone lines in favor of wireless services like cell phone towers. Why bother going through all of the stages leading up to a technology, they reason, when it is possible to jump right to the cutting edge? Similarly, many countries that are just starting to build their face-to-face ADR networks are expressing a desire to go straight to ODR. Countries such as Singapore and Argentina are building online dispute resolution resources into their new dispute resolution programs, so that when disputants are introduced to ADR they are exposed to ODR at the same time. The United Nations held a two-day conference on ODR in Geneva, June 6–7, 2002, that focused on the issue of expanding ODR to developing economies. The premise of the gathering was that ODR networks can provide legal infrastructure in developing countries that do not have robust legal institutions, removing a barrier to receiving more foreign investment.

Perhaps the most exciting initiative is the emerging e-Parliament, which plans to use ODR technology to bring together thousands of elected representatives around the world to address global issues, such as the spread of AIDS and global warming. William Ury, one of the co-authors of *Getting to Yes,* is coordinating the project through the Program on Negotiation at Harvard Law School.

THE END OF THE INTERNET?

In late 2000 the Internet expansion began to slow. The rosy projections for a "long boom" economic expansion were tarnished by companies not hitting their growth projections. Investors began to slow down on their commitments, and some formerly high-flying Internet companies began to run out of money. By the spring of 2001 there was a sense that the economy was moving toward recession, and in April 2001 the stock market started to put serious pressure on technology stocks. Venture investors began to feel the heat, and they decided to close down some of the weaker companies they had invested in to preserve capital to support the stronger ones. Eventually the technology sector experienced a major correction, pulling down even established market stalwarts like Intel, Cisco, and Hewlett-Packard. The September 2001 terrorist attacks in the United States weakened confidence even further. Some ODR companies that were dependent on investment, such as Montreal-based eResolution, ran out of money and were forced to close their doors.

The perception, stemming from a backlash against the heady dot-com boom days, was that the Internet was over. Having been promised the moon and the stars, pundits seemed ready to declare the Internet a fad like CB radios in the 1970s and to go back to buying their slacks at Wal-Mart.

Fortunately, the world had already been changed. More than half of the United States (over 145 million people) is now wired into the Internet. Instead of the old stereotype of the Internet being the domain of pasty computer geeks, women came to outnumber men online in 2001, and seniors and young children were logging on in huge numbers. Homeless shelters began giving out email addresses and voice mail boxes along with hot meals and beds.

ODR is in a process of institution building, and even if it takes longer than originally assumed, everything is still in place to develop a global ODR system. Many of the projections made in advance of the economic slowdown still hold true, but their timeframe has been pushed out further into the future. Now that the economy appears to be turning around, the environment is once again ripe for the ODR field to continue its growth.

CHAPTER TWO

How ODR Works

For many people the idea of dispute resolution is appealing, but the practicalities of how it works are less clear. There is a stereotype that dispute resolution is all about people holding hands and singing "Kumbaya." Some business leaders have been heard to agree to participate in a dispute resolution process, only to warn the neutral that they are "not going to do any of that huggy-huggy stuff."

In reality dispute resolution is based on decades of practical work crafting tools and techniques that can help move parties toward agreement. There are dozens and dozens of these techniques, each of which has different advantages and disadvantages and each of which applies to different types of disputes. Processes can be as "huggy-huggy" or as unemotional as the participants desire. Some of the conflicts dealt with by dispute resolution techniques are as un-"huggy-huggy" as they come, like intransigent ethnic conflict or high-pressure labor management negotiations under the threat of a large-scale strike. The value of "Kumbaya" in such situations is highly debatable.

Many of the techniques that have been developed to help parties resolve their dispute display great creativity. The CEO of Southwest Airlines, when confronted with a dispute over an advertising slogan that was also being used by an aviation company in Florida, decided to challenge the other CEO to an arm wrestling contest to resolve the matter. Being somewhat scrawny, the CEO of Southwest Airlines was reasonably sure he would lose the contest, and therefore the slogan. But by turning the event into a media extravaganza, both companies received a lot of free advertising above and beyond the persuasive power of the disputed slogan. The creativity of the dispute resolution process chosen also helped to bolster the image of Southwest Airlines as a creative and fun company. Dealing with the conflict this way created value for both parties and turned a challenge into an opportunity.

The best way to describe how ODR works is to begin with the tools and techniques of ADR and to explain how those face-to-face techniques translate into the online environment. Some face-to-face concepts transfer easily to online practice, and others don't translate at all. ODR has also led to the development of wholly new tools and techniques for resolving disputes. This chapter details some of the new online practices and explains how they provide useful new tools in helping parties reach agreement. Arm wrestling is not one of the dispute resolution mechanisms described here, but creative approaches toward resolving disputes are often precisely what is required in achieving optimal outcomes to difficult disputes.

HOW DOES ADR WORK?

Put simply, practitioners of dispute resolution attempt to work out conflicts between individuals and organizations without resorting to the courts. Dispute resolution is sometimes referred to as "private justice" because it is a private alternative to the courts. ADR also focuses on having participants feel that a just resolution was achieved in their particular situation.

Dispute resolution practitioners put a very high priority on ethics in their service delivery because their credibility as an impartial and fair way to resolve disputes is essential to parties continuing to utilize them. Most organizations are scrupulous about hunting down any conflicts of interest because reputation is everything in dispute resolution. If a sense develops that a particular dispute resolution service provider is biased in one direction or another it can severely damage its credibility. This credibility is essential for the neutral to gain the confidence of disputants, and once damaged it is very difficult to repair.

A common misconception about ADR is that it just comes down to having the parties split the difference. Dispute resolution is not about achieving a compromise where the disputants merely meet in the middle. A core tenet of dispute resolution practice is that through *integrative* problem-solving (as opposed to *distributive* problem-solving) parties can often work together to "expand the pie" or to generate new value for both sides. The arm wrestling contest is an excellent example of integrative problem solving. Disputes are frequently framed as zero-sum, me-versus-you affairs where any gain enjoyed by one party comes at the expense of the other party. Dispute resolution programs and practitioners attempt to clarify the underlying needs of the parties to ensure that each side has their core concerns addressed in any agreed-upon resolution, which often leads to resolutions that are not purely zero-sum.

The tools and techniques of dispute resolution can be envisioned along a spectrum, ranging from options where the parties are totally in control of the process and the outcome to options where a third-party decision-maker is totally in control of both the process and the outcome. Almost every dispute resolution technique can be placed somewhere in between these extremes. Some of the tools are very prescriptive and regimented, and the decision-making power resides within a neutral third party who acts very much like a judge. In the tools on the other side of the spectrum, the parties retain all the control, though they might bring in a neutral third party to help them work out an agreement, even though that third party retains no decision-making authority (as you'll see in the figure below).

Over the years many different dispute resolution methods have been crafted to match the incredible variety of disputes and disputants that exist. The most basic dispute resolution techniques are:

- *Negotiation,* in which parties try to work out their dispute between themselves without outside assistance.

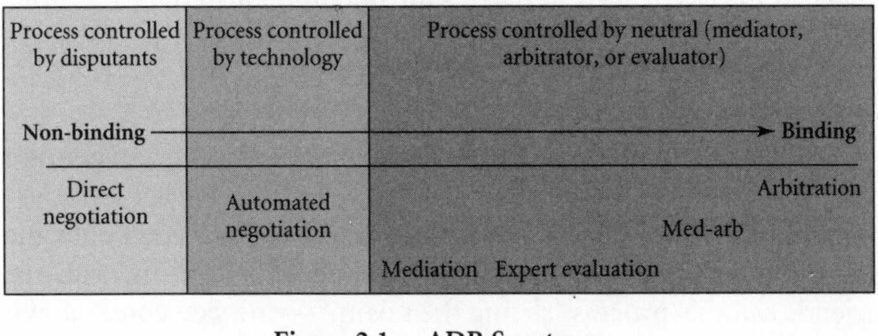

Process controlled by disputants	Process controlled by technology	Process controlled by neutral (mediator, arbitrator, or evaluator)
Non-binding ——————————————————————————————————————→ Binding		
Direct negotiation	Automated negotiation	Arbitration Med-arb Mediation Expert evaluation

Figure 2.1.   ADR Spectrum

- *Mediation,* in which parties work to resolve their disagreements with the assistance of a neutral third party who has no decision-making authority.

- *Arbitration,* in which parties make their case to a neutral third party who has decision-making authority.

These three mechanisms are the basic building blocks of almost all dispute resolution processes, so it's worthwhile to go into each in some detail.

Negotiation

Negotiation is the most simple and common form of dispute resolution. You negotiate with your kids about their bedtime, you negotiate with your boss about your raise, you negotiate with the car dealer about the purchase price for your new minivan. Negotiation is so common in day-to-day life that most of us don't even think about the fact that we're negotiating. Only in formal situations, like a business meeting or a house purchase, do we think strategically about how to negotiate most effectively. Even so, each one of us has a negotiating style that we use with others all day long. As the saying goes, in work as in life, you don't get what you deserve, you get what you negotiate.

All business deals involve some sort of negotiation, even if it's an internal dialogue. If the price for the can of peas is stuck right on the can in the grocery store the consumer still needs to make the internal decision that the price is an acceptable one. If they don't like it, they can go down the street to another store.

Negotiation is the root of all non-binding dispute resolution procedures. Negotiation theory provides the foundation for dispute resolution theory. The Harvard Program on Negotiation, a research institute at Harvard Law School, has housed the scholars that authored many of the classic texts in the dispute resolution field such as *Getting to Yes* (1991) by Roger Fisher and William Ury, the *Art and Science of Negotiation* (1985) by Howard Raiffa, and *Getting Past No* (1993) by William Ury.

In a pure negotiation, where there is no neutral body helping the disputants reach agreement, the two sides likely engage in a give-and-take discussion to move toward a mutually agreed-upon outcome (a price acceptable to both sides, for example). Some of my mediator friends call this process "slicing the salami"—one side comes down five dollars, the other side goes up five dollars. After a while, if the discussion goes well, the two sides meet somewhere in the middle.

This process seems almost laughably inefficient, as it would be much easier for some third party to just come in and choose a reasonable price between the two offers. But this give-and-take process is important to give the parties a sense that they are controlling their own destiny. If one side gets what it asks for too easily it can be the victim of the "winner's curse"—the thought that maybe their demand wasn't high enough and that they could have gotten more if they had started higher. If either party starts the bidding at a ridiculously high or low value they risk that the other side will be insulted and walk away from the negotiation. The back and forth, along with the posturing and strategy, assures the negotiators that they are doing everything they can to extract value from the situation. It gives them ownership of the outcome and buy-in to the process.

Face-to-face negotiation is usually fairly simple. Whether it's haggling in a Middle Eastern market or figuring out the sale price for a billion-dollar corporate acquisition, most negotiations follow roughly the same pattern. Researchers have discovered slight cultural differences in the way people negotiate, and those slight differences can result in major differences in outcomes if people don't understand them. For instance, there was a significant amount of research in the 1980s as to Japanese negotiating styles, as western businesspeople were engaging in a lot of negotiations with Japanese businesspeople. Putting time into learning about the negotiation styles of the other side can be time well spent. Planning your negotiation strategy before a negotiation begins (deciding on your target price and absolute reserve price, for example) can also pay off in getting good outcomes from your negotiations.

Mediation

Put simply, mediation is assisted negotiation. In a private disagreement the disputants always have the right to sit down unassisted to attempt to negotiate a resolution to their dispute. Quite often, though, the parties are unable to come to a satisfying agreement through negotiation, particularly in complex or high-stakes disputes. Because emotions can run high, and because both sides are being strategic in the way they conduct themselves in the negotiating process, it is very easy for a negotiation to run off the rails and for the participants to find themselves unable to reach agreement. In mediation, the parties retain the same decision-making power that they have in a negotiation process, but they involve a third party who helps manage the process. This third party, the mediator, has no decision-making power over the disputants and can't issue a binding decision. Instead, mediators work with the parties to facilitate communication, brainstorm ideas, and move the discussion toward agreement. No resolution is possible unless both parties agree to it, so both sides have veto power. The mediator's role is to keep the discussion focused and productive, so as to increase the likelihood that effective communication will take place and a resolution will be achieved.

The mediator is not affiliated with one side or the other in the dispute, so they have no vested interest in the outcome. This impartiality is a core function of the role of the mediator. The disputants will only accept the involvement of the mediator if they truly believe there is no bias toward one party or the other. The mediator has no decision-making power in the dispute, because his or her only role is to help focus the discussion on the key issues and minimize the unproductive communication so that the parties can achieve agreement. Because the mediator is there purely by consent of the parties, and the mediator has no decision-making authority, the parties can leave the mediation process or fire the mediator at any time with no penalty.

The mediator's task is a delicate one, as he or she is there only by consent of the parties and can be replaced at any time. Many mediators are very careful not to push the parties too hard in one direction or the other for fear that the parties will not feel ownership over the eventual resolution reached in the dispute. The mediator is often in charge of the process, and in that role serves primarily to facilitate communication between the parties but does not contribute substantive suggestions or evaluations of either side's points.

There are many different types of mediation, and each type of mediation has its own subtleties and particular way the process is conducted. However, most mediations follow the same basic blueprint. The mediator usually introduces the process to the disputants and lays down some basic ground rules about how the discussion will be conducted. Then the parties are given an opportunity to describe the situation from their perspectives. This first description is often uninterrupted, meaning the participants on one side can say everything they would like to say without being interrupted until they indicate that they are finished. Then the other side has the same opportunity, and they can describe the situation from their perspective without being interrupted. After each side says everything they want to say the mediator then engages in "assisted storytelling," where he or she asks questions of the disputants to gain more clarity on key aspects of the dispute. The goal of the mediator is to reveal the underlying issues in the dispute and help the parties reframe their positions so that a mutually satisfying outcome can be crafted. Once the issues in the dispute are brought to light, the parties can begin to propose possible resolutions to the disagreement, which the mediator can help to reality-test, ensuring that the solutions will hold up in the real world.

No resolution to the dispute can be adopted unless all of the participants in the process agreed to it. Mediation resolutions always require unanimous consent. A common misconception among disputants is that the mediator will be able to step in and make a decision for the parties if the process breaks down, or that the mediator will advocate for one perspective or another based on what he or she perceives to be correct. This is not the mediator's role. The mediator is there only to assist the parties in crafting their own resolution to the disputes, and the mediator has no decision-making authority. Mediators will scrupulously avoid any appearance that they are biased toward one side or the other, because it doesn't really matter what the mediator thinks is right or wrong. What matters is what the disputants think, because they are the ones who have to make the decision about how the matter will be resolved.

Being a mediator is not a simple task. The job is often described as equal parts art and science. It is not easy to work with two angry parties, who probably don't trust each other very much, in an attempt to get them to develop a robust and sustainable agreement. Some mediators have an innate ability to help people understand each other, and their involvement can be the catalyst that enables resolutions to emerge when there seems no possibility an agreement could ever be achieved. There is no ideal mediation style. Some mediators are very aggressive and challenging, like trial lawyers, focusing on the details in the dispute and pushing disputants on inconsistencies. Other mediators are much more reflective, like therapists or counselors, letting the parties go through their own exploration of the issues, and focusing on the relationship between the parties. Different styles fit different types of disputes and different types of disputants.

Arbitration

Arbitration can be most easily described as private judging. In an arbitration process, the disputants agree to transfer their decision-making authority to a neutral third party, who then determines the outcome to the dispute. The neutral third party hears the arguments from each side in the dispute, asks a few questions or examines a few pieces of evidence, and then renders a binding decision that resolves the matter in question.

Arbitration often works very much like the process in courtrooms, which means arbitrators often rely to a very great degree on the applicable law, relevant legal documents and contracts, and other precedent-setting decisions. For this reason, arbitrators are usually lawyers with legal expertise in the matters on which they are called in to decide.

Because the disputants have control over the arbitration process, they can make process choices that ensure that the arbitration is more efficient, effective, and tailored to the individual needs of the disputants than a court proceeding would be. Another advantage of utilizing an arbitrator is that the parties can choose a neutral who has extensive expertise in the subject matter at hand, which significantly lessens the amount of time required to bring an uninformed judge (or jury) up to speed in the matter. Arbitration processes can also be designed in a streamlined way, focusing the discussions immediately down to the core issues that need to be decided as opposed to playing many of the delay games that are inevitably a part of court proceedings. Some arbitrations are documents only, cutting off much of the posturing and positioning that takes place in face-to-face hearings.

Arbitrators play a very different role than mediators. Instead of merely facilitating the process, arbitrators are invested with the authority to eventually decide the outcome of the dispute. Each of the parties therefore needs to persuade the arbitrator that their position is correct so that the arbitrator will decide in their favor. Arbitrators may reality-test different outcomes with the disputants during the process, and they may even encourage the parties to try to resolve the matter themselves before the arbitrator issues a binding decision. But once the arbitrator takes it upon him or herself to render an opinion, the parties are often precommitted to abide by whatever the arbitrator decides. This leads to very different dynamic in an arbitration session than in a mediation session.

Sometimes arbitrators agree to render a decision that is not binding on the disputants. In these circumstances the arbitrator acts as more of an expert evaluator, hearing both sides of the dispute and rendering a nonbinding decision that the parties can choose to implement or ignore. Often expert evaluators are used in preparation for an eventual court proceeding, because the opinion of the expert evaluator may indicate the relative strengths and weaknesses of each side's position and foreshadow how a judge might interpret those arguments in a courtroom.

Med-Arb

Each of these techniques can be changed and adapted into different forms. Recently there has been a surge in the use of med-arb, which involves a neutral third party acting as a mediator through the early stages of a dispute, and then becoming an arbitrator at a later stage if the parties are unable to reach agreement during the mediation component. Some have expressed concerns about this technique, because parties work very differently with a mediator if they suspect that their mediator will at some point be evaluating their case and issuing a binding decision. Some dispute resolution systems are med-arb, but the arbitration decision rendered by the initial mediator is a nonbinding decision, and a different neutral needs to be secured if the parties elect to begin a binding arbitration process.

There are a great many specific techniques that can be applied in different types of disputes: expert evaluation, facilitation, mediation, evaluative mediation, bracketed arbitration, fact-findings, arb-med, and med-arb, just to name a few. All of these methods can be plotted on the graph in Figure 2.1. Each technique has its own strengths and weaknesses, and the best dispute resolution practitioners can mix and match these methods to create the optimal approach for resolving any particular dispute.

FROM ADR TO ODR

All of the tools, techniques, and roles described in the previous section on ADR are focused on one goal: helping people resolve their disputes out of court. Put simply, ODR is the application of technology to achieve the same goal. ODR can be as rudimentary as using email to set up a face-to-face meeting with a neutral, or as extensive as empaneling an online jury to hear a full set of formal arguments from attorneys representing the disputants. ODR can involve automated negotiation processes administered by a computer, or it can provide world-class experts to administer binding arbitration procedures. ODR systems can be legalistic and precedent-based, like the courts, or flexible exception-handling mechanisms to act as an extension to customer service efforts. ODR can be a multimillion dollar customer relationship management system or a $75 website set up to aid a mediator with the administration of a small case. Any use of technology to complement, support, or administer a dispute resolution process falls into the world of ODR.

ODR started out as the administration of ADR processes online. If the face-to-face mediation process involved three stages (such as unassisted storytelling, then assisted storytelling, then joint problem solving), then that was exactly what early online neutrals attempted to do. ODR was seen as a way to replicate face-to-face interaction when such interaction was not possible. In this framework, audio conferencing and videoconferencing were the logical next steps for the technology, as they more accurately replicated face-to-face interaction. As the technology improved (bandwidth became cheaper and more widely available, for example) ODR would improve, because the services would get closer to replicating "true" dispute resolution procedures.

Just like face-to-face ADR, ODR services represented the gamut of ADR possibilities, from direct negotiation to binding arbitration. Sometimes the neutral played a facilitative, non-judgmental role, and other times the neutral had absolute decision-making authority. The key tasks of the online mediator were the key tasks of the offline mediator: reframing the discussion, keeping the parties on track, and reality-testing proposed solutions. Arbitrations were even simpler: submit your briefs, examine the evidence, and render a decision. Documents-only arbitrations could take place without the benefit of a single face-to-face conversation between the neutral and the parties.

DIFFERENCES BETWEEN ODR AND ADR

As ODR services began to roll out, some new wrinkles to the technology emerged. Some of the mainstays of face-to-face dispute resolution practice did not translate well into the online environment, and some capabilities of online dispute resolution were entirely new. As researchers began to consider some of the new possibilities online dispute resolution presented for neutrals and disputants, technological innovations began to push the envelope for what was possible online.

In face-to-face dispute resolution all communication happens by voice, either in the same room or over the telephone. Occasionally one side or the other will submit a brief, such as in an arbitration, but the vast majority of communications are voice-based. Online it became clear that there were many different communication options available to neutrals and disputants, and each option had its own strengths and weaknesses. Technological platforms to support online dispute resolution procedures could often put a wide variety of these communication options at the disposal of the neutral to be mixed and matched as the neutral saw fit. Technological innovation was also constantly improving and adding features to each of these components. Soon it was clear that online dispute resolution had a rich array of component tools that could be combined into a custom process to meet the needs of a particular dispute.

Some dispute resolution professionals came to realize that ODR opened completely new possibilities for dispute resolution. Some of the functions that were relatively simple to conduct online were impractical at best for face-to-face dispute resolution, and probably functionally impossible. Technology-mediated dispute resolution was also impractical in a face-to-face setting. Online interaction opened up new possibilities by fundamentally changing the equation of how dispute resolution services could be administered.

Computer-Mediated Communication

The main difference between ODR and ADR was the role of technology in mediating the communication between the parties. In a face-to-face interaction there is a very familiar interface through which people can communicate, and the mediator or arbitrator has very little control over it. The parties look into each other's faces and read their expressions.

Online, the neutral is given much greater control over the process. The platform might allow for video and audio conferencing or it might limit the parties to static pictures of each other's faces. It might make the communication between the parties public, or involve the participation of neutral third parties. It might use mathematical algorithms to help the parties focus on their underlying needs as opposed to their positions. It also might give them access to reference materials relevant to the dispute to ensure that they are informed about the facts under discussion.

The role of technology in administering a dispute resolution process was almost entirely new in dispute resolution. It had been contemplated in earlier computer programs intended to supplement face-to-face procedures, but once the parties interacted primarily through computers there was the potential to build an entirely new environment to frame the parties' movement toward resolution. Before, the neutral could do little more than arrange the room and table as everyone liked and ask questions to help the parties make progress. Online, however, the neutral could completely redesign and reshape the environment the parties found themselves in. The burdens of this responsibility were both exciting and overwhelming, as few neutrals had any idea how to build an online environment that would help their parties come to agreement.

TYPES OF ONLINE COMMUNICATION

The first challenge confronting ODR platform designers and neutrals is choosing among the different types of online communication. Each option creates a very different dynamic in the dispute resolution process. It could be that the parties agree that mediation is the best methodological approach for resolving their particular dispute, but the neutral still needs to determine which communication options would best fit with the needs of the disputants and would most effectively urge the process toward resolution. Mediation over email is qualitatively different than mediation in a chat room, which are both entirely different than mediation over a videoconference.

Understanding the different online communication options is essential to being able to design appropriate ODR systems. The range of dispute resolution types and the multiple tools that have arisen to match different dispute needs parallel the range of online communication types. Instead of merely choosing an ADR process, ODR designers need to choose both a process and a communication venue. Different online dispute resolution platform designers have chosen different communication options, and the resulting systems are almost entirely different from a practice perspective.

The different ways people can communicate online can be viewed along a spectrum, ranging from low-bandwidth asynchronous to high-bandwidth synchronous (see Figure 2.2).

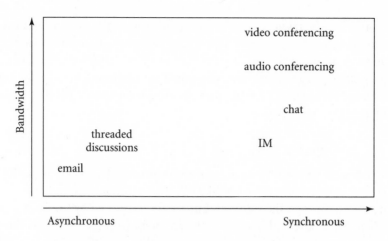

Figure 2.2.   Online Communication Options

Synchronous and Asynchronous Communications

One way that online interaction completely changed the dispute resolution process was in the way it changed the participant's notion of time. Most people don't interact at the same time over the Internet. Many of the communication technologies used online were actually designed to allow people to log on as they like throughout the day. Email, for instance, allows parties to send and receive messages whenever it's convenient for them to do so, as opposed to the phone, which requires you to use it at the same time the other party is using it.

These two communication methods are synchronous and asynchronous communication. *Synchronous* is when you and the other party are communicating in "real-time," and you are expected to respond to the other side as soon as they finish making their comments. Phone and face-to-face interactions are both synchronous communications.

Asynchronous communication is when you and the other party are not communicating at the same time. When you get a message from the other side you are not expected to respond immediately. Sending letters back and forth through the mail is asynchronous, and posting messages on an online bulletin board or discussion forum is also asynchronous.

In face-to-face dispute resolution processes, there is no choice about how the parties will communicate. The only option used is in-person or over-the-telephone synchronous voice communication. When online, however, selecting which type of communication mechanism should be used becomes an important part of the neutral's planning and design process. The basic types of online communication each have strengths and weaknesses that neutrals can evaluate in designing an online dispute resolution process most appropriate for the needs of a particular dispute.

Email

The lowest bandwith online communication option is email. Email messages operate very much like offline written letters, but they are delivered through the Internet. Emails are composed by the sender at his or her leisure and sent off to the recipient with the understanding that the messages will get there eventually. As every user of email knows, sometimes an email can reach the recipient in a minute or two, but occasionally an email takes hours if not days to arrive.

Email is the most popular Internet application for several reasons:

- It is very easy to understand and use, as most people understand how it compares to the traditional postal mail system.
- Content that comes in through email is usually very personalized, as it is intended for a single recipient.
- Email does not require a high bandwidth connection. Most messages are text-only, which means they require little time to download.
- It's easy to send emails, so users can establish networks where they are exchanging messages among their friends and family on a weekly or daily basis.
- Unlimited email is included for free with most Internet access plans.

Email is usually sent between two people, but it is easy to add others into the "To:" field of an email message, so email can also serve a simple conferencing function. Increasingly newsletters are being sent out over email, which essentially means a long distribution list of email addresses (hundreds if not thousands) are being inserted into the "To:" field.

Another aspect of email that many users like is that the recipient is in charge of deciding when email will be handled. In contrast, when the phone rings, the expectation is usually that the recipient of the call will pick it up, regardless of what they are doing at that moment. When email comes in there is no immediate expectation that the user will stop whatever they are doing to check on the new messages.

Email is a low-bandwidth, asynchronous communication option. It is much closer to the exchanging of postcards than to a face-to-face conversation. Its use has dominated Web traffic since the beginning of networking, so clearly users have found that communication through email is engaging, enjoyable, and valuable. Because so many alternatives to email have been developed email clearly does not meet every need.

Discussion Environments

Email programs are capable of supporting communication between multiple parties, but beyond three or four participants things can get very confusing. Messages often cross over each other, leading to confusion about which line of conversation is the active one. Documents can be included with emails, but if two people edit a document at the same time and circulate their edits it becomes difficult to figure out which is the most up-to-date copy. It also starts to get confusing as to which message is intended for the whole group and which message is intended for a particular person or group of people.

The way most multiparty conversations are handled on the Internet is through a discussion environment. Many of these environments work either hand-in-hand with or through email, such as Listservs or Usenet groups. These solutions are often chosen or supported because they allow anyone on the Internet to participate, as they require little bandwidth and are easy to maintain and access. More powerful discussion environments are presented as Web pages where information is aggregated into a framework organized by topic and time.

Discussion environments often look like a string of email messages placed one after another. The easiest way to do this is to post the messages in order, ranked by when they were written. This results in a list of messages arranged first to last. There are some problems with this structure, however. If a user wants to reply to a point raised in a message that was posted several messages ago, they have to explain to what they are referring, which can get complicated. The conversation may have moved on, and when one message is referring to a thread from four messages back, and the next is addressing a different point, the discussion quickly becomes difficult to follow.

This problem was addressed through the creation of threaded discussion environments (see below). In a threaded environment, it is possible for many different topics to sit side-by-side in a discussion, grouped apart from the other topics. For example, if someone raises a point of interest, you can respond directly to that message, even if other messages have been posted since the point was made. Your response stays connected to the message it was replying to, so there's no need to explain how to find the message you are addressing. Even if a thousand new messages are posted in the discussion, your reply will always stay connected to the message you were addressing.

Threaded discussions are powerful because they keep a record of an entire line of conversation. If a newcomer joins a discussion halfway through it is easy for her to start at the beginning and to read all of the messages that have already been posted, allowing her to get up to speed. Threaded discussions also allow parties in a dispute to break out all of the individual components of their conflict into different areas, so each can be addressed on its own merits. Segmenting a face-to-face conversation into different components can be very difficult.

Discussion environments are as asynchronous as email, but may require more bandwidth because they use Web pages with graphics.

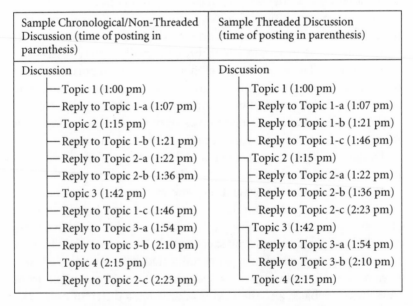

Sample Chronological/Non-Threaded Discussion (time of posting in parenthesis)	Sample Threaded Discussion (time of posting in parenthesis)
Discussion — Topic 1 (1:00 pm) — Reply to Topic 1-a (1:07 pm) — Topic 2 (1:15 pm) — Reply to Topic 1-b (1:21 pm) — Reply to Topic 2-a (1:22 pm) — Reply to Topic 2-b (1:36 pm) — Topic 3 (1:42 pm) — Reply to Topic 1-c (1:46 pm) — Reply to Topic 3-a (1:54 pm) — Reply to Topic 3-b (2:10 pm) — Topic 4 (2:15 pm) — Reply to Topic 2-c (2:23 pm)	Discussion Topic 1 (1:00 pm) — Reply to Topic 1-a (1:07 pm) — Reply to Topic 1-b (1:21 pm) — Reply to Topic 1-c (1:46 pm) Topic 2 (1:15 pm) — Reply to Topic 2-a (1:22 pm) — Reply to Topic 2-b (1:36 pm) — Reply to Topic 2-c (2:23 pm) Topic 3 (1:42 pm) — Reply to Topic 3-a (1:54 pm) — Reply to Topic 3-b (2:10 pm) — Topic 4 (2:15 pm)

Figure 2.3.   Comparison between Non-threaded and Threaded Discussion

Discussion environments also usually contain much more information than email exchanges, because one discussion can have dozens and dozens of participants.

Instant Messaging

A step up the synchronous ladder from email and discussion forums is instant messaging (IM). Popular instant messaging programs include AOL Instant Messenger, ICQ (pronounced *I-seek-you*), and MSN Messenger. These programs are similar to email in that they allow text messages to be sent between users. However, instant messaging programs take much less time to get the communication from one party to another. Most often the recipient will see the sender's message within a few seconds of its being sent. This allows for much more back-and-forth than in an email exchange. The expectation of the sender of an instant message is that they will get back an immediate response, whereas email senders rarely expect an immediate response.

Unlike email, in which a user has to start up his email program and check for new messages to see if anything has come in, IM programs often run in the background of a user's computer system, waiting silently for new messages. Once a message does arrive, the program can either notify the user that a new message is waiting (either with a flashing icon on the screen or a sound) or just pop the message up on the user's screen. This allows a back-and-forth exchange to begin.

A side application to IM are buddy lists. Because IM senders often want to know who is online and available to receive a message, all of the major IM programs allow users to see a list of their frequent IM exchange partners with an icon indicating their status (for example, not logged in, logged in but away from her desk, not accepting instant messages, or logged in and ready to receive messages). This list allows Internet users to gather around a "virtual watercooler" where conversations can start up among the people who are available.

Usage statistics on IM programs show that they are starting to get enough traffic to rival email as the communication tool of choice. Conversations frequently arise from IM sessions, which leads to a much more in-depth exchange of information than can be communicated through one or two email exchanges. IM programs also require more bandwidth than email programs, and they take a heavier toll on Web servers (though still almost nothing compared with multimedia applications like audio and video).

Chat Rooms

The line is blurring between instant messaging (IM) and chatting, as many IM programs now have a button a user can push if they would like to begin a chat session with the other side. From a communication dynamics standpoint, however, chat rooms are significantly different than IM.

In most IM interactions a user receives a message, composes a reply, and clicks "send" to transmit the reply to the other side. The other side then receives the fully composed message. In chat sessions, the other side can usually watch you compose your reply keystroke-by-keystroke. Often they will be able to start responding to your message before you even finish it. Even if the other side can't see each keystroke as it is typed, the exchanges are usually depicted in a single window, one after another.

Chat exchanges are more synchronous than IM exchanges because they happen in real time. There is no delay between messages exchanged, or even during message composition, so it is closer to a face-to-face conversation than an IM exchange. Chat communications are still textual, though, which makes synchronous communication more complicated. There is an incentive to make one's points short, as the other side can start responding before the prior message is sent. Chat interactions quickly deteriorate into short, clipped, back-and-forth exchanges as opposed to more well thought out, fully developed exchanges.

Another aspect of chat communication is that the person who types faster has a major advantage. If one side types thirty words per minute and the other types ninety words per minute the latter party can get in three words for every one of the other side. There will undoubtedly be delays as one side or the other makes their points, but the thirty-words-per-minute party will probably get frustrated as he struggles to keep up with all the points coming from the other side. This frustration will likely degrade the quality of the discussion as well, as the parties become more focused on getting their points in than thinking through what they really want to say.

Audio Conferencing

The telephone is widely used in face-to-face dispute resolution because of its convenience. While there are no visual cues available over a telephone conversation, much can be gleaned from voice-only meetings. Many mediators and arbitrators rely on the phone for in-between meetings, or for short discussions focusing on a single point. The telephone is completely synchronous, meaning all communication happens in real time. Participants on a telephone call are expected to respond immediately, much like a face-to-face interaction. In addition, telephone calls can be quite expensive, especially teleconferences involving multiple parties.

Audio conferencing over the Internet isn't quite as good as the traditional telephone. Audio requires quite a bit of bandwidth, and many Internet users still do not have access to adequate bandwidth connections that might enable them to use audio conferencing software effectively. The Internet also suffers from latency, so when one user makes a comment it takes a few seconds for that comment to reach the other side. This results in participants stepping on each other's comments and talking over one another. When parties are emotional or angry this slight time disconnect can be very frustrating to all involved, and it can prevent the parties from listening to each other.

Video Conferencing

Video has been considered the ultimate ODR technology. Once parties can see each other and the neutral, some observers have reasoned, little incentive remains to ever bother getting together face-to-face.

Having experimented with videoconferencing extensively, it is important to be honest and to observe that even at the high end it lags far behind a face-to-face interaction. Perhaps it's the color difference when someone appears on a monitor, or just the distance of having the other side flat on a screen in front of you instead of in flesh-and-blood, but even the best video conferencing does not replace the need for face-to-face interaction.

Internet-based video conferencing is still fairly primitive, though it has been around for almost a decade. Bandwidth limitations and data latency, both of which are frustrating in audio conferencing, are even more frustrating in video conferencing. Video cameras that can be attached to computers have become very cheap, costing between $50 and $100. It is important to note that the cameras are not the problem. Fundamental shortcomings in the current architecture of the Web make Internet Protocol (IP)-based videoconferencing impractical for application in most professional dispute resolution processes.

Dedicated videoconferencing hardware from companies like PictureTel and Polycom provide a much higher-quality video conferencing experience. Instead of relying exclusively on the Internet, these dedicated pieces of hardware can often use other networks (like ISDN connections) to circumvent the latency problem. These solutions are usually much more expensive than IP-based videoconferencing. Entry-level, set-top units often cost $500 or more, with conference-room systems reaching into the tens of thousands of dollars. These solutions may be appropriate between businesses or inside corporations, but most individual consumers would not be able or willing to pay these costs for videoconferencing.

The technology of video conferencing is also not yet seamless. Time is frequently spent figuring out someone's microphone, or adjusting a camera, or configuring a computer to operate effectively. Advances have been made in this technology, but fundamental shortcomings of the Internet will likely keep video conferencing a niche technology for some time.

Video is the ultimate synchronous, high-bandwidth online communication mechanism. Once the Internet is capable of supporting full-motion, thirty-frames-per-second video there will undoubtedly be demands for larger screens and sharper resolution. One video conference can take up the same amount of bandwidth as tens of thousands of email interactions.

Matching Communication Options with Disputes

The primary change online dispute resolution brings to ADR is the ability to control the communication environment within which the parties interact. The application of different online communication options to dispute resolution changed the nature of the interaction between the parties and created new options that neutrals need to consider when they design a dispute resolution process for a particular dispute.

However, the spectrum of communication options, as dramatic a change as it represented for the practice of ADR, was not the only change technology brought to the practice of dispute resolution. Those experimenting with ODR began to understand that technology could play an even greater role in helping parties move toward agreement, one that in the past had been reserved only for humans.

ENVISIONING THE "FOURTH PARTY"

Ethan Katsh and Janet Rifkin introduced the concept of technology as the "fourth party" in their book *Online Dispute Resolution* (2001). Neutrals are often referred to as "third parties" in a dispute because they are the third participants in the process, in addition to the two disputants. When ODR is introduced, the technology can also play a major role in managing the process and setting the agenda, so in a metaphorical sense the technology becomes the fourth party.

This idea is important because it indicates the significant role technology can play in guiding disputants toward agreement. Technology is not just about replicating face-to-face interactions as accurately as possible. There are many benefits to face-to-face communication, but sometimes other modes of communication may be a better fit with the needs of the disputants. In addition to facilitating the process, as face-to-face neutrals do, online practitioners need to think through the various communication options available and design a communication environment that can best address the issues under discussion and the dynamic between the parties.

ODR system designers came to realize that in addition to playing a crucial role in shaping the environment housing the parties' interaction, ODR technology could also play a facilitative role in and of itself. New methods for helping parties reach agreement began to appear online, methods that didn't require a human's involvement to operate. This development was significant because many of the rules that had been developed regarding effective and efficient ADR practice presumed that the process was being run by a human. The rules were constructed the way they were in order to combat human tendencies to be biased, inefficient, erratic, or to make snap decisions. If the process instead was being run by a machine, and that machine was merely working through the steps in a program, then the challenges were entirely different. The machine would execute the steps programmed into it, but the program and the programmer took on a new significance. There was less of a problem with bias arising during the dispute resolution process and more a problem of bias in the way the program was constructed.

Automated Negotiation

While face-to-face negotiations are usually fairly uniform, online negotiations can vary widely. ODR environments have the power to change the frame of the negotiation significantly. Online negotiation can parallel face-to-face negotiation by putting the parties into an unstructured communication environment, which simply uses technology as the communication medium for a traditional process. Online negotiation can also place parties into automated negotiation procedures, which use algorithms to drive the negotiation process. If both parties assent to using an automated algorithm to handle their dispute, sometimes resolution can be reached much more quickly than would be possible under any face-to-face process.

Offline automated negotiation is very rare because it is difficult to conduct, and usually it doesn't have much value for the participants. Online automated processes, on the other hand, can be very effective and efficient, because they create a structure for the negotiation and can help to focus deliberations on the crux of dispute, stripping out posturing and delay tactics that do little more than waste time.

Solution Set Databases

Mediators are often reluctant to suggest possible resolutions to disputants because it may put them in the situation of advocating a particular solution to the dispute. Later, if the solution doesn't work out, the parties might blame the mediator for pushing the option on them. As a result, parties are often left to their own devices to come up with resolutions to their disputes, even if the mediator has seen dozens of similar disputes before.

Computers are less concerned with perceptions of bias in situations like this one. Because the computer is just following its programming instructions there is little concern that advancing a particular solution will result in a perception of "bias" on the part of the technology. A computer will put options on the table, but because it is incapable of playing any advocacy role in the dispute resolution process it need not be concerned with being blamed later for pushing an option on the disputants.

One result of this dynamic is the integration of solution set databases into ODR platforms. In the simplest incarnation, solution set programs merely ask disputants what type of dispute they are engaged in. When the disputant specifies a dispute type, the ODR platform can display a list of common resolutions to that type of dispute. The disputant can then indicate which of the solutions would be acceptable to them, and then the platform can share that information with the other party. If the other party agrees to one of the proposed resolutions, then the matter is settled.

In their advanced incarnations, these solution set databases are learning systems. New dispute types can be continuously entered into the database, and new resolutions can be added as well. When new disputes enter the platform, the system can ask questions about dispute types it has never heard of before, and then match resolutions achieved with the new dispute types. In this manner the database is constantly growing and evolving, and the lessons learned over multiple disputes can benefit future disputants.

This type of function could not be played by a human mediator because of concerns about bias, misrepresentation, advocacy, and impartiality. But a computer can easily play this role. Once a system such as this one grows sophisticated, it may replace the need for many human mediators. SquareTrade, the ODR provider working with eBay, has reported that a simple solution set system they have deployed, working roughly as described here, resolves almost 80 percent of their incoming disputes without requiring human intervention.

Blind Bidding or Automated Arbitration

Some ODR companies have emerged to offer a single kind of dispute resolution process: a blind-bidding process, in which an automated algorithm evaluates bids from each party and if the two bids are within a prescribed range (for example, 30 percent) then the case settles for the median. If the cases are not within the prescribed amount, then the bids are destroyed and neither side knows what the other proposed. Both parties are fully informed as to the way the process works before it begins, and they agree to abide by the outcome if one is reached.

Blind-bidding processes can work better on the Internet than they do face-to face. In a courtroom or mediation, the mediator can give information away by his or her facial expressions, or even a meaningful sigh. On the Internet, once the process is automated in a software program, there is no opportunity for that type of secondary communication. Parties can submit bids and get outcomes without tipping their hand at all; if no resolution is reached, neither side has any more information than they had before the process began.

Most ethical rules for dispute resolution practice argue that the fee charged for a dispute resolution process cannot be contingent on the outcome of the case. It is not difficult to see how the actions of a mediator could be affected by such conditional compensation. A mediator may have an incentive to push for an inequitable settlement because she will only be paid if agreement is reached. Mediators might also attempt to lower the expectations of parties to make agreement more likely.

In an automated system, however, the rationale behind this rule is weakened. If the process is coded into software, then it will always be the same, no matter how the pricing is structured. Incentives that may create problems in a human-managed ADR process may not cause problems in software-coded online processes. Online ADR providers offering blind-bidding mechanisms have used this defense, combined with complete up-front disclosure, to justify the conditional pricing model. If the system is always the same, as a human mediator cannot be, then the concern raised in traditional ADR standards should not apply.

There is much less unpredictability in an automated, algorithm-based arbitration process than in a process reliant on a human arbitrator. There is also much less flexibility. The participants must be willing to have their dispute reduced to a single variable, money, to participate in this process. If the participants are willing to make that sacrifice, however, blind-bidding systems can be very efficient and effective.

Multivariable Resolution Optimization Programs

The most sophisticated fourth parties currently in use are the multivariable resolution optimization programs. These programs allow disputants to detail all of the issues in their dispute, and then to weigh their relative importance. They also elicit the value of swaps between the different items, numerically tracking all of this information on both sides of the dispute. The programs then allow the disputants to generate different proposals to be presented to the other side. After several proposals, armed with all of the relative preference and valuation data from both sides, the platform can deliver a mathematically optimal solution to the dispute, maximizing the benefit that can be achieved for both parties based on the preferences they registered. This is the best resolution that can be achieved, something that no human mediator or arbitrator could ever identify without the assistance of technology.

The most developed and easiest to use of all of these programs is SmartSettle, though SmartSettle still advises disputants to work with a human mediator who administers the program and helps to facilitate the preference registration and proposal exchanges. SmartSettle has come a long way toward user-friendliness over the years, but it is still too complicated for the average user to easily understand. Once a user takes the time to learn how the program works, however, it is staggering in its ramifications. Eventually technology such as Smart-Settle will be repackaged in a way that is simple and user-friendly, and such tools may revolutionize dispute resolution.

Online Transactions Are Disputes, and Marketplaces Are Dispute Resolvers

Taken a step higher, all online commercial transactions can be viewed as disputes. Buyers and sellers have diverging interests, yet they do want to complete their transactions. The incredible variety of transaction models that has emerged on the Web can all be viewed as dispute resolution mechanisms for getting buyers and sellers to come to agreement on a mutually acceptable set of terms for their transaction. An excellent paper by Christopher Hobson in the July 1999 *Negotiation Journal* analyzed a variety of online commerce websites from the perspective of negotiation theory and found a staggering array of possibilities.

Take eBay, for example, the largest auction in the world. At any given time eBay can have more than two million items for sale on its website. The company's negotiation environment is very simple. Sellers post items for sale that are bid upon by a large pool of buyers. Sellers can post their minimum reserve price, below which they are not willing to sell the item, or they can have no reserve, meaning they will sell it at the lowest price no matter what that price is. Buyers then bid against each other over a period of days or weeks, with the item going to the highest bidder. In this environment, the seller and the buyer are not negotiating directly—the seller is having buyers negotiate against each other in a structured transaction environment.

Priceline.com, another e-commerce site, is a different negotiation example. On Priceline, buyers post the price that they want to pay for an item and Priceline tries to find the item at that price. Priceline insists on a certain amount of flexibility in the item to be delivered, however. For instance, if a buyer posts a price for an airline ticket, Priceline requires that a) the buyer be bound to accept any ticket that Priceline comes up with that matches the expressed needs of the buyer, and b) the buyer does not have the ability to choose what times the flight takes off and lands, only the day of arrival and departure. In this negotiation system the power to set a price, usually held by the seller, is transferred to the buyer, but the seller then has more flexibility as to the specifics of the delivered good.

When viewed from the perspective of dispute analysis, the possibilities for structuring online transactions appear almost infinite. The innovations in online marketplace design can all be viewed as innovations in online dispute resolution. By engaging in this type of analysis, designers of online transaction environments can shape their processes to leverage the positive aspects of commercial conflict (moving toward efficient market outcomes and more accurate pricing) and avoid the negative aspects (irrational escalation, retaliation, and participant withdrawal).

The Fourth Party Is Brand New

While the field of ODR has made significant progress thinking through the ramifications of different communication options on the delivery of dispute resolution services, the consideration of this second application area of technology to dispute resolution, technology as the fourth party, has only just begun. Whether we will ever see computer programs capable of adjudicating complex disputes, or walking parties through a mediation to resolution, seems like the stuff of science fiction at this point. But even with the primitive state of our current technology we have seen some very effective first steps in this direction. One day our courtrooms may have a computer in the judge's chair.

Just like the challenges facing dispute resolution practitioners, the challenges facing designers of ODR processes are subtle and complex. If ODR technology is carefully designed and thoughtfully applied, it can be an essential component in helping parties reach optimal resolutions to their disputes. If it is misapplied and poorly designed, it can be a major obstacle to reaching agreement. In the next chapter we analyze some of the powerful advantages of well done ODR, as well as some of the pitfalls that can haunt applications of technology to ADR that are not as carefully thought out and executed.

CHAPTER THREE

Advantages of ODR

T he key factor motivating disputants, neutrals, businesses, non-profits, governments, and international organizations to call for ODR are the clear benefits it offers them. As the tools and technology underlying ODR continue to evolve, and as awareness of ODR continues to spread, the inertia behind its implementation builds. The more the promise of online dispute resolution is examined the clearer its benefits become.

It is important to note that online dispute resolution offers many of the advantages of traditional face-to-face dispute resolution. Resolutions can be reached more quickly, and at less cost. Matters can be kept confidential. Costs are much lower. Future complaints are avoided because relationships are maintained and strengthened. Disputants are more satisfied with both the process and the outcome. Resolutions are more creative. Enforcement is less of a challenge, because the disputants have ownership over the resolution. All of these benefits are as true in face-to-face dispute resolution as they are in online dispute resolution. As they have been exhaustively covered elsewhere, and bolstered by extensive research, I won't go into detail about them here, but they are important and compelling reasons on their own to implement ODR.

In addition to those benefits of dispute resolution generally, however, ODR offers important new benefits to everyone involved in a dispute:

- Disputants benefit from online dispute resolution environments custom tailored to the needs of their particular situation. They have more time to think about how they want to respond, they are not as easily intimidated or bullied, they have easy access to information, and they can spend as much time as they like working individually with the neutral.

- Neutrals are given a whole new set of tools they can use in helping their parties reach agreement. They can hold private caucuses at the same time the joint meeting is occurring. Their coaching and reframing can be much more effective, as they can work with the disputants before, during, and after key communications, as opposed to just reacting to developments after they've taken place. They can constantly gauge their parties to determine how close the dispute is to resolution, as opposed to playing guessing games.

- Businesses benefit from an ability to address disputes much earlier than is possible through traditional face-to-face dispute resolution. ODR creates feedback loops that help businesses continuously improve their transaction models and customer service. It also helps to shield them from frivolous litigation, and to demonstrate an intention to "do right" by customers and partners.

This chapter discusses the many benefits ODR can bring to all players in a dispute resolution process, as well as some of the pitfalls. ODR has the power to completely transform the landscape of a dispute, and when used effectively, that power can be the difference between the parties reaching agreement or reaching an impasse.

ADVANTAGES FOR DISPUTANTS

First and foremost, ODR must provide significant advantages to disputants. If disputants sense that ODR only benefits neutrals and organizations then disputants will stay away, and the tools will never be used. Fortunately, ODR has many clear and compelling advantages for parties.

Speed

The main advantage of online dispute resolution, and the one that brings the majority of parties to it, is speed. On the Internet, people have come to expect that everything they need should be available to them twenty-four hours a day, seven days a week. When someone wants information or services or support they often expect that on the Internet they should be able to get it whenever they want, even if it's 2 A.M. on Sunday. Traditional judicial systems are built with the exact opposite intention. Delay is used intentionally to encourage people to reflect, or to ensure that people are serious and determined to reach a resolution. Even face-to-face dispute resolution systems have begun to take longer and longer, particularly formal procedures like arbitration.

Online dispute resolution, on the other hand, can move very quickly because scheduling meetings and planning for travel and finding space are not necessary to convening and beginning an online process. A virtual meeting room can be opened instantaneously and a neutral can be engaged from anywhere around the world. This means that in online dispute resolution the parties' expectation of instant availability and fast, efficient service can be met. For most disputants, this is the most compelling reason to utilize online dispute resolution, because their overriding desire is to resolve the matter quickly.

Asynchronous Interaction

Face-to-face dispute resolution must happen in "real time" as each side reacts immediately to new developments. A mediator can call a "time out" or use a caucus to break up this flow, but in most joint meetings and discussions disputants must engage in a give-and-take where their responses are expected right away. In the lingo of computer-mediated communication, this is *synchronous* interaction, as was discussed in the prior chapter.

Online parties, however, have the possibility of *asynchronous* interaction, where their response is not expected immediately. Disputants can connect to the ongoing discussion at different times, and even defer their response until after they've had time to consult with others, do some research, or just contemplate the situation.

As Jim Melamed has observed, this ability to interact asynchronously can help parties to "be at their best" in a mediation.[1] Instead of reacting emotionally to a new development or escalating a discussion out of surprise, parties can consider an issue and communicate in a considered way. They can still react emotionally, but they have the option of stepping back and reflecting before they respond.

Power Differentials

One of the most interesting advantages online dispute resolution can offer disputants is the way it changes the nature of their communication. When a dispute arises between two people who have a relationship from a prior context the disputants can get into certain communication patterns that reinforce the disagreement they find themselves involved in. Usually relationships reflect some sort of power equation between the participants, such as between a supervisor and supervisee, between husband and wife, or between a professor and student. This power dynamic affects the communication between the two parties. It may be that the more powerful party is accustomed to speaking uninterrupted, or is accustomed to not having her points aggressively questioned. The party that perceives himself as less powerful may unconsciously participate in this communication dynamic. Or, alternatively, the party that feels less powerful may feel the need to be more aggressive or very defensive to counteract what he perceives as the advantages of the more powerful opponent.

Online communication often changes this dynamic. Research into the use of email in organizations has found that lower-level employees are willing to send emails to upper management with comments and observations that they would be uncomfortable saying in person. I've spoken with parents who had a very difficult time communicating with their children when they are in the same house, yet after they send their children off to college, a rich email correspondence began. The parent and child were not able to communicate face-to-face partially because of the power dynamic between the two of them. Many husbands and wives get into similar communication patterns based on the relative power in their relationship, and when they begin to communicate textually through an online interface it's different enough from the normal modes of communication that they're able to break out of those patterns.

Neutrals can learn to use the newness of online communication patterns to the process's advantage by helping people reevaluate unproductive modes of communication and build new communication channels in conjunction with their exploration of online communication options. Skilled facilitators can exploit ODR tools to combat calcified relationships and repair broken lines of communication. People in relationships based on past power differentials can communicate on more of a level playing field when online communication options are brought into the picture.

Research

In a face-to-face dispute resolution process, the two parties are often sitting at a table looking at each other over little more than a pad, a pencil, and a few documents. In the course of that dispute resolution process, the disputants will exchange lots of facts. Sometimes it is very difficult for one side or the other to confirm or deny the veracity of the facts provided by the other side. For example, in a dispute between a computer supplier and a business owner, the computer supplier could say in a face-to-face dispute resolution process that the cost of the raw motherboard in each of the machines provided to the business was $500 apiece. The business owner who purchased these machines may not have any idea if that number is wildly high or wildly low. In a face-to-face dispute resolution process, that business owner would probably have to respond to that estimate with a guess about its veracity. If that valuation is crucial to crafting a resolution to the dispute, it may be that later when the business owner finds out that price was inaccurate, he or she will feel that they agreed to an unfair resolution.

In an online dispute resolution process, however, it's a simple matter for participants to conduct research in the middle of the process. If a representation is made by one side about the cost of a component or the value of an item, the other side can easily verify the cost over the Internet. Once that research is conducted, she can even share that research with the other participants by providing a Web address. This ability to conduct research as the dispute resolution process is occurring provides an important reality check to any resolutions that are being considered by the disputants. It also guarantees that any agreements that are reached will stand up to later scrutiny because the parties were fully informed at the time the agreement was being crafted.

Cooling Distance

Because of the asynchronous nature of online communication and the lack of face-to-face immediacy, online communication is often less likely to escalate to accusations, name calling, and violence than face-to-face communication. In addition to simply having more time to think about what you want to say, the emotional heat that can be generated by face-to-face confrontation is less intense in online interaction. This dynamic has come to be called *cooling distance*. In online interactions, the temporal and physical distance between the parties can help to cool hot tempers and to keep disputes from escalating.

The only time I ever feared for my safety in a mediation was when I oversaw a dispute between two couples over a luxury car that one couple had sold to the other. Tempers escalated in the room and snide comments were passed between people when it wasn't their turn to speak, even though I was doing my best to stop the interruptions. Soon insults were hurled, accusations were thrown, and the two husbands got up to throw some punches. Like any good mediator, I positioned myself between them and mentioned the fact that I wore glasses and they wouldn't want to punch me, or something similarly brave. The heat in that room was impossible to control. The parties were ready to fight when they came into the room.

In an online process, this type of provocative finger pointing and snide commentary is not possible. Because communications are textual, communications must be delivered directly. Also, because physical violence is impossible through online communication, that ultimate threat is removed. It is of course possible for parties to be insulting in online communication, but the heat and the immediacy that leads to rapid escalation, along with the risk of violence, is much less likely. This is a result of the cooling distance provided by online, textual, asynchronous communication. In certain types of disputes, this cooling distance can be invaluable if not essential to helping the parties maintain a respectful dialogue.

More Reflective Communication

One of the goals of the dispute resolution profession is to help disputants reflect on why they feel the way they do in a particular dispute situation, why they want what they're asking for, and what they really need to be satisfied with the resolution to the matter. Sometimes it's very difficult to get the parties to communicate why they are frustrated in a particular situation. Often the disputant walks in with a particular demand and refuses to rethink that demand. The only thing that will satisfy him, he says, is getting that one thing. Much of the work a mediator does may be asking the party to step back and think more broadly about other ways the matter can be resolved. Online communication, by its very nature, encourages this kind of reflection. As people draft their written comments they are naturally forced to answer the question "why?"

In writing, people have more of the tendency to explain why they are saying what they're saying, whereas in face-to-face communications people often just state their position and cross their arms, refusing to elaborate further. Because online communication encourages reflection, mediators often find it easier to have parties think about why the dispute came about and what they really need to resolve the matter at hand.

Self-disclosure—Race, Sex, and Age

One of the most difficult aspects of human nature to deal with is the problem of bias. Different people are biased by different things. For example, some people may be biased on the basis of race. For others, it may be sex, or sexual orientation, or age. Sometimes one's physical characteristics may lead to certain assumptions on the part of others that are untrue. This is not only a challenge for disputants; neutrals need to be cognizant of their own vulnerabilities to bias. Not all biases are negative. Some people may find themselves favorably predisposed to others who share a common physical or ethnic characteristic.

The problem of bias in human relations is well documented, but bias remains very difficult to address. If a neutral is confronted with a party who is biased against the other party, it can often be difficult or impossible to address that bias within the limited time frame of the dispute resolution process. Many dispute resolution professionals would argue that even attempting to address such bias within a dispute resolution process would be difficult if not impossible.

Online dispute resolution is powerful because it enables parties to self-represent. There is an oft-cited cartoon from the *New Yorker* depicting a dog sitting at a computer speaking to another dog, saying, "On the Internet no one knows you're a dog."[2] This is true in online dispute resolution. It is not immediately obvious in an online interaction if the other party or neutral is male or female, black or white, gay or straight, or old or young. In many circumstances, the parties can choose what they want to share about themselves or what they want to hide. It is even possible for the parties to misrepresent themselves, or to leave certain characteristics unaddressed.

The challenge of bias is a very difficult one to address in mediation practice. But online dispute resolution creates an environment where bias can be removed as a factor in building an agreement between two disputants. This is impossible in face-to-face interactions.

Anonymous Communication

The advantages of self-representation can even be taken a step further in online dispute resolution. Procedures can be designed in which disputants can participate anonymously. In a face-to-face interaction, it is highly impractical to design a dispute resolution process where the identity of one party remains unknown to the other party. However, there are situations in which such an arrangement might make sense and might allow for a dispute to be addressed much earlier than it might otherwise be confronted. In a workplace situation, for example, in which one of the parties is reluctant to come forward with incriminating information because they fear reprisals, an anonymous process might allow for a situation to be addressed without risking negative outcomes.

Anonymous information can also be valuable in addressing situations before they worsen or before significant damage is done. Some processes may start out with an anonymous participant because he or she refuses to engage in the process on any other terms. Over the course of the process, however, the participant may eventually agree to reveal his or her identity. A process could even be conducted in which the two disputants know each other, but their identities remain concealed from the mediator. In each of these situations anonymous participation may allow for dispute resolution where it would otherwise be impossible.

Convenience

The most obvious advantage of an online dispute resolution process is its convenience. In a face-to-face process, the participants must dress up, take time off of work, travel perhaps long distances to the meeting place, and spend hours discussing the issues underlying the dispute. The time spent on all of these activities has a clear cost, which is sometimes called the *convening penalty*. The convening penalty is the time, money, and energy required to merely get the parties to sit down at the table. In some circumstances, the convening penalty outweighs the desire of the participants to resolve the dispute.

In an online process the convening penalty is almost eliminated. Participants can login whenever and wherever it is convenient for them to do so. The disputant can login from his desk at work, or from home sitting in front of the computer in his pajamas. There is no necessity to synchronize everyone's schedules and to find acceptable meeting times because the parties and the neutral can simply login whenever they have time available. For many people with busy schedules this type of flexibility is what makes their participation in a dispute resolution process possible. For them, face-to-face dispute resolution may not even be an option.

Access to Better Neutrals, with More Subject Area Expertise

For many face-to-face dispute resolution processes there are not many options as to who will serve as the mediator or arbitrator. Neutral availability is often dictated by the neutral's case schedule, her geographic proximity, and applicable conflicts of interest. If the disputants decide to go to court, the judge assigned to the case will most likely know nothing about the case's subject matter and the parties will have the responsibility to educate him or her from scratch. Should the case ever go in front of the jury, that education process will likely take even longer. In complex disputes involving lots of data or requiring certain background subject area or scientific understanding, the education process can be very costly and time-consuming.

The advantage of online dispute resolution is that geography, schedule, and expertise are no longer major concerns. The parties can choose any neutral they like to help them resolve their dispute, regardless of where that neutral is in the world, his time zone, or even his other commitments. This ability to have the best neutral in the world for your case is a major advantage to online dispute resolution procedures.

Text-Based Communication

Voice-based communication has many benefits, in terms of ease of use, speed, and inflection. Many ODR platforms are moving toward the integration of voice communication to capture some of these benefits. However, text-based communication, which provides the foundation for many current ODR platforms, also has benefits that shouldn't be overlooked. Aside from encouraging reflection and contributing to the cooling distance of ODR environments, text-based communication also makes the drafting of documents much easier. As many mediators have found, sitting around a table with a pen and a pad can be a difficult way to draft a document. People speak very differently than they write, so while some parties can easily express verbally what they want it can be very difficult to translate those preferences into text acceptable to both parties.

Text-based communication has the advantage that people are forced to translate their preferences into text from the beginning of the process. When the time comes to draft an agreement, the mediator can lift actual language from past postings to ensure that the parties will approve of the phrasing. It also helps people be more specific in their comments, as it is difficult to finish other people's sentences online or to rely on generic language. It is harder to be reticent online, as silence in text connotes absence more than sullenness or passive-aggressiveness, so there may be more of an incentive for parties to express their feelings, interests, or desires.

Efficient Automated Negotiation Processes

In many mediations I have administered, the process ends up "slicing the salami," in which one side and then the other make monetary bids in an attempt to agree on an acceptable number. When online, an automated tool, such as a blind-bidding algorithm, can be used when the parties reach that particular stage in order to more efficiently find the amount in question, without the time-consuming back-and-forth negotiation that characterizes most "salami-slicing" procedures. In fact, some mediations fail as the fragile agreement that has been built through the session is broken by the strain of the back-and-forth monetary negotiation.

In an online environment, a wide variety of these automated negotiation tools, separate and apart from the mediator, can be brought in to a mediation session to help parties resolve discrete issues efficiently. The software algorithm can be described in detail so that the parties understand the method, and purely distributive issues (such as monetary settlements) can be settled through the software while the parties focus instead on the more complex relationship-based issues.

ADVANTAGES FOR NEUTRALS

Neutrals benefit in a variety of ways by using ODR, as well.

Asynchronous Communication

Asynchronous communication can also be a valuable tool for mediators and facilitators. Just as disputants can react emotionally to new developments, neutrals can get caught up in the immediacy of a face-to-face session. Third parties can benefit from the cooling distance provided by asynchronous interaction, allowing them to pay greater attention to their own biases and perhaps enabling them to become more reflective practitioners. They can set notifications so that they are instantly informed of new postings, allowing them to discuss postings with the author before the other side sees them. The features of asynchronous communication lead to many of the process benefits described in the following sections.

Pre-communication Reframing

Reframing is an important part of any mediator's skill set. Helping parties frame their communications in a way that the other side can best hear and understand them is an essential component of moving a dispute toward resolution. However, in a face-to-face interaction, reframing must be done in front of both parties. Once a name is called or an accusation leveled it can't be pulled back, even if the mediator does manage to work with the disputant to reframe the sentiment in a more productive way. Many mediators have had the experience of parties making progress and moving in a productive direction when suddenly one side makes an inopportune comment that derails the discussion and yanks parties back into name-calling.

A mediator has a variety of options online. If one party posts a comment that is accusatory in tone or violates ground rules about insults, a mediator can discuss the sentiments expressed with the poster and help her reframe the posting before the other side has seen it. A mediator can even take the comment off of the live site and discuss it in caucus with the author before jointly posting a reframed version. In extreme cases, a mediator can even set the system to require mediator approval of each posting between parties, allowing the mediator to control each communication in a system along the lines of shuttle diplomacy.

These options allow the mediator to reframe communications unseen by the intended recipient, so that the initial unproductive outburst and any resistance to reframing can be dealt with behind the scenes. Then, only the reframed comment actually makes it to the recipient.

Concurrent Caucusing

While some mediators refuse to caucus with individual parties during mediation sessions, others rely on it quite heavily. The ability to talk about issues with one side in a confidential way can be extremely valuable in moving parties toward a resolution. Interests and motivations that would never be expressed in a joint discussion can come out in caucuses, allowing parties to be heard and enabling the mediator to get a better sense of the underlying issues in a dispute.

Caucusing can be a crude tool in face-to-face mediation sessions, however. The mediator usually has to call the joint discussion to a stop, and then has to decide which of the parties should caucus first. The other party is then sent into the hallway to wait while the mediator caucuses. Then, usually to preserve the sense of even-handedness, the parties switch and the mediator caucuses with the other side. Finally, after a relatively short amount of time (because the mediator is cognizant of the other party waiting outside the meeting room) the parties are reconvened. Hopefully the delay hasn't derailed the progress that was being made before the caucus; often, mediators only call caucuses when discussions hit a stalemate because they don't want to disrupt productive discussions.

Online, caucusing can be much more flexible. Mediators can caucus with parties at the same time the joint discussion is going on. In the joint discussion, postings reach all participants, but in caucus discussions the mediator interacts with one side or the other. This allows the mediator to caucus through the entire mediation, even when the discussion is progressing well. It also prevents the other side from having to wait during caucusing, or to wonder what secrets are being passed while they are out of the room.

It should be noted that maintaining three different concurrent discussions (joint, caucus A, and caucus B) can be a little confusing at times. However, this kind of mediator multitasking can be very effective. It's similar to having several documents open in a word processor. Managing these different threads (and making sure communications go in the right places) is one of the new skills ODR professionals need to master.

Ongoing Consensus Evaluation

Consensus building processes often involve multiple parties discussing a wide variety of issues. Facilitators of these processes frequently have many balls to juggle, as each party is at a different stage in accepting or rejecting proposals at hand. Often facilitators will evaluate the consensus of a group by going around the table and getting a sense of where people stand on an issue. This is a time-consuming process that must be done judiciously, as parties can become frustrated with multiple consensus evaluations when they don't perceive that any progress toward agreement is being made. In addition, these consensus evaluations are frequently public, meaning that individuals must make open pronouncements of their positions even though they may be wrestling with different and conflicting desires. Once a statement is made in public many individuals feel the need to defend the position they've taken instead of continuing to consider alternatives.

Online consensus evaluation can be carried out simultaneous to the discussion. Mediators and facilitators can poll participants to determine the extent to which they agree with certain statements, or to express what they see as the key obstacles to agreement. These results (who voted for what, or what the "average" agreement number is) can be confidential, viewed only by the facilitator, or they can be made public while keeping the identities of individual voters confidential.

This information can be very helpful to the mediators and facilitators, giving them a sense of how close or far the group as a whole may be to agreement. Parties are not forced to defend their opinions in public, which allows them to be more honest and less defensive.

Invisible Mentoring

Most of the mediation programs I have worked with use a variation on the co-mediation model. Having two mediators can be an effective way to deal with many different ADR challenges, especially when inexperienced mediators are just starting out and don't have total confidence in their abilities to move parties toward resolution effectively. Such mentoring relationships are a good way to expose new mediators to various ADR techniques and to get them sure of their footing in the mediator role.

However, mentoring can only go so far in a face-to-face context. Experienced co-mediators are tempted to take over when the process gets complicated, and inexperienced mediators are more likely to rely on their expert co-mediators in difficult situations. As an alternative, the experienced mediator can be a silent observer in the back of the room, but the silent watcher can also affect the ways that disputants interact with each other.

Monitoring mediator performance over time is also very difficult. Mediators that go through their training phase and continue working solo often get very little ongoing supervision. It is hard for program administrators to monitor both the new trainees and also keep tabs on the more experienced panelists.

Online dispute resolution environments allow observers and mentors to be in the virtual room monitoring the proceedings, and even communicating with the mediator in a caucus closed to the parties, without the parties feeling uneasy because of the presence of a stranger. The monitoring role must be cleared with the parties in advance of the session, so that they know that there is the possibility of a program representative visiting the room at some point. Once that approval is given the mentor (participating in the online meeting room as an observer, able to see what's going on but not able to participate in any way) does not affect the dynamics of the process as much as a live body in the back of the room might.

Archived Communication

An extension of text-based communication is that postings in an online context are usually archived, either just for the length of the mediation or even beyond the end of the mediation. If parties prefer not to have a record of their discussions after the close of their session, the file can be deleted and no record will exist. If parties prefer to have the text of the session available to revisit, they can save all the text of their discussions into a file that can be reopened at a future date.

Mediators can revisit archived communications to help clarify issues, or to remind people of statements they had made earlier in the discussion. In a face-to-face session, once a party says something, it's gone. Later a mediator can remind a party of a statement that had been made earlier and the party can deny it, portray it in a different context, or reinterpret its meaning. Each side may remember earlier conversations very differently, and unless the discussions were tape recorded (which creates a very different tone for the mediation) there is no right or wrong recollection.

Archived communications allow the mediator (and the parties, if they retain access to the archive) to actually copy out the words from a party's posting and remind them of the sentiment or preference expressed. It is as if the mediator had an instant recording of everything that had been said in a mediation session ready to play back at a moment's notice, but without the self-consciousness of a tape recorder.

Reusable Language

Many mediators memorize their opening statements so that they don't forget basic ground rules and so all of the necessary disclosures about their role in the mediation process are made clear to the participants upfront. However, mediators can't easily memorize whole blocks of discussions from the middle of mediations, or reuse well-phrased questions or detailed reframing techniques between sessions.

Online mediators can copy particular passages from discussions with parties that they think do a particularly good job in moving the parties toward resolution or clarifying key issues. Once they take out information specific to the parties, those passages can be reused in future mediations. They can even share the language with fellow medi-' ators to get constructive criticism, or let others use the language when they find it helpful.

Some ODR platforms have a folder accessible only to the mediators with resources useful to them in providing effective dispute resolution services. There is suggested language for different stages of the mediation process developed by expert dispute resolution practitioners. Mediators can also consult training material or suggested steps for parties to move through in an attempt to reach resolution, all in the middle of their ADR process. In a face-to-face session, consulting materials such as these might delay the process or make parties question the experience of their neutral. Online access to these resources, especially effective language worked out ahead of time, can aid the work of the mediator transparent to the disputants.

Modularity of ODR Environments

It is important to note that mediators who prefer not to use these capabilities (for instance, caucusing, approving postings, archiving communications, or even interacting asynchronously) can also remove one or more of them from their online meeting space. Each online process can be completely customized by the mediator to include or exclude the elements they choose, which allows for easier integration into face-to-face processes. All the more reason why dispute resolution professionals must become more familiar with these capabilities so that they can decide how they want to practice online and how best to meet the particular needs of their parties. Over time, mediators will probably come to mix-and-match various online techniques to best address the challenges of each individual dispute.

ADVANTAGES FOR BUSINESSES

The interests of neutrals and parties in online dispute resolution usually focus on one particular dispute. For most consumers, online dispute resolution is something they might experience once or twice over a five-year period. Neutrals may be involved with dozens of cases in a single year, but their focus is usually on maximizing the effectiveness of each individual case. Businesses, on the other hand, have more systemic interests in online dispute resolution. A business may be involved with hundreds of formal complaints in a single year. Businesses need to concern themselves with efficient and effective dispute resolution systems designed to adequately address their concerns in resolving those disputes before they escalate. Many of the benefits that businesses realize from online dispute resolution happen in the aggregate, whereas the benefits individual consumers and customers realize from dispute resolution happen on a case-by-case basis.

Early Intervention

Because of the convenience, ODR can often be called into disputes much earlier than traditional face-to-face ADR. As a general rule, the earlier that dispute resolution efforts begin in a matter the better. The longer time the dispute has to escalate the harder it is to resolve it, and the greater the potential exposure.

Online dispute resolution, when appropriately integrated into the business processes of organizations, can uncover and surface potential disputes at a much earlier stage in their development. Because consumers, customers, and partners have an easy way to register their frustrations they will often take action to resolve them far in advance of the development of a formal grievance. Recognizing these complaints early on is a major advantage to businesses, because grievances can be proactively addressed before they evolve into formal conflicts that may end up in court. This early access also enables the business to prevent escalation as a result of mishandled grievances, delays in response, and perceived inadequate access to redress options on the part of the consumer.

Cost Effectiveness

Another major benefit of online dispute resolution from a business perspective is the cost-effectiveness of the tools. Because there is no convening penalty, travel and time expenses are significantly minimized. Top-quality neutrals often charge less for online dispute resolution procedures because they do not have to spend as much time traveling to meetings, scheduling and synchronizing people's calendars, and locating and reserving meeting rooms.

In addition, the significant negative exposure that can come from unresolved disputes makes the financial calculus behind implementing online dispute resolution even more obvious. Even if only one claim out of one thousand makes it all the way to a courtroom hearing, the financial exposure on the part of the company may be enormous. Effective and efficient online dispute resolution services, provided early in the development of the business-consumer relationship, can significantly decrease such legal exposure, if not erase it completely.

Customer Retention

Studies of consumer behavior have determined that customers who have a dispute with a business and then resolve that dispute effectively are more loyal to that business than consumers who never experienced a dispute at all.[3] Studies have also determined that a negative experience with a business will be related to others ten times more than a positive experience. The baseline expectation of many consumers and customers is that their transaction should be seamless, and that they should come out of the transaction fully satisfied. If the transaction does not live up to this standard, customers are often frustrated and might even feel a little betrayed. Providing a fair, effective online dispute resolution process demonstrates to customers that a business is committed to their satisfaction. A resolved dispute can also make a customer feel that she has time and energy invested in the relationship with the business, making her less likely to go elsewhere to receive services. Viewed from this perspective, complaints and disputes are opportunities for businesses, because they present the business with a chance to demonstrate its willingness to go the extra mile for the customer.

As an example, my wife recently received an appliance as a gift that she did not want to keep. The appliance did not come with the receipt, nor was it packaged in its original box. However, the giver mentioned that the appliance had been purchased at a major department store. On a whim, my wife brought the appliance back to the department store and mentioned that she had received it as a gift, though she had no evidence that the appliance had actually been purchased from that department store. Regardless, the store accepted the return with no questions asked. Now my wife insists on making purchases from that department store even though their prices are slightly higher because she was so impressed with the degree to which they accommodated her. Online disputes present a similar opportunity for businesses offering services and goods over the Internet. If disputes are handled in an expedient, accommodating, and flexible way, businesses can build loyalty among their customer base more effectively than they could with expensive advertising campaigns targeted solely at new consumers.

Better Feedback Loops

The one factor that often separates the failures from the successes in e-commerce is the degree to which the company pays attention to feedback from its customers and partners. Often it is difficult to motivate customers to provide detailed feedback on the performance of business, particularly if the overall experience was positive. Wise corporations focus like a laser on the needs and desires of their customers. Determining these needs and desires through market surveys and educated guesses is much more difficult than simply gathering the information directly from the customers themselves. Online dispute resolution systems can be very helpful in gathering feedback from customers and partners. ODR systems are often designed as learning systems that can detect patterns and trends in user experiences and report aggregated information back to the businesses themselves.

For instance, if one component of an e-commerce website is causing confusion or errors in the orders placed by customers, an online dispute resolution process can detect the common source of this confusion and recommend back to the business that the matter be proactively addressed to minimize the risk of future disputes. For example, let's say that when an online dispute resolution tool is integrated into a website 3 to 5 percent of the transactions flowing through that website may result in complaints. If the feedback loops built into the online dispute resolution system are effective, over time the percentage of transactions that result in disputes will decrease. After one year, the percentage of transactions that result in disputes may decrease to only 1 to 2 percent of the transactions. Building in effective feedback mechanisms can enable a business to better target its customers as well as bolster loyalty among those customers.

A Litigation Safety Net

The primary motivation for many businesses to integrate online dispute resolution into their transaction processes is the desire to decrease the risk of litigation. The person in a business or corporation who is the strongest advocate of online dispute resolution is often the risk manager, who has the responsibility of minimizing the business's legal exposure. There are many kinds of insurance policies that businesses can purchase to manage their financial exposure in different circumstances. Online dispute resolution can be viewed as insurance against litigation because its adoption can significantly reduce if not eliminate legal exposure to complaints from customers and partners. As the price tags for legal settlements in various customer claims, such as class actions, continue to rise, the importance of this type of legal insurance grows. Effectively implemented online dispute resolution can insulate businesses from damaging court action, which can harm hard-earned reputations just as much as hard-earned profits.

Favorable Government Treatment

The final benefit online dispute resolution can offer businesses is favorable treatment from government and regulatory bodies. The integration of effective third-party dispute resolution into business methods signals a business's intention to play fair, not only with consumers but with governments. Increasingly legislatures and international organizations are calling for the application of online dispute resolution into e-commerce as an attempt to provide viable redress options for consumers. Standards calling for online dispute resolution have been adopted by a wide variety of government bodies, advocacy groups, and industry consortia. If businesses voluntarily abide by these standards and institute an online dispute resolution program, they will benefit from the presumption of good faith on the part of regulators and perhaps even the courts. If a business is eventually involved in a formal judicial process with regard to a failed transaction, the early availability of a fair and effective dispute resolution option in the transaction process can significantly work to its advantage by showing that the business participated in the transaction in good faith. The benefits that can be realized from this predisposition on the part of governments and judges may be difficult to quantify but are undeniably important.

ODR DISADVANTAGES

Online dispute resolution can radically change the communication dynamics in a dispute, which can lead to many of the advantages listed in the previous sections. It is important to note, however, that these changed communication dynamics can also result in disadvantages as well. Many of the characteristics of ODR processes are double-edged, with both plusses and minuses. They can enable parties and neutrals to make significant progress if used appropriately and correctly, but they can also create new problems and challenges if mishandled.

The Downside of Archived Communication

For instance, the fact that every communication is recorded can be a liability. Many people are understandably cautious about what they type in emails or documents. It is much easier to capture and save textual communications than verbal communications. Many people have had the experience of an email written months (if not years) before coming back and later embarrassing them. Putting sensitive, confidential information into text form can cause concern because one doesn't know where the information is going to end up. It may be intended for a single party, but once the intended recipient receives it, there's no guarantee that the information will not be passed along to someone else.

In ODR processes archived communications can also be a problem if the parties engage in harsh words and then refuse to move on. Parties can insist upon going back and re-reading the harsh words over and over again. If insults and accusations are traded between the parties at the beginning of the dispute resolution process it is easy to return to those insults again and again, and to reopen old wounds. In a face-to-face communication process, once something is said it immediately begins to recede into the past; as progress is made in the dispute resolution process it's easy to forget about earlier insults that had been exchanged. In an online process, all the communication is archived, so it is a relatively easy thing to revisit past topics, particularly when communication starts to slow down, which makes it difficult to keep the earlier harsh words in the past. There are ways that online neutrals can combat these tendencies (by removing old discussion threads, for instance) but this aspect of online communication is always a challenge to be kept in mind.

Privacy and Confidentiality Concerns

Another shortcoming that grows out of archived communication is concerns about privacy and confidentiality. They can be a major barrier in getting parties to participate in an online process. If the parties are not 100 percent sure that communications will remain confidential they will refuse to participate in a process where they would be required to put sensitive information down in text form. Online dispute resolution technology platforms usually rely on Web-based interactivity as opposed to email because email is inherently insecure. It is easier to protect the confidentiality of information that is maintained in a Web-based environment and provided only to users who have logged on with the appropriate password and username. However, there is no foolproof way to prevent parties from copying information off of their screen for later use. Even if the parties are prevented from cutting and pasting text, they can still take a screen capture of the text. In a face-to-face dispute resolution process it is much harder to surreptitiously capture communications through the use of voice recording devices or similar techniques.

For this reason, it is of the utmost importance that online dispute resolution service providers maintain the security of their platforms, and that they build adequate protections to ensure that private information stays private. If a party comes to a dispute resolution process because she is frustrated with what she perceives to be a violation of her privacy, she will feel doubly wronged if the dispute resolution platform cannot protect her privacy and ensure confidentiality as well.

Dropping Out and Stonewalling

Another shortcoming of online communication is that it is very easy for parties to drop out or stonewall the other side. Because the neutral cannot compel any participant to log into the environment and respond when a response is required, parties can easily drop out of the process if they feel it is not in their interest to continue participating, or stonewall by not posting comments or responding to questions in order to put pressure on the other side. In a face-to-face process, once the parties are in the room, the neutral usually has their undivided attention and can even lock the door as a way to keep the parties focused on the matters at hand. In an online dispute resolution process there is no such way to ensure that the parties stay engaged with the process. Online dispute resolution platforms can provide incentives for parties to continue participating and maybe even penalties for those who drop out of a process, but there is no way to compel parties to continue participating in an online interaction if they don't want to. This is another reason why it is important for online neutrals to stay in close contact with the parties and keep them engaged with the process so that they stay focused and interested in resolving the dispute.

Strategic Communication

Research into online communication has also shown that people are more likely to lie during online communication. It takes a special kind of person to be able to look into his opponent's eyes in a face-to-face interaction and to knowingly tell him something that is untrue. Most people are confident that they can tell when another person is lying if they can observe them face-to-face. The way that they make this determination is to read the body language of the other side. In an online interaction, there is no body language to give a cue to the intentions of the other side. If someone looks you in the eye and says, "Yes, I sent the check," most people believe that they will be able to tell if that person is being truthful. In an online interaction, that person could be laughing while he typed, "Yes, I sent the check," and the other side would never know.

Because it is so much easier to lie online, people are also less trusting of information that they receive online. People are often much more skeptical of facts, assertions, and apologies that they receive in online communication than they are when the same information is presented face-to-face. Fortunately, the ability for parties to do research online and to verify facts during the dispute resolution process can help to build confidence in information exchange between the parties online. In some dispute situations this skepticism can be a good thing, as it prevents one side from manipulating or pulling the wool over the other side's eyes. The ease with which people can misrepresent or be strategic in what they say, and the resultant skepticism on the part of the listener, can undermine communications and interfere with the development of understanding between the parties.

Lack of Body Language and Nonverbal Cues

Because online communication is primarily textual, most of the nonverbal cues that people use to communicate are lost. In a face-to-face dispute resolution process, skilled neutrals can almost learn more about the true feelings of the disputants from watching the way they sit in their chair, talk with the other party, or react to points made. If someone crosses their arms or shakes their head no while listening to someone speak, or if they look exasperated or sigh in frustration, important communication is taking place. In an online interaction this communication is not possible. Every bit of communication between the neutrals and the parties has to be typed in and sent deliberately, which makes communication much more intentional but also filters out many of these nonverbal cues. Many dispute resolution professionals rely so heavily on these nonverbal cues that they are skeptical that any meaningful communication can happen in a text-only environment. This is taking things a bit far, as it is possible to have rich communication online (see Chapter Sixteen for more on this), and there are ways to replicate nonverbal communication. But the point is well taken that the lack of body language is a disadvantage to online interaction.

Building Rapport

It is also much harder to build rapport between the parties in an online environment than it is in a face-to-face interaction. Many of the things that people talk about with each other when they first meet are not intended to communicate meaningful or important information. They are intended only to establish a friendly relationship. Often when strangers meet they have a discussion about the weather, or the upcoming weekend, or the performance of local sports teams. This communication can be very important in establishing a friendly environment for future communications, even though no real information is being passed. In online communications, this type of friendly banter is very rare. Such communications come off very differently when typed in and posted in a discussion environment.

People are usually much more businesslike in textual communications, which means they don't devote as much time as they would in a face-to-face communication toward building that rapport and establishing a friendly environment for the interaction. There are ways that technology designers can combat this tendency to be overly businesslike, and neutrals can encourage parties to begin their discussion with some rapport building, but it often does not come as naturally online as it might face-to-face. Friendly, gregarious participants oftentimes will begin online interactions by jumping right into the issues, whereas in a face-to-face interaction they would have taken the time to ask about the other side's interests, family, or make small talk.

Power Corrupts

Dispute resolution professionals often assume that they will not have as much power in an online dispute resolution environment to control the agenda and keep parties focused on the goals of the process. In reality, the opposite is usually the case: online neutrals have much more power in their ability to direct parties to focus on a particular issue, and often this power is unintentionally abused or misused. Parties can feel bossed around by technology that forces them to go to a particular place or answer a particular question. In a more prescriptive process, like blind bidding or arbitration, parties may expect this type of treatment, but in a negotiation-based process, like a mediation, parties can easily chafe under technology or neutrals that are overly aggressive. I have seen online disputants rebel against bossy neutrals and upend the process in frustration. Once an online process devolves to this level it is nearly impossible to get the discussion back on track.

Like in any dispute resolution process, online or face-to-face, neutrals need to be cognizant of both the positive powers of the tools available to them and the negative potential of those same tools. Training neutrals about how not to use online environments is as important as training them in best practices for ODR. Effective ODR practice and systems design understand both the pros and the cons of online interactivity, and can steer disputants toward effective agreements while at the same time steering them away from the pitfalls that exist.

PART II

ODR and Business

CHAPTER FOUR

ODR: Essential to E-Commerce

A global alternative dispute resolution system is necessary to encourage cross-border electronic commerce.

Carly Fiorina, CEO, Hewlett-Packard.[1]

T he rapid expansion of e-commerce has created vast numbers of online disputes: between buyers and sellers, between consumers and services, and between users themselves. These disputes undermine the credibility of online marketplaces, making customers and businesses less willing to engage in online transactions.

ODR builds trust in transactions, keeps customers satisfied, preserves relationships, and shields companies from liability. The first wave of e-commerce created online marketplaces for businesses and consumers and made a huge splash trumpeting their possibilities. Then, once the hype died down, the shortcomings of online markets became clear. The second wave of e-commerce will build the services buyers and sellers need to sustain their involvement in online marketplaces, dispute resolution first of all. Only after users of online marketplaces can obtain redress will the real potential of e-commerce be achieved.

Online dispute resolution brings efficiencies to inefficient online markets by removing the risk of failed transactions. Without this functionality, users quickly discern the shortcomings of engaging in transactions online.

Businesses that understand this need and proactively address it by integrating online dispute resolution services into their websites will benefit from increased customer loyalty, higher transaction volumes, and significantly greater profits. Those businesses that do not offer such services, or that develop mechanisms that do not provide a fair forum for resolving disputes, will lose credibility with their customers and partners and be penalized with declining usage over time.

THE PROMISE OF E-COMMERCE

The Internet revolution was triggered by a single development: the application of global computer networks to commerce. Networks had been growing for more than a dozen years without sparking much commercial activity at all, but then Tim Berners-Lee came up with the notion of the World Wide Web, and suddenly entrepreneurs and investors around the world could see what was coming. With the introduction of Mosaic, the first browser, the potential was there to build a worldwide, always-on commercial environment where the traditional inefficiencies of the marketplace were removed. Information could flow freely from buyer to seller, prices for a single item could instantly be compared to hundreds of sellers around the world, and every storefront on the Web could access every buyer on the planet. The benefits to commerce were clear and overwhelming, and the money, millions and millions of dollars of it, started to roll in.

Business analysts (Gartner Research, Forrester Research, Jupiter Research, and the like) seemed to be competing as to who could come up with the biggest projections for global e-commerce. The consensus seemed to be that global e-commerce would top $6 trillion worldwide by 2005.[2] The analysts also asserted that the Internet would shake up every industry, bringing old market leaders down and raising new companies in their place. The Internet, they argued, was the "greatest wealth creation boom in history."[3]

To paraphrase Homer, that sentiment was "the face that launched a thousand ships." Once the marketplace began to hear the estimates of how much business was going to be done over the Web, entrepreneurs were off to the races. Everything from toothbrushes to pet supplies to private jets were sold online, by a staggering array of start-up companies all jostling to get their IPO pay-off date, at which point their stock valuations would shoot into the stratosphere. New companies without any profits were bidding against General Motors for advertisements during the Super Bowl. Five-year-old Web companies like Yahoo! were so flush with cash that they contemplated purchases of old-media stalwarts like CBS. It seemed for a time that maybe the projections were correct and that the world was in fact about to be changed forever.

The Crash

In retrospect, of course, it was inevitable that the bubble would burst. In a stark example of Schumpeter's notion of "creative destruction,"[4] hundreds if not thousands of these Internet companies fell to earth after the stock market started to decline in spring 2000. Scores of companies declared bankruptcy in the first half of 2001, laying off tens of thousands of people. Magazines began to refer to dot-coms as "dot-bombs," and former Internet employees held pink-slip parties around the country to ease the pain of their terminations.

It was inevitable that such a rapid rise in the e-commerce world would spark such a drastic backlash. The number of foolish business plans that had received outrageous sums of investment created a sense that the Internet was all hype and no substance. The Web media outlets, supported by advertising revenues from Internet companies, had announced the coming dominance of the Internet over the old world, and once the house of cards started to fall apart traditional media and business units gloried in the unraveling of the upstarts.

The collapse of the publication *Industry Standard,* considered by many in Silicon Valley to be the bible of the Internet revolution, cemented the sense that the dot-com bubble had truly burst, and now it was back to business as usual. At that point the familiar mnemonics B2C and B2B were sarcastically redefined to mean "back-to-consulting" and "back-to-banking."

THE UNFORESEEN CHALLENGES OF E-COMMERCE

Now that we're on the other side of the first wave of Internet enthusiasm, it's clear to see that the initial hopeful vision for what the Web could have become was not achieved. As was noted on the *PC Magazine* website, we were promised a network nirvana where all our desires could be met, and what we got instead was a "wasteland for spammers and a graveyard for dead websites."[5] Internet retailers have come and gone, and the projections for e-commerce growth that had been accepted as gospel now seem extremely unrealistic.

What went wrong? Very early on it was obvious that there were significant problems with e-commerce that had not been foreseen in the rosy scenarios. It was very hard in the unregulated anarchy of the Internet to control unethical people who used the infrastructure for their own benefit without considering the overall systemic impact. The Internet gained a reputation, however undeserved, as the definitive source for spam, porn, and fraud. Users began to get the impression, drawn largely from the large quanities of uninvited mail in their inbox, that most of the people out there on the Net were perverts and scam artists. Who wants to do business with those types of people?

The Trust Problem

The main problem with transactions over the Internet was a lack of trust. How could you pick out the good transaction partners from the bad? How could you be sure that any problems that arose online would be worked out in good faith? In the face-to-face world there are ways you can make sure that the business you're working with is genuine. There are also ways you can work out any problems that arise. For online transactions to be as trusted as offline transactions these types of services need to be made available on the Internet. Without them consumers and businesses are vulnerable to being taken advantage of by undesirables.

Frances Fukiyama, the prominent political scientist, tells a story about attending a lecture at the height of the Internet boom where the speaker, a riled-up techno-futurist, described an idyllic future in which teenagers in their basements could put up slick websites that were indistinguishable from large companies. Small regional banks could compete on equal footing with the massive banks like Citibank and Fleet because instead of having marble buildings and billions of dollars in assets they just had to have an intuitive, sophisticated Web presence. All of this was presented in the lecture as a good thing, the Web as giant-killer. Fukiyama's reaction was the exact opposite. If you don't know who you're working with on the other side of the computer screen, how can you ever trust them to do what they say? It's all well and good if a teenager can set up a hedge fund in his or her basement, but would you want to invest your money in that hedge fund if you knew that was the way it was operated? You gather important information when you walk into a huge bank building and look at their marble floors and velvet drapes. You know they're not going anywhere, most likely, and that they have a history of taking care of enough customers to stay in business. If those pieces of information are removed from the transaction process the customer is most likely flying blind, and they're bound to be disappointed when the depth of service they'd come to expect isn't available from their new relationships.[6]

It is crucial for the Internet to develop a trust infrastructure to support the building of confidence between transaction partners. Online dispute resolution is an essential part of that trust infrastructure. If consumers and businesses know that they will be able to work out their problems then they will be willing to engage in transactions. If they think that they'll be left holding the bag should any problems arise then they'll stay off of the Internet when they do their buying and selling.

TRANSBOUNDARY TRANSACTIONS

The primary reason why so many organizations have called for the development of ODR to support e-commerce is the number of cross-border transactions that are taking place online.

When buyers and sellers transact in the face-to-face world almost all transactions happen in the same geographic area out of convenience. Many consumers and businesses feel that it's too much of a headache to do business outside your hometown. Even if the price is higher most transactions take place locally.

Online, that disincentive is removed. If the best shoes are made in Italy there is little incentive not to visit an Italian shoe store online and to make the purchase. If a business can get a better price on bulk materials from a supplier overseas then they might as well go for it. The cost of shipping is often offset by the savings in sales taxes. The Internet is remarkably efficient at bridging distance.

These widespread transboundary transactions are a new phenomenon, and consumers and businesses are only starting to wrestle with the challenges presented by them. For one thing, it's harder to know if the buyer or seller you're working with on the other side of the planet can be trusted, as was discussed previously. More significant, it is unclear what happens if something goes wrong with the sale. If your purchase was from Herb's Shoe Shack on the other side of town you can drive over and get Herb to come out of the back office to work things out. If you're still waiting for your shoes to arrive two months later from Milan it's a little more complicated to figure out what your next step should be. Booking a plane ticket usually isn't an option.

The law surrounding these transboundary transactions is complex. Just figuring out which law applies to a transaction can cost a lot of money. Getting legal representation or even just advice from another country can be frustrating and expensive. Legal systems don't really know how to handle disputes that straddle borders very well. Paying lawyers to put the time into figuring it all out really doesn't make that much sense, especially if the transaction value is less than a couple thousand dollars.

Some legal scholars have suggested that disputes should legally reside in the country of origin, meaning in the e-commerce context where the purchaser resides who made the purchase. For example, if a business in Little Rock, Arkansas, bought a product off of a German company's website, the legal location for that dispute is Arkansas. This works to the advantage of buyers, because if a dispute arose the buyer could handle it in his local jurisdiction, but it works to the disadvantage of sellers, who would have legal exposure all over the world. In the example, the German website might then have legal action initiated against it in Arkansas, where it has no representation or even awareness about local laws and regulations. It also means that the German website could be violating laws it knows nothing about, simply because the buyer lives in a region governed by those laws.

The prospect of being liable in countries around the world is terrifying to most businesses. Even if the business is not clearly in the wrong it is very expensive to retain legal counsel, respond with whatever filings are required by the court, or even to travel to defend against such actions. I know of a lawyer working in England who ordered flowers to be sent to her mother on Mother's Day from a popular online florist located in the United States. When the flowers did not arrive she complained to the florist, and threatened to file suit against the florist in England. Terrified of legal exposure in another country, the florist then offered the lawyer a huge discount on any future purchase from the website, just to make her drop the threat of an international lawsuit. Even if all of the future purchases resulted in a loss to the florist it would be much less than the cost of defending against such an action. This is an indicator of the fear many e-commerce businesses have of getting entangled in legal actions around the world.

The other option being considered by the treaty, country of destination, has its own problems as well. Under this option the legal location for the transaction would be the seller's location. To extend our original example, the Arkansas buyer would have to initiate legal action in Germany to get redress for the problematic transaction. This may work in the favor of the German company, as it will only have to defend against complaints in its local courthouse, but it transfers the burden of the transaction onto the buyer. Not too many consumers will have the ability to travel to the physical location of the e-commerce companies they patronize to engage in legal action.

This illustrates the primary reason why ODR is a better fit in resolving e-commerce disputes. In an ODR process, the legal location of the dispute doesn't matter, because the resolution is crafted based on either the preferences of the parties or some other standards administered by an arbitrator. It's not necessary to get legal counsel in the other country, because the decision isn't going to be based on the law. You can also select a neutral that has the expertise most appropriate to the nature of your dispute. Whatever decision is made regarding the legal location of disputes, there will still be compelling reasons for all e-commerce disputes to be resolved through online dispute resolution.

The Two Types of E-Commerce: B2C and B2B

All e-commerce is normally put into one of two categories: business-to-consumer or business-to-business. While both deal with basically the same thing, the transfer of goods from one party to another, they are very different in practice.

B2C transactions usually take the form of an individual consumer buying something from a large business. Think of your next-door neighbor buying a stereo from Circuit City, or your father buying a book from Amazon.com. These transactions are characterized by a significant power and information gap between the parties. The large business may have a vested interest in keeping its customers happy, but it has many thousands of customers to worry about. The business has teams of lawyers and sizable resources it can devote to a particular problem if it chooses to do so. The challenge is that it probably has thousands of problems at any given time to worry about. The customer is in a very different situation. He probably just wants to get the problem solved. He doesn't have an unlimited amount of time, energy, or resources to devote to the matter.

B2B transactions are different. Most transactions between businesses involve two parties that are roughly equivalent in terms of money, power, and business savvy. Both sides probably have lawyers they can consult on legal issues, as well as resources to pursue the matter should it escalate. Sometimes small businesses are really little more than individuals with a corporate identity, so it's not wholly accurate to say that every B2B transaction involves parties with equal stature and resources, but in most cases B2B transaction partners are on equal footing.

The differences in B2C and B2B transactions mean that ODR systems built to serve these two different types of e-commerce face very different challenges. The key considerations in building a B2C e-commerce ODR system are much different than the key considerations involved with the construction of a B2B ODR system.

As a result, the analysis of e-commerce ODR in this book has been split into two chapters, one focusing on B2C and one focusing on B2B. Some of the observations made will apply to both, but the differences outnumber the commonalities. Ironically, B2C ODR is the focus of much more international attention and effort than B2B ODR, even though B2B ODR has a much more attractive revenue model.

E-commerce disputes were the motivation for the creation of the ODR field. With e-commerce came the sense that there was money to be made. If you bought the $7 trillion Internet projection and you applied the rule of thumb that 1 to 3 percent of transactions end up in some kind of dispute, then you were looking at hundreds of billions of dollars tied up in disputes needing resolution. Those numbers may not occur as quickly as the analysts originally thought, but everyone agrees that they're coming.

CHAPTER FIVE

Providing Online Redress
ODR and B2C E-Commerce

*Online merchants should seek to resolve customer
complaints and disputes in a fair, timely, and effective
manner. . . . Online merchants shall also offer a fair method
for resolving differences with regard to a transaction by
offering either an unconditional money-back guarantee or
third-party dispute resolution.*

*The Better Business Bureau Code
of Online Business Practices*

T he recent economic slowdown not withstanding,
B2C e-commerce is here to stay. People are using the Internet to
engage in transactions with other people who are not in the same
county, country, or even on the same continent. These new marketplaces are now embedded into the way things work, and they will continue to grow slowly and steadily over time.

When problems arise in these transactions, as they inevitably do,
there needs to be a way for the buyers and sellers to work them out.
The choice is a stark one: either redress will soon become available
online or customers will start to steer clear of online transactions.

Consumers need to have the same support structure for transactions that take place online that they have offline. People need to be
confident before, during, and after the transaction if they are going to
patronize a business. They need to know that they're going to get what
they paid for, and that they won't be victimized by fraud.

Governments, international organizations, large non-profits, industry associations, and consumer advocacy groups have all examined this problem and they have reached a common conclusion. The best way to provide redress to online consumers is to create effective and ethical online dispute resolution services.

A sizable consensus is growing behind this conclusion. Standards calling for quality ODR have been issued by the Better Business Bureau (the definitive business-consumer standards organization in the United States), the Trans-Atlantic Consumer Dialogue (TACD, a consumer advocacy body), the Global Business Dialogue on e-Commerce (GBDe, an industry consortium), and the Organization for Economic Cooperation and Development (a European international organization). Former Secretary of Commerce Bill Daley has stated, "Given the global nature of e-commerce and the small dollar value of most consumer transactions, trying to settle disputes in court is probably not a practical option for most consumers and businesses. I believe ADR can provide this option."[1] The Electronic Commerce and Consumer Protection Group (which includes AOL Time Warner, AT&T, Dell, Microsoft, and Network Solutions) put it simply in their *Guidelines for Merchant-to-Consumer Transactions:* "Merchants should provide Consumers with fair, timely, and affordable means to settle disputes and obtain redress."[2] In their *Guidelines for Consumer Protection in Electronic Commerce,* the OECD also concluded that "Consumers should be provided meaningful access to fair and timely alternative dispute resolution and redress without undue cost or burden."[3] The list goes on and on.

There is continuing disagreement among some constituencies regarding what B2C ODR services should look like, how they should be regulated, what standards they should live up to, and how the rights of consumers can best be protected within them. But the clear consensus is that the courts are not going to provide a system that will effectively meet the needs of consumers in the new global marketplace, and that a global ODR network is the best solution to the problem.

THE SHORTCOMING OF B2C
E-COMMERCE: A LACK OF TRUST

Online merchants have come very quickly to the realization that transactions require trust, and the Internet is woefully low on trust. It's easy to lie online, and it didn't take long for everyone using the Internet to understand that fact. As a result, users of the Internet are much more skeptical of online promises. They are also very reluctant to trust any merchant they don't already know.

In the face-to-face world, consumers have come to rely on a variety of services that make them feel more comfortable. First, buyers can usually hold the item they are thinking about purchasing in their hands before they actually purchase it. This gives them a chance to check out the quality in advance of making the commitment. Second, sellers usually have a physical presence, so if a buyer has a problem with an item the buyer knows how to return to the store to address it. Third, if the seller refuses to resolve the problem, the consumer can contact supervisory bodies like the BBB or local government agencies to put pressure on the seller to provide redress. Fourth, should all other attempts at getting the problem solved fail, there is always the courts. A consumer can take a business to small claims court and make a case in front of a judge.

In reality, few buyers take advantage of all of these services. A very small percentage of transactions turn into formal complaints with the BBB, and even fewer make it to small claims court. However, it isn't necessary for face-to-face ADR services to actually be used for them to make consumers more trusting of the overall system. Sellers have come to understand that making customers happy makes good business sense, and some stores now offer full money-back guarantees or accept returns for store credit without asking questions. These offers clearly increase the trust of consumers, making them more likely to make purchases. Even if the policies result in some lost income, the sellers reason, it is more than compensated for by the additional transactions that take place because of the policies.

Before ODR was available the online transaction dynamic was quite different. The services that consumers rely on to make them feel comfortable in the face-to-face world were lacking or absent altogether. First, buyers could almost never see the item they were thinking about purchasing before they bought it. There could be lots of information about the item posted on a website, with close-up pictures and in-depth presentations of features, but the buyer could not actually put their hands on the item in advance of a purchase. Second, most sellers did not have a physical store where buyers could go if they had a problem. Some online retailers were connected to real-world stores, but often the real-world store had nothing to do with the online store, and they would refuse to accept returns or to handle complaints. If the buyer had a problem most likely they would be forced to work it out through the website. Buyers also quickly learned that websites could disappear overnight, or force customers with problems into unresponsive customer service departments. Third, the supervisory agencies that took user complaints offline did not have the same reach and power online. You could file a complaint with the BBB online, but it did not have the same effect as a complaint in the real world. The seller could be located anywhere in the world. The vast majority of customers would never hear about the complaint, so the seller could essentially continue unaffected. Local government agencies, and even federal ones, also seemed overwhelmed by the size and scope of the Internet marketplace. They could barely stay on top of all the complaints coming in, much less act on them. Fourth, as has been noted previously, the courts were not an option for most online consumers. There was no small claims court a buyer could use to get redress for an online transaction. Even if the buyer went through the trouble of getting a court date, showing up, and winning a verdict, it probably wouldn't be worth the paper it was written on. The local authorities would not put the work into finding the seller someplace out on the Internet and bringing them to justice, especially not for a low-value transaction.

Buyers quickly came to realize that if they were involved in a transaction they weren't satisfied with, or even if they were the victim of a fraudulent transaction, they had little option other than to just accept the loss and move on. Some retailers developed a good reputation for taking care of their customers, and they continued to acquire business. For most retailers who did not have a widely recognized brand, however, this problem of trust became a major obstacle to making sales.

Instituting ODR is an effective way to combat these problems. When businesses make ODR available to their customers it generates profits. It also helps them hold on to their customers, as was discussed in Chapter Three. When a company institutes ODR they will see an improvement in their bottom line. As Orna Rabinovich-Einy observes, "The online market could grow substantially if users were confident that any problems or conflicts arising from transactions on commercial websites would be resolved with relative ease and speed and in a fair manner."[4]

TYPES OF B2C TRANSACTIONS

The most common consumer transaction involves the direct sale of a good or service from a business to a customer through a physical storefront. Mail order and catalog services moved transactions beyond face-to-face exchanges. These traditional models were replicated in the online environment, but the new transaction dynamics also contributed to the creation of wholly new transaction types.

The Internet and New Transaction Models

The Internet has created an unbelievable variety of transaction models, some of which are even more vulnerable to this type of post-transaction disappointment. Standard customer-purchase-from-large-retailer models (such as Wal-Mart in the offline world and Amazon.com in the online world) are certainly common. New models, such as Priceline.com (where the buyer states the price they want to pay for an item or service and the sellers compete to meet it) or Togetherwesave.com (where the price goes down as more people order a product) are rewriting the rules for how transactions should take place.

Some game theorists are experimenting with new transaction models, such as time-limited negotiation periods or multivariable price matrices (for example, trading time of delivery, payment options, or quality against price at the time of purchase). These experiments are retooling the traditional ways buyers and sellers make purchases. Each of these mechanisms can be viewed as a different type of predispute ODR, as the two parties brainstorm and experiment with different solutions to the problem (crafting acceptable terms for the transaction) and then determine how the preferred solution will be carried out. Then, as with all resolutions, there needs to be some enforcement or follow-up mechanism put in place to handle the transactions where something goes awry.

Auctions

The first e-commerce environment to make use of online dispute resolution was auction websites. These sites are particularly vulnerable to conflict because the transaction environment usually connects the buyers and sellers and then leaves them alone to work out the details.

It is difficult to find out who is on the other side of the transaction, and whether or not they are telling the truth about the item they want to sell you. There are rarely repeat relationships between buyers and sellers, so most of the exchanges take place between strangers. Because of this lack of personal contact it is difficult to trust that the other side is telling the truth.

Auction sites have developed a variety of tools to reassure buyers and sellers. Escrow accounts, where money is held by a neutral third party until the good is delivered, help to solve the problem of fraudulent sellers. Ratings help transaction partners who do not know each other to see a record of the other side's positive or negative feedback from prior transactions. Auctions have also developed online dispute resolution programs to help work out any problems that arise.

PROVIDER PROFILE: SQUARETRADE

In December 1998 the Online Ombuds Office at the University of Massachusetts-Amherst was approached to conduct a mediation pilot program for the online auction site Up4Sale. The proposed structure was to make mediation available to buyers and sellers in the auction so that any disputes that arose could be resolved purely online, working with a mediator from the office. Up4Sale had been purchased by the online auction giant eBay in the summer of 1998. When eBay absorbed Up4Sale they also took on the online dispute resolution pilot.

Working with Ethan Katsh, the program designer and head of the Online Ombuds Office, eBay agreed to put up a link to a mediation service on one of their customer service pages for two weeks in early spring 1999. The link was not featured on any of eBay's top pages, but eBay was one of the most heavily trafficked sites in the world. During the two weeks the link was active 150 cases were filed with the Online Ombuds Office regarding disputes arising off of eBay. All of the cases were handled by Mark Eckstein, who as a result is probably the most experienced online mediator in the world. The program was considered a success, and in a follow-up conducted by eBay the users expressed satisfaction with the service and argued that it should be available on a permanent basis.

At the same time, a group of consultants at McKinsey, a prestigious management consulting firm, were looking into possible startups they could create and manage. Steve Abernathy, Ahmed Khaishgi, and

Lalitha Vaidyanathan were all working in the New York office of McKinsey, and they began to explore the idea of some sort of trust-in-transactions company to increase confidence in e-commerce. They had some introductory discussions with Ethan Katsh in the fall of 1999 and learned of the pilot with eBay. eBay had a record of working with promising startups on services it thought were useful to its core business, and then acquiring those companies at generous margins. So after some discussions Katsh decided to sign on with the group of consultants as an advisor and to roll the eBay pilot project over to the new company.

The name chosen for the company at inception was Transecure, which captured the sense of securing transactions over the Internet. The initial pool of mediators was drawn from a list compiled by Katsh from a series of announcements on the DisRes listserv, which Katsh maintained, and which was hosted by the Online Ombuds Office. Mark Eckstein also joined the company to contribute his expertise to the new enterprise.

A few months later, the name of the company was changed to SquareTrade, which did a better job communicating the ideas of both fairness and trade. SquareTrade received some seed investment from some prominent angel investors in the Bay Area and eventually raised significant investment to support its growth. The new SquareTrade website was launched in March 2000 and the service was fully integrated into eBay.

SquareTrade's methodology is simple. Any buyer or seller with a complaint contacts SquareTrade and files a complaint. They are asked certain questions about the nature of their dispute, and common solutions to frequent dispute types are presented to the complainant along with an inquiry into whether the complainant would be amenable to any of the suggested resolutions. Then the other party to the dispute is contacted and provided with some information about the nature of the SquareTrade process. They, too, are presented with some common resolutions and asked if they would be amenable to any of the resolutions. If each side selects the same suggested resolution, the Square-Trade system recommends that the parties resolve the dispute in that manner.

If an agreed-upon resolution is not forthcoming, the two parties are put into a negotiation environment where they can discuss their problem without the assistance of a mediator. This environment is made available to the parties at no cost. If the parties cannot reach agreement on their own in the negotiation environment, they can request the assistance of a mediator for a nominal fee. If a mediator is brought in, the mediator then works with the parties to resolve the issue at hand. If they are unable to resolve the dispute, then the mediator can make a suggestion to the parties as to how they think the dispute should be resolved, in sort of an expert evaluation role. However, the suggestion is not binding.

Starting with the list provided by Katsh and Eckstein of dispute resolvers interested in handling cases online, word spread quickly about SquareTrade's services, and many mediators got involved. Eventually SquareTrade capped their panel at about three hundred neutrals.

Ethan Katsh and Janet Rifkin both signed on as initial advisors to SquareTrade, and the advisory board soon boasted a very prestigious list of members: Roger Fisher, author of the seminal dispute resolution book *Getting to Yes* (1983); David Johnson, the Washington, D.C., cyberlaw expert and originator of the Virtual Magistrate project; and Jonathan Zittrain, professor at Harvard Law School and faculty member at the Berkman Center for Internet and Society, to name only a few.

SquareTrade initially focused on these B2C cases from eBay, and there was no shortage of work. Caseloads grew quickly as awareness of the SquareTrade solution spread among eBay users. In the first year of SquareTrade's existence it handled more than 100,000 cases, the vast majority of which came from eBay. Soon SquareTrade expanded its focus to include other types of disputes, such as business-to-business matters. A panel of more business-focused neutrals was put together, including Linda Singer and Michael Lewis of ADR Associates, a prominent alternative dispute resolution firm in Washington, D.C.

SquareTrade's core competency lies in their experience with B2C dispute resolution on a large scale. The SquareTrade platform has supported the largest volume of ODR cases anywhere in the world.

GETTING CONSUMERS TO TRUST ONLINE TRANSACTIONS

For most people who think about and design e-commerce systems, dispute resolution is one discrete piece of an overall trust-in-transactions architecture. On its own, dispute resolution has value, but more often it's considered to be a component of a broader schema. Users on a website will not be assured purely by a notice that the website offers dispute resolution services. It may raise other questions in your mind, such as: Why do they offer a dispute resolution service? Does that mean I'm likely to be involved in a dispute if I engage in transactions on this site? You don't just want to use dispute resolution to resolve problems that have already occurred. Ideally, you want to solve the problems before they occur.

As a result, B2C ODR makes more sense in the context of other confidence-building programs. A seal at the bottom of a website promoting dispute resolution will not mean as much to a user as a seal at the bottom of a website promoting the website's participation in a comprehensive trust-in-transaction program of which dispute resolution is a component.

Ratings

A logical way to build trust-in-transactions is to connect buyers and sellers to some sort of system that keeps track of their transaction history. Every time a business takes part in a transaction, for example, the system could invite the other side to offer their perspective on how well the business performed. Over time a comprehensive history of the business's transactions would develop, a history that new customers could consult before they decided to buy or sell something with that business.

The most comprehensive ratings program along these lines is eBay's feedback system. Feedback on eBay allows former transaction partners to "rate" the buyers and sellers with whom they transact. These feedback ratings are taken very seriously, because future buyers and sellers rely heavily on these numerical ratings to decide who they will and will not buy from and sell to. Therefore, the number-one motivation for participating in a SquareTrade dispute resolution process is to protect against an unfavorable rating from the other side.

Efforts at creating a Web-wide rating system have had mixed results. The most successful, Open Ratings and BizRate, have not been able to create a critical mass. They also have not been integrated into e-commerce sites, particularly those that have had negative comments lodged against them in the system. Some sites like PlanetFeedback have less a ratings system than an open complaints process, where any user anywhere on the Web can post their horror stories for other consumers to read. The problem with these types of sites is that they don't have any context. American Airlines may have fifty complaints lodged against it on a complaint site, but how many people fly on its planes every day? A small regional airline may have only a handful of complaints, but proportionally it might be a much greater percentage of their passengers. Consumers often make decisions about which sites to patronize and which sites to avoid based on non-scientific, non-representative analyses. Most businesses are reluctant to promote ratings or feedback sites that may spread stories that the businesses feel are inappropriate or inaccurate.

If a ratings website was to gain significant penetration into the Web's user base then it might come to have the incentive effect of urging businesses to use ODR to prevent negative feedback. In the meantime, however, Web businesses may be content merely ignoring these types of ratings and feedback programs or arguing that the information posted on them is not representative of customer experiences as a whole. These types of enforcement mechanisms will need to grow beyond the bounds of a single site to range across the Internet if they are to be broadly effective in getting businesses to implement ODR programs.

Trustmarks

Much of the energy in the B2C ODR space is currently devoted to discussions of trustmarks. ADR and ODR providers, such as the BBB and SquareTrade, currently sell Web seals that sellers can put on their sites, to let buyers know that they are certified by a third party as being a trustworthy transaction partner. These seals are provided to websites who meet certain criteria and pay dues to the trustmark issuer.

ODR providers are tempted to issue trustmarks because it is an easy way for the website that posts the trustmark to advertise its participation in a dispute resolution program. It is also a way for ODR providers to get revenue, as trustmark holders have to pay a certain amount per month or per year to have the right to display the mark. The argument is that because customers are more willing to buy when they see a trustmark on a website, the merchant paying for the mark will more than recoup its investment over time.

On the surface, trustmarks appear to be a very sensible way for e-commerce websites to put consumers at ease. In practice, however, trustmarks can be a very difficult solution. In order to be effective, a trustmark needs to reach critical mass. Consumers need to know what a trustmark means if it is to be a useful way to set their mind at ease. Logos from organizations like the BBB or TRUSTe have reached this level of critical mass, as most users have seen these marks repeatedly on other sites and have some sense of what they signify. New marks, however, have a difficult time reaching that level of penetration. Because the Web is so diverse, with a wide variety of certification bodies, there has developed something like a trustmark glut. Some Web vendors have six or seven trustmarks appended on the bottom of their homepages. There are marks for privacy, for secure transactions, for good consumer feedback, and for various Web quality awards. There are so many marks that most consumers have little idea what any of them mean, and few are likely to take the time to bother figuring any of them out.

Websites are increasingly reluctant to post trustmarks on their homepage for several reasons. First, some feel it cheapens the design of the site to have a cluster of trustmarks at the bottom of their pages, none of which are designed to fit in with the site's color palette. Second, trustmarks often look like advertisements for the site that issues them. If a user clicks on a trustmark, they are often transported to the website of the trustmark issuer. Why give up valuable Web real estate to a link that may take a user away from your site? Third, putting a trustmark on your website may seem a little defensive. If a user comes to your site and the first thing they see is a brightly colored icon assuring them that there's redress in case any disputes arise, they may wonder to themselves, does this site generate a lot of disputes? Many companies feel the best trustmark is their brand. Coca-Cola doesn't need a trustmark attesting that it's a good product. The reputation of the brand sells consumers on the product.

The best trustmarks are the ones that customers have come to accept, such as the BBB seal, the TRUSTe logo, and the VeriSign logo. Consumers might not even pay any attention to those seals because they exist on so many sites, but if they do notice them, they are assured by their presence. Trustmarks that appear only on a few sites that the consumer visits may make the consumer question how meaningful the trustmark really is, which may raise more of the user's concerns than they assuage.

It is also important to note that trustmarks can work within particular constituencies and user groups. Not every trustmark has to penetrate the entire Internet to become useful. SquareTrade, for example, put its efforts into penetrating the eBay market, and they were very successful. SquareTrade's seal is now meaningful to those consumers who frequent eBay because SquareTrade focused their energy on building awareness in that particular marketplace. A user who has never shopped on eBay might not immediately know the significance of the SquareTrade seal, but once they see it on a variety of auctions and see eBay's page explaining its value they can quickly come to understand its meaning. For new entrants into the trustmark space, finding a smaller constituency to target might make more sense than going after the whole Internet. Creating seals for a particular country or region might make more sense than trying to create another TRUSTe, for example.

E-Commerce Insurance

One solution that e-commerce companies are using to put the minds of their customers at ease is insurance. Insurance companies have stepped into the trust-in-transactions space by providing policies that guarantee that a user will not be the victim of fraud. By collecting a small premium payment from every seller in a marketplace, or by taking a tiny percentage of each transaction, insurance companies can aggregate the risk of bad transactions among all the participants. By calculating the likely percentage of bad transactions, estimating the monetary exposure from those transactions, and then collecting enough of a premium to cover those transactions, insurance companies can guarantee that any buyer or seller who is the victim of fraud will be able to get his or her money back, even if the fraudulent transaction partner can't be found. Other insurance packages may guarantee that a buyer will always be able to get her product from a seller, even if the seller goes out of business.

Insurance may not solve the root causes of fraud, but it does treat the symptoms. Consumers will feel more comfortable if they know they can recover their money. However, it may provide an incentive for sellers to engage in fraud if they know the people they defraud can get their money back from the insurance company. Insurance providers need to match these types of programs with aggressive dispute resolution efforts if they are to be successful. (For more information on e-commerce insurance and ODR, see Chapter Seven.)

Unconditional Money-Back Guarantees

In the BBB's standards for e-commerce providers the initial require-ment was for all e-commerce sellers to have dispute resolution options available for their customers. However, some of the sellers balked at that requirement. They reasoned that if they offered an unconditional money-back guarantee for all products sold then there would never be a reason to have a dispute resolution process. The BBB thought about that point and eventually agreed, changing their standards to call for dispute resolution availability or an unconditional money-back guarantee. However, the guarantee needs to be fully unconditional or the need for dispute resolution remains.

On the Web the logic for these types of programs is weakened. Because there is a cost involved with getting the good back to the seller, there is an additional cost to the return beyond the write-off of the merchandise. If the seller removes the obligation from the buyer to return the item after the money-back guarantee is granted, that cre-ates an incentive for the buyer to engage in fraud, because they think that they will be able to keep the item even after getting their money back.

KEY CONSIDERATIONS FOR B2C ODR PROGRAMS

Face-to-face consumer complaint mechanisms are not highly regarded. In fact, as Laura Nader has pointed out, dispute resolution mechanisms for consumer complaints are notorious for discouraging consumers while being advantageous to businesses.[5] Consumers often lack the resources to put up a good fight with the company, while the company (as a repeat player) has an incentive to keep customers in the dark in order to make it harder for them to prove their cases. Cor-porations often have an incentive to wage a war of attrition with cus-tomers because they have more resources. Most consumer complaint mechanisms have not been able to bridge this gap.

The Internet has somewhat changed this power balance. Con-sumers can more easily exchange information, which allows them to become informed before they get into a transaction. Online com-plaint filing is also proving much more effective than in-person filing. The Federal Trade Commission (FTC) and BBB both have noted that the ability to file complaints online has led to an increase in the num-ber of complaints. Businesses have proven less willing to wage wars of attrition because it is easier for customers to take their grievances public over the Web. This has led to an increase in the use of dispute resolution by companies in an attempt to head off the circulation of negative stories over the Internet.

While they may be better than face-to-face redress systems in some respects, B2C online dispute resolution systems have their own pressure points and weaknesses. Systems designers need to be cognizant of these considerations when they are contemplating what type of ODR they should make available to consumers.

CREDIT CARDS AND CHARGEBACKS

The number-one way funds are transferred online is by credit card. Most credit card companies resolve complaints against the system through the use of a mechanism called chargebacks. Chargebacks enable the credit card holder to protest any charge on their card, putting the burden of proof back onto the merchant. The credit card companies urge buyers and sellers to sort out confusion themselves before they use chargebacks, but if a complaint is lodged the amount is "charged back" to the merchant and the merchant then justifies the charge to get it reprocessed. In practice, this often means that the buyer has the power.

Credit cards in the face-to-face world experience chargebacks extremely rarely—as low as .001 percent of transactions are charged back in the face-to-face world. This probably is accounted for by the fact that most products or services are purchased first hand in the real world, or the service at a restaurant is provided before the charge, so the quality of a purchase can be determined before the card is charged. The real-time nature of the face-to-face world removes much of the uncertainty that can necessitate a chargeback.

Online experience is proving to be quite different. By some accounts, online chargebacks are occuring in up to 6 percent of transactions. While being stuck with the cost of a product .001 percent of the time in the real world may be acceptable to a merchant for the convenience of using charge cards and making customers feel secure, it is almost certainly not enough to compensate merchants for being stuck with the cost of 6 percent of their inventory. Investing all of the power in the buyer through chargebacks can skew ODR systems, because the buyer's alternative to a negotiated agreement is just to stop payment. Online merchants are increasingly calling for credit card companies to offer alternate forms of redress to credit card users online, forms that are fairer to both parties in a transaction. Dispute resolution clearly fits this need.

POWER DIFFERENTIALS BETWEEN CUSTOMERS AND BUSINESSES

Businesses and consumers use ODR in very different ways. Consumers may utilize ODR once or twice a year, whereas companies could have more than a dozen processes going at any given time. Companies can also insert binding clauses into click-through agreements at the top of a site where it is very unlikely that consumers will read them. Individual consumers will also be at a major disadvantage when it comes to enforcing agreements, or even understanding their rights in online transactions. Businesses are more likely to make informed choices about ODR providers, while consumers are vulnerable to having particular ODR providers imposed upon them. As a result it is much more important for outside bodies to set standards ensuring procedural fairness in B2C processes.

The differing perspectives of business groups and consumer groups heavily influence the current debate over standards for B2C ODR. Business groups argue that e-commerce is just in its infancy and burdening it with regulations will crush its ability to attain its full potential. Governments that put requirements on e-commerce companies will put those companies at a competitive disadvantage to e-commerce companies in less regulation-heavy countries. Over the long term, this will push e-commerce profits and firms to the areas of the globe that have the fewest regulations. Businesses also argue that the marketplace is creating incentives for companies to adopt dispute resolution programs into the way they do business, as consumers will increasingly come to expect that such services are available. As Peter Phillips of the CPR Institute for Dispute Resolution has argued, quality businesses will select quality ODR providers, so there is little incentive to start forcing the issue with regulations.[6]

Consumer groups have a different perspective. Because businesses often choose which ODR provider they and their customers will work with, ODR providers know where their bread is buttered. ODR companies will work to keep business interests happy, because the businesses choose which ODR providers will get work. Also, consumers do not have extensive experience with ODR, as they may only be involved with a couple of ODR procedures every few years. Businesses, on the other hand, are repeat players, and they quickly learn the subtleties of the process. A process that appears fair through one or two uses may have built into it a systemic bias in favor of business interests that no one consumer can see but that becomes obvious over time. Relationships may grow between ODR providers, their neutrals, and the business representatives that participate in many of these processes.

Business groups like the E-Commerce Working Group (representing companies like Dell, Microsoft, IBM, and Hewlett-Packard) have also argued for mandatory ODR processes, even when they are nonbinding, like mediation. They argue that such a requirement is necessary to get consumers to utilize the services, even when they are in the consumer's best interest. Consumer groups (such as the Trans-Atlantic Consumer Working Group, the Consumer Federation, and Consumers International) have responded that such required processes are simply an additional hurdle for consumers to jump through so that they can obtain redress, and if such mechanisms are required then a certain number of consumers will simply decide that redress isn't worth the effort, which is in the interest of the businesses. These consumer groups have argued against industry self-regulation, as they do not believe that businesses will voluntarily work in the best interest of consumers.

There is a long history of suspicion between these two constituencies, one which won't be easily resolved in the debate over ODR. What is clear is that any effective ODR provider must be aware of the sensitivities on both sides of the issue, and work to reach buy-in from both business and consumer groups to avoid accusations of bias.

Predispute Binding Arbitration Clauses

Many businesses have shown an affinity for binding dispute resolution techniques, mostly because the finality that comes with arbitration is appealing to corporations. The number-one reason for this is because finality completely removes the threat of a lawsuit. Many businesses, such as credit card companies, have even resorted to predispute binding arbitration clauses in their service agreements, effectively preventing customers from suing in court. These techniques have been decried by consumer groups, who believe that such predispute clauses are abusive. Most consumers do not think about future disputes that might arise when they sign a service agreement with a bank or with a credit card company. However, post-dispute binding arbitration agreements, provided that parties are fully informed of their rights, can be very effective and rarely are questioned by consumer advocates. Online dispute resolution service providers need to stand firm on ethical service delivery grounds and not give corporations whatever they ask for if those requests violate basic tenets of dispute resolution practice. (For more information about predispute binding arbitration clauses, see Chapter Fifteen.)

WHAT IS HAPPENING NOW

The Federal Trade Commission/Department of Commerce conference on B2C online dispute resolution was a watershed event in crystallizing the issue of B2C ODR in the United States. The conference was motivated by European moves, coming as early as 1997, to regulate ODR and ODR providers. Europe is more favorably predisposed toward both non-binding dispute resolution and ODR standardization. Most European countries are more comfortable with regulating businesses than the United States. The B2C ODR conference in The Hague made this distinction even clearer. Consumer advocates are much more forceful in their calls for government intervention in Europe. Concerns over privacy and systemic bias are more pronounced in the European context.

The International Chamber of Commerce B2C ODR Clearinghouse

The International Chamber of Commerce (ICC), which calls itself "the World's Business Organization," houses the most prestigious international court of arbitration. This court of arbitration usually handles only a couple hundred business-to-business cases a year, but cases usually focus on disputes with very large monetary amounts at stake, some in excess of hundreds of millions of dollars. In an interesting change of role, the ICC has announced that it is in discussion with a variety of institutions (notably Consumers International, one of the largest international consumer advocacy groups) regarding the creation of a global B2C ODR clearinghouse. The clearinghouse would take in consumer disputes from around the world and then refer them to ODR providers deemed appropriate on a case-by-case basis. In this clearinghouse role, the ICC would establish strict standards for the ODR providers to which it referred cases. Every provider that wished to participate would have to prove that it met the ICC's ODR standards on an ongoing basis. If it ever fell out of compliance the ICC would refuse to send it any further cases.

While this idea does appear to have its merits, particularly as a non-regulatory mechanism for ensuring that ODR providers meet a certain set of baseline standards for practice, its success depends on several things. First, while the ICC is very prestigious in business-to-business circles, it does not have much of a reputation with global consumers. For consumers to trust the ICC's case intake and management role there would need to be a major media push to spread the word. The effort would need to be branded in a compelling way, and the services would have to be simple enough for consumers to understand without too much difficulty. The ICC needs to become much more than a middleman passing cases around if they are to have enough value to merit their central position. Second, the number of global B2C e-commerce disputes could soon reach into the millions. The ICC is going to need to build the technological and administrative capacity to handle all of these cases, in a wide variety of languages, if it is to stay on top of the tidal wave. It is also going to need a way to fund this infrastructure. It will be difficult, if not impossible, for the ICC to make money off of this referral role. It is already hard to see how ODR providers will make enough money to resolve these low-value disputes, much less where additional funds to support the case administration might come from.

The BBB/Eurochambres/FEDMA Global B2C ODR Network

Another major development in B2C ODR is the development of a global trustmark network involving the Better Business Bureau in the United States and the Federation of Direct Marketers (FEDMA) and Eurochambres in Europe. Between the three organizations, the network could cover more than eighteen million businesses across Europe and the United States. Many other global consumer complaint organizations, including some from Asia and South America, have also expressed interest in joining this initiative.

The BBB in the United States is the premier private business complaint-handling body. Most consumers have instant brand recognition for the BBB's logo, as they've seen it in shop windows and advertisements for many years. The BBB is supported by some of the largest businesses in the United States, including IBM, Microsoft, Hewlett-Packard, and Proctor & Gamble. The BBB also has more than a hundred branch offices in cities and towns across the country, giving them a regional presence no other organization can match.

The BBB serves as the default consumer complaint handling service in the United States. If a consumer has a problem with a car dealer, plumber, or airline, they can take that complaint to the BBB to have it addressed. Outside of North America, however, there is not much awareness of the BBB. In Europe the chambers of commerce are the primary providers of consumer complaint functions. In the United States businesses voluntarily join regional chambers of commerce, but in some areas of Europe, membership in the chamber is required of all businesses. This reach positions the chambers perfectly for the role of consumer complaint administrators.

The vision is for each participating organization to coordinate the sale of a jointly branded trustmark to businesses within its region. The trustmark would have a uniform look and logo to it, though it would be offered by a variety of different organizations around the world. Should a consumer have a problem with an online transaction they could click on the logo and be directed to a complaint form in their language. Once the complaint was registered the network of participating organizations would coordinate the involvement of the responding business, and eventually facilitate the resolution of the complaint. If a dispute was between a buyer and seller in different regions the two organizations that govern those regions would work together to share complaint information, provide translation, and assign appropriate neutrals. The technology employed by all of the participating regional organizations would facilitate this type of information exchange through data connectors that allowed the easy exchange of complaint data.

This system has many potential benefits. First, it leverages the position of the default consumer complaint bodies around the world to get maximum consumer awareness of the network. Whatever organization traditionally handles the consumer complaint role in a particular region can join the network to provide trustmark and dispute resolution services. Second, it adjusts much more flexibly to the different legal requirements of countries and regions around the world. Instead of a single organization monitoring the various legal requirements placed on ODR providers around the world, each individual organization can stay abreast of the developments in its region. Third, this design is much more sensitive to cultural and language differences.

Such a system is sprawling to design and difficult to maintain. The quality of one regional organization's technology or customer support infrastructure may deteriorate and the other providers would not have the authority to address the situation. Fees to support the system, presumably to be drawn from dues paid for the trustmark placed on business web sites, may not generate enough revenue in some regions to support the system. Also, power struggles could erupt between the participating organizations, each of which might prefer its particular technology to the other platforms being utilized.

The American Bar Association e-Commerce ADR Task Force

A comprehensive effort to think through the challenges of ODR in the B2C context is being conducted by a task force set up by the American Bar Association (ABA). The task force has convened meetings in New York, San Diego, London, Paris, Washington, D.C., and Toronto in an effort to gather feedback relating to e-commerce dispute resolution. The members of the task force represent many of the ABA's sections, including the business law, international, and dispute resolution sections. A website to support the work of the committee was set up in early 2001, providing a variety of surveys intended to gather more in-depth feedback about e-commerce ODR from ODR providers, neutrals, users, and businesses.

The first product to come out of the task force was a white paper draft that offered several suggestions to ensure that ODR services remain effective and ethical. The primary idea was for the creation of an ODR provider seal that could be issued by a central authority. This seal would certify that the website displaying the seal met certain standards for ODR service provision. The ABA has no intention of enforcing or maintaining such a seal system, but perhaps the BBB or ICC efforts would be willing to take on those obligations. The task force also began to make some recommendations for what standards ODR providers should be expected to meet.

The final white paper detailing the task force's recommendations will be issued in 2002. Based on the range of input collected by the task force it should do a good job balancing the interests of both consumers and businesses, but how much influence the report will have in changing the way B2C ODR services are regulated and administered is an open question.

Electronic Consumer Dispute Resolution (ECODIR)

Another transboundary ODR system currently being developed is the European Union-funded ECODIR project based out of the University of Namur in Belgium. Powered by ODR technology originally provided by eResolution in Montreal, ECODIR was built by a coalition of French, Irish, and Belgian academics. The EU has allocated funds to several different ODR efforts, including one in Italy, but the ECODIR effort is the first EU-funded platform to launch as a publicly available service. Eurochambres, one of the partners in the BBB-sponsored B2C ODR network, may use this platform to handle its cases.

Institutional Emphasis

Both the BBB/Eurochambres/FEDMA network and the ICC clearinghouse indicate the amount of international planning that is going into the development of these global B2C ODR systems. Of all the areas in which ODR is being applied it is B2C e-commerce that has garnered the most attention from governments, non-profits, international institutions, and providers. B2C ODR has the most institutional emphasis from across the spectrum, which both burdens it with conflict over how it should function and blesses it with more resources, stakeholders, and participant interest. Whatever network emerges to meet the redress needs of consumers will likely be the most comprehensive global ODR system ever created. Whether or not it will be a success story or a battleground remains to be seen.

Case Study: B2C Auction

During a fast-finger auction hosted by biggieauctions.com, Arthur purchased an original, mint set of John Lennon portrait stamps from different countries around the world. The photograph of the stamp set showed at least sixteen stamps with popular paintings and drawings of John Lennon from different stages of his career. Long a connoisseur of stamps depicting famous pop music characters, the photo had two stamps Arthur was particularly excited about: a stamp from Guyana with a black-and-white rendering of the *Revolver*-era John, and a close-up of John's face on a stamp from the Antilles from the *Imagine* time period.

Three weeks later, the stamps arrived, but Arthur was disappointed to see that the stamps in the set he received were not the same stamps that were depicted on the website. In particular, Arthur received multiple copies of some of the less desirable stamps, and neither the Guyana nor the Antilles stamps were included in the package. What's more, the stamps had been sealed in plastic wrap against a cardboard backing that had gotten bent in the mail, so many of the stamps were creased, or the serrations along the edge of the stamps had been blunted, making them unmountable.

Arthur contacted the seller of the stamps, who still had the product listed on biggieauctions.com—in fact, Arthur later learned, the product was perpetually listed by this seller, who seemingly had an endless supply of these stamp collections. Arthur communicated his dismay about the lack of selection in the shipment he received, and how more choice stamps had been depicted on the Web description of the product. Upon revisiting the listing on biggieauctions.com, however, Arthur did notice in the fine print that no guarantee was offered that the depicted stamps would actually be in the shipped orders.

Arthur heard nothing back from the seller, so he sent two more messages. The third message did generate a reply, but it was little more than an automated message saying that the seller's company (Celebrity Stamps of Des Moines, Iowa) took customer satisfaction very seriously and that a representative would contact him soon. Unfortunately, after another week, no representative had contacted Arthur.

After consulting biggieauctions.com's customer service pages, Arthur sent a message complaining about the misrepresentation in the seller's posting. Very quickly, biggieauctions.com sent a reply stating that their responsibility was matching buyer and seller through their innovative time-based bidding process and that in that role biggieauctions.com had no responsibility for problems that arose out of the transactions it facilitated.

Arthur was becoming so frustrated that he was tempted to give up. The collection had only cost him $27.75, so there was a strong inclination to just live with the disappointment. However, he was angry at the misrepresentation, and convinced that Celebrity Stamps had the stamps that he really wanted. After visiting a resource site with information pertaining to biggieauctions.com, Arthur stumbled upon an online dispute resolution service provider that helped buyers and sellers resolve disputes arising out of auctions. Arthur filled out the case intake form and waited for a reply.

He received an automated message stating that the other party (Celebrity Stamps) would be contacted about the matter, and that he would know whether or not the case was initiated in three days. On the second day, an automated notice came back from the online dispute resolution site informing him that the other side had in fact logged on and agreed to initiate the case. The email also provided a URL for the space where the initial negotiation would take place, and informed Arthur that there was no cost for the service.

Arthur logged onto the site with the username and password provided to him in the email. It was fairly intuitive how to post his initial message, in which he detailed the history of the situation and expressed his desire—to get a refund or to get a new set of stamps including the ones he most wanted.

For two days there was no reply on the site. Finally, Arthur received an email notifying him that new content had been posted in the negotiation space. Arthur logged into the negotiation space and was dismayed with what waited for him there: a very angry tirade from someone referred to as stamps128@stampfan.com berating Arthur for threatening his business and giving him low feedback on biggieauctions.com, and also explaining that he had sold hundreds of these sets and had never had a problem. There was neither acknowledgement of Arthur's proposal nor a willingness expressed to make the situation right.

Arthur wasn't sure how to respond, so he sent an email to the support address specified on the dispute resolution website. He soon received a response from someone named "Karen" who suggested that he repropose his preferred solution, or he could involve a live mediator in the discussion for a payment of $15. Arthur was reluctant to pay the $15, especially as the set of stamps had only cost about $30, so he re-posted his proposal, along with an assurance that if the stamps were resent he would not lodge any negative feedback ratings on biggieauctions.com in regard to Celebrity Stamps.

The next day, a single message was posted in the negotiation room on the online dispute resolution site: "Fine." A week later, Arthur received another packet of Lennon stamps, this one also bent, but with the Guyana and Antilles stamps included in the collection. Between the two shipments Arthur had approximately fifteen stamps in good enough condition to mount them in his stamp book.

Analysis

The low dollar value of many B2C transactions make finding a sustainable revenue model a challenge. Automated negotiation environments, or processes with minimal human interaction, are sometimes the most appropriate response to B2C disputes. The cost for the dispute resolution process might be borne by the marketplace (in this example, biggieauctions.com) as a way to build confidence in the trading environment. However, a low filing fee is often wise to discourage frivolous claims.

Sellers often create conflicts with their customers simply because they are overburdened. The lack of a response magnifies the frustration of the buyer and makes resolution more difficult. Most merchants who have built any brand at all in a particular space understand that being flexible in making customers happy is usually a good investment, even if it involves a modest cost. Because customers are usually satisfied with a replacement product as opposed to a cash reimbursement, the merchant can often settle the matter at a much lower out-of-pocket cost. In our case study, each set of stamps sold probably cost the seller less than $3, though the value to the customer was approximately $30.

Conclusion

It is not an easy thing to change the buying habits of consumers, and e-commerce is going to take a much longer time to perfect than all the original dot-com business plans had predicted. Eventually the backlash against businesses doing e-commerce on the Internet will ease. Already B2C e-commerce has become a fixture of the global economy, with U.S. e-commerce retailers completing several billion dollars worth of transactions a year.

Online dispute resolution does for B2C e-commerce marketplaces what the returns desk and small claims court does for offline marketplaces: it lets customers know that they can buy with confidence. As Orna Rabinovich-Einy has observed, "Offering links to reputable external ODR services will, in time, become an industry standard among major commercial websites as a means of assuring customer satisfaction and confidence."[7] Without that assurance, consumers know that they might as well go to the mall.

CHAPTER SIX

A Well-Lighted Place
ODR and B2B E-Commerce

. . . a simple and affordable global resolution process for inevitable disputes is essential.

> *Jean Monty, CEO, Bell Canada*[1]

While business-to-consumer e-commerce grabbed the early headlines in the Internet revolution, business-to-business e-commerce eventually emerged as the real heavy hitter. Businesses may not buy as exciting items online as consumers (think a ton of fresh fish as opposed to a DVD player), but their transaction volumes are much higher. While B2C e-commerce is limited by low transaction values (usually less than $500) B2B transactions are usually between $1,000 and $50,000.

By some estimates B2B e-commerce will account for ten times more transaction volume than business-to-consumer e-commerce by 2006, generating more than six trillion dollars in global B2B e-commerce volume. Business-to-business transactions, because of their higher value and savvy participants, may even be a better fit for the full range of online dispute resolution services than B2C or consumer-to-consumer (C2C) e-commerce.

B2B MARKETPLACES: THE RISE AND FALL

Similar to the B2C companies, B2B marketplaces have had a wild ride through the expansion and contraction of the Internet economy.

Once considered unglamorous and ungainly, B2B markets became the exclusive focus of entrepreneurs and investors for a good timespan of the Internet craze. Once the definition of what was a B2B transaction was clarified, and the staggering size of the overall market was comprehended, the appeal of the consumer-only business models (like Amazon.com) quickly evaporated.

The Development of Online Exchanges

The original design for B2B transactions focused on the creation of radical new online marketplaces, often called exchanges, where suppliers and buyers from all over the world would come together to sell their wares. These exchanges would be like huge bazaars with everything for sale in the world, and the sellers with the lowest prices could get immediate attention from buyers on the other side of the planet. Economists predicted a "frictionless commerce" space where the cost of going out to find the best deal was so close to zero as to be meaningless. The efficiencies that would come from such an environment would lead to higher growth rates and eliminate the need for warehousing and stockpiling goods.

The companies that were created to enact these marketplaces were often started by entrepreneurs looking to capitalize on the expansion of the Internet. Thousands of these online exchanges targeting a wide variety of business "verticals" (meaning specific market spaces) sprung up almost overnight. Some of these companies were legendary "category killers" that promised to change whole industries. One famous exchange involved Chemdex, in the bulk chemicals industry. Instead of pouring through shelves of thick catalogs to find the one supplier who had the chemical you needed, Chemdex promised to aggregate all the suppliers in one online marketplace so that chemicals could be ordered quickly and easily. All the suppliers would join this marketplace to get the largest number of potential buyers, and the efficiencies would convince all buyers to partake as well.

Venture capitalists loved these new online exchanges because they saw them taking over huge pieces of commerce. Speed was thought to be the key determinant of success, so many of them raised huge mounds of cash and raced to be the top player in the space. The thought was that in each vertical market there would be one "winner" who became the default marketplace, and the key was to get enough people into your marketplace as early as possible so as to increase the chances that people would come to think of your exchange as the default. That's why so many millions were spent on Super Bowl advertisements by companies trying to get their name into the minds of millions of Americans. The sense was that the faster a company could build its brand the greater its chance of success in becoming the default.

Network Value

Online marketplaces work similarly to fax machines. The first person who bought a fax machine had a worthless device. Once the second person bought a machine, however, the value of the first person's machine increased, because now he could send a document to someone else. From then on, every fax machine that was sold increased the value of the machines that had already been purchsed. By the time every office in the country had a fax machine, it had almost become an essential piece of business equipment. This type of network value is one of the key concepts of the Internet, and most of the most successful e-commerce sites (eBay, for instance) make use of this dynamic.

A good example of network value in B2B transactions is the growth of PurchasePro, an online exchange in Las Vegas. PurchasePro had started out as a marketplace focusing on the entertainment industry in Las Vegas, namely the hotels and resorts along the Vegas Strip. They signed up the kitchens and front offices of the resorts and then got the suppliers (bulk food providers, office supply companies, manufacturers of linens, and so on) to join the marketplace as well, touting their service as a way for the suppliers to access new customers. The customers liked it because they could order from a centralized interface whenever they needed new supplies, and it was easy for them to see which companies had the lowest prices. PurchasePro got paid a small transaction fee for each sale that went through their platform. Soon after the service started to grow, the suppliers to the hotels started to urge *their* suppliers to use the platform (for example, the linen company urged their supplier of cotton to log on, or the office supply company urged their pencil manufacturer to log on). The hotels and resorts began to offer their services through the marketplace as well. Soon PurchasePro was expanding its user base through something called viral marketing, where each new participant gets "infected" with the idea and then goes out and passes it on to others.

PurchasePro became a very large company, drawing in new suppliers around the country and earning significant transaction fees. Eventually they had so much power as the marketplace operator that they could make money selling ad banners on their system.

While watching the PurchasePros and Chemdexes of the world expand, the more traditional power players in these vertical markets got scared that they were going to be cut out of the loop on many of the transactions they had facilitated in the past. Buyers and sellers might be able to find each other on the Web, ending their reliance on large players to make the connections. As a response, the larger players started to formulate their own marketplaces. Instead of signing up with a hot young start-up trying to be the default marketplace for auto parts, large auto makers like Ford eventually decided to go their own way. Major companies that had been competitors for years came together to create their own online marketplaces to compete with the upstarts. In the auto parts arena, for instance, six of the world's largest automobile manufacturers came together to create Covisint.com, a global online exchange for auto parts. Other online exchanges created by the established players are sites like Orbitz, an alliance of sixty airlines into one huge travel site, and Transora, an exchange focused on comestibles that involves the largest food-producing companies.

The Crash

Once the established players got off the mark and began creating their own exchanges, the start-ups were in trouble. Very few of them had garnered the critical mass necessary to compete with the market leaders. Soon the hype about the dot-com economy started to fade, and many companies found it hard to preserve their cash. Venture capitalists were less enthusiastic about putting large amounts of money into exchanges that were competing with the traditional market leaders. Even poster child companies of the new economy like Chemdex had to throw in the towel. However, many of those early companies transformed themselves into technology providers who then sold their online marketplace software to the more established companies moving into the space.

Eventually even the established players began to have a hard time making money in online exchanges. It was very expensive to get new buyers and sellers into the system, and even those that did use the new marketplaces didn't return to use it again and again. The predictions for how fast B2B e-commerce would grow didn't prove to be accurate. Many of the near-zero transaction costs and "frictionless commerce" visions never came true. One major reason why was the lack of effective redress options. A significant percentage of transactions occurring through the exchanges resulted in problems, and no mechanism existed to easily address those problems. B2B e-commerce didn't live up to its promise partially because online dispute resolution options were not available to businesses when the transactions went awry.

The Issue of Trust

Similar to B2C transactions, online exchanges soon discovered that they had an issue with trust. It was very difficult to determine anything about a potential trading partner found in an online exchange. The international scale of many B2B trading environments, with the related language, shipping, and currency problems, compounded the difficulties.

For example, a company could log onto a B2B fabric exchange and place an order for bulk fabric. The names of different suppliers offering the fabric requested by the buyer then would appear on the screen. Who are these suppliers? What is the quality of their product? In a face-to-face context you could visit the office of the supplier and put your hands on the fabric, but in an online context you don't have that ability. Maybe at best you can visit their website and see some photos of their product. Have other users had a good experience with that seller? You don't know if you can trust the testimonials on their home page. Will they deliver on time? If you do have a problem with your order, will they address your concern quickly and courteously? Online it is almost impossible to get reliable answers to these questions.

Some companies, such as GeoTrust (a leading business-to-business trust-in-transactions company) are working on developing this very type of trust architecture. ODR provides dispute resolution for transactions that go awry so that disputants don't have to resort to calling lawyers. GeoTrust provides True Credentials, a service that allows buyers and sellers to check out the transaction partners they're contemplating working with, information such as: how long they've been around, where they're located, how many people they employ, their credit rating, and so on. This information can help buyers and sellers avoid transaction partners who seem more likely to generate a disputed transaction. GeoTrust also plans to track complaints about businesses, so that if a business refuses to participate in an ODR process, future transaction partners will be able to see that in the True Credentials record. In this sense, GeoTrust is a global credit rating company for the B2B space.

Private Exchanges

The area of online marketplaces that has had more success in dealing with the trust problem in B2B transactions is private exchanges. In these arrangements, a large company (such as IBM or Dell) sets up a private exchange in which everyone who wants to do business with the sponsor must sign up. When IBM wants to buy hard drive platters, it goes onto its private exchange and finds a seller from whom it wants to buy. Then the architecture of the private exchange makes ordering and fulfillment a snap. Many buyers and suppliers set up their repeated relationships in private exchanges, so the buyer can set a profile that says "I need 500 hard drive platters delivered to this office every Tuesday afternoon" and the exchange platform can execute that instruction at the same time every week, always getting the lowest price.

B2B ONLINE EXCHANGES NEED ODR

B2B exchanges are perfect candidates for online dispute resolution. In B2B transactions the two sides are more likely to be equals, with parity in access to counsel, experience in online marketplaces, and ability to enforce agreements. Buyers and sellers in B2B transactions are also usually repeat players, so they have an incentive to participate in good faith so that they don't jeopardize their future desirability as a transaction partner. Repeat players have much more effective outcomes from dispute resolution, because there is a greater penalty to not abiding by agreements. It's also more difficult for businesses to disappear, because they have a legal identity, established markets and partnerships, and sizable physical locations.

B2B transaction partners also have a mutual interest in keeping their dispute confidential. Most businesses feel that putting company information into the public domain should be avoided, because it cues competitors about internal business decisions and may send the wrong message to other potential transaction partners.

One of the major challenges of ethical dispute resolution service delivery is figuring out who pays the mediator. If the seller pays the cost of the mediator, then there is a risk of bias in the mediator's actions. On the other hand, many buyers cannot afford or are not willing to pay for the services of a mediator. Online exchanges are perfect customers for online dispute resolution because they are neither the buyer or seller in a transaction that they facilitate. Therefore, if they pay the bill for the ODR service (as they should, because ODR increases the credibility of their marketplace and makes future visitors more likely to buy) there is no risk of bias in the actions of the mediator.

ODR in Public and Private Exchanges

Online dispute resolution in a public exchange looks quite different than in a private exchange. In a public exchange, the participants may know nothing about each other. The administrator of the exchange may have approved the participation of both organizations, but there is no guarantee that any two market participants will have an awareness of each other. Most transactions that happen in a public exchange take place between relative strangers, so the importance of a trust architecture is accentuated. If you are going to purchase several tons of bauxite from another company you want to know that company's background and reputation, to ensure that you will be satisfied with the outcome of the transaction.

In a private exchange the transaction partners are much less likely to be strangers. If the exchange is hosted by a single company, like IBM, then IBM likely approved the participation of each individual buyer and seller. Even if there is not comprehensive information about the background of each market participant, IBM has the ability to eject any supplier that it does not like from the marketplace, decreasing the risk of repeatedly unsatisfactory or fraudulent transactions.

If a dispute resolution process is initiated, then it must operate in line with the expectations of the disputants. In a public exchange the dispute resolution process is likely to be more formal, as there is less trust between the parties. Fact finding will probably be more in depth as each side has very little information about the performance or circumstances of the other side. In a private exchange, however, automated dispute resolution procedures are more feasible. Because there

is likely a history of satisfactory transactions between the two partners, protocols may already have been worked out for various transaction problems that have arisen. If a computer is damaged in
shipping, for example, a brief fact-finding as to the nature of the damage may be all that is required for a resolution to take place. Private
exchanges can build on the accumulated goodwill that exists between
the participants, and that can result in more streamlined ODR
mechanisms.

Advancing B2B Technology Supports ODR

The technology behind online exchanges has also experienced major
advances in the past couple of years. The rise of XML (extensible
markup language) has enabled exchange participants to share data
seamlessly between computer platforms, leading to much closer integration of corporate procurement and accounting systems. Electronic
document interchange (EDI) has also gone a long way toward stan-
dardizing transaction flows between businesses.

So many phases of the transaction process have been automated
that soon dispute filing could be largely automated as well. The Joint
Research Center of the European Commission has developed an XML
standard for e-commerce disputes that they are promoting for adoption among ODR service providers. Accounting systems could monitor transactions and then notify system administrators only when
something appears out of order. Then dispute resolution could be
brought in as an exception-handling mechanism to be instituted
only when the system does not operate as planned. The day will
never come when technology can handle every possible dispute, but
technological systems with built-in error checking can go a long
way toward minimizing mistaken orders and miscommunicated
expectations.

Online exchange technology is increasingly being updated to
include automated case filing and management. Coordination with
online dispute resolution service providers can easily be built into the
technology supporting the online marketplaces. In the TradePro
platform (a large B2B online exchange serving the Southeast Asian
marketplace) background information is available on all of the businesses participating in the marketplace, and a dispute can be initiated
with any trading partner by clicking a button next to their name.
This level of integration streamlines the ODR process by instantly

providing all relevant contact information and transaction records to the ODR provider (and, by extension, the neutral), resulting in an even faster resolution of the dispute.

One additional strategy for minimizing B2B disputes is detailed transaction tracking. Tower Technology, an Australian company specializing in unformatted data storage, has created a product that operates like a Web security camera. When a transaction takes place online, Tower's product takes snapshots of every stage, recording all of the submissions from both the buyer and the seller. If a dispute arises later about what information was communicated between the transaction partners they can look into the records that were captured by the security camera and determine exactly what information was entered. The records can also easily be made available to a neutral mediator or arbitrator if an ODR process is initiated. This product will be very useful in certain types of disputes where there is confusion over specific information passed from one party to another.

Provider Profile: Online Resolution

Online Resolution was started by John Helie, Jim Melamed, and myself in the fall of 1999. I was working as the general manager of Mediate.com, the most popular mediation information resource on the Web. John and Jim had founded Mediate.com in the mid-1990s and hired me to help coordinate the construction of many of the websites Mediate.com (and its parent company, Resourceful Internet Solutions) had been contracted to create. The people behind Mediate, including John and Jim, but also its pool of investors, had been involved with the dispute resolution field for decades. John had founded ConflictNet, the first online ADR resource, back in the late 1980s. Many mediators host their homepages on Mediate.com and check the headlines there on a weekly or daily basis. Mediate.com was a great place to find out about all the emerging issues in dispute resolution and technology.

In 1999 the Internet really started to take off, and Mediate.com was doing very well building websites and helping organizations craft their Internet strategies. However, the buzz surrounding online dispute resolution was starting to grow. Blind-bidding sites like ClickNsettle and Cybersettle sprang into prominence through the first half of the year, and there was a sense in the ADR field that this new online component of dispute resolution was going to grow in importance.

Many of our users started to ask us what Mediate.com was planning to do in the area of ODR.

John, Jim, and I had a discussion in the fall of 1999 at Jim's house in Eugene, Oregon, where we talked about the trend. I was very excited about the growth of ODR, and all three of us felt that Mediate.com was perfectly positioned to play a leadership role in developing ODR. So the decision was made to spend some of Mediate.com's time and energy on the development of an online dispute resolution program. It was at that meeting we registered the name Online Resolution.

The project started out as Online Mediators, as we weren't yet ready to offer all of the service elements necessary to call ourselves Online Resolution. In the fall and early winter of 1999 the lead programmer for Mediate.com, Carol Knapp, built the foundation of the Online Mediators case intake and processing system. We made the decision to focus our project on B2B disputes, both because the disputants were more likely to be roughly equal in terms of power and resources, and because there was a clearer business model in working with higher-value disputes.

After garnering some positive press in the spring of 2000 we made the decision to spin Online Resolution off of Mediate.com as a separate company. On May 1, 2000, Online Resolution was incorporated and I took over as CEO. In September 2000, we relaunched the site with a new design and the capacity to support four service types: mediation, arbitration, expert evaluation, and automated negotiation.

Our platform made use of the technology of another company, eRoom, who was right up the road from us in Cambridge, Massachusetts. eRoom had invested millions of dollars in its online collaborative groupware, and we partnered with them so that we could customize their technology for online dispute resolution. The platform was quite sophisticated, so that gave us a major leg up over the other start-ups just entering the space. We renamed our customized technology Resolution Room and began adding new features to it and altering the structure and language so that it would be more appropriate for dispute resolution.

Our initial business focused on business-to-business disputes in excess of $10,000. We spent a lot of time working with e-commerce marketplaces, which were riding high at the time. Our major relationships through the first year included the Korean World Trade Center Association and their online marketplace, TradePro; GeoTrust, a prominent business-to-business trust-in-transactions company; and the CPR Institute for Dispute Resolution, the most prominent B2B ADR think tank in the United States.

We wanted our reputation in the field to be defined by a close association with the face-to-face dispute resolution community, so we went about building a panel of highly experienced mediators and arbitrators drawn from our personal contacts and the Mediate.com mediator database. Very quickly, we had signed on more than six hundred mediators and arbitrators to our panel. We charged hourly rates based on the value under dispute, largely because we wanted to ensure that OR panelists would be paid fairly for their time. Eventually we hired David Steele, the former president of Chevron Latin America, as our CEO, and I shifted to president. Later, David transitioned to the board of directors and Dana Haviland, a prestigious international arbitrator and Silicon Valley lawyer (who left her partnership at Wilson Sonsini to come to OR) took over the CEO role.

We were able to start some promising pilots with B2B exchanges through the end of 2000 and into the spring of 2001, but when the economy turned sour many of our B2B partners began to struggle. Resources that had been devoted to building trust in transactions were reallocated to operational costs. The exchanges were never able to generate enough transactions to feed us a steady stream of cases.

We expanded our services to focus on B2C and B2B e-commerce, as well as workplace disputes and insurance cases. Eventually our platform was adapted for use in multiparty public dispute resolution processes because of its ability to support complex, multifaceted discussions with extensive document management. We eventually retooled OR to offer technology services in addition to dispute resolution services, licensing our platform to ADR service providers and individual neutrals for use in their own cases. We remain convinced that the B2B market is a strong one, however, and once the economy starts to grow again we will refocus on providing ODR to the B2B marketplace.

Case Study: B2B Transaction

A buyer for a major department store in the United States placed a request for eight thousand plastic laundry drying racks on a business-to-business exchange specializing in molded plastic goods. After several bids came in from suppliers in North America and around the world, the buyer selected a Chinese company that posted specifications for a collapsible drying rack that sat on the floor. The photo posted in the company's bid on the website appeared very modern and attractive, and the buyer noted that the type of plastic used in producing the racks was high-quality. The buyer notified the Chinese company that the bid was accepted.

Using the trade facilitation mechanisms of the business-to-business exchange, the two parties agreed on a delivery date and estimated the cost of shipping expenses. The buyer approved the transfer of money to the business-to-business exchange, which acted as an escrow account for the funds. After the two weeks of production time and the two weeks of shipping had passed, the buyer's warehouse was ready to receive the shipment.

Unfortunately, the shipment did not arrive on time. The buyer contacted the business-to-business exchange that hosted the transaction and asked them to not release the money in escrow because of the late delivery. Finally, the shipment arrived, and the buyer was called down to the warehouse to examine the product. The five sample racks that the buyer opened were very disappointing. When opened, the racks did not sit flat on the ground, so they appeared very unstable. Also, although the plastic used in making the racks was high quality, the mold had not been cleaned adequately between pressings, so the plastic had bubbles in some places and did not have a uniformly smooth finish.

The buyer contacted the business-to-business exchange and notified them of the problem. When the representative of the business-to-business exchange notified the Chinese company that had supplied the racks that there was a problem, the producing company was very angry. The delay in arrival was not the fault of the producer, they argued; the shipping company had made a mistake in delivery, so the producer should not be penalized for that. In addition, the racks met all of the specifications provided in the bid that was accepted by the buyer. Based on those facts, the supplier insisted that the full value of the transaction be released from escrow.

The business-to-business exchange referred the dispute to the online dispute resolution company that was specified in the terms and conditions posted on the exchange's website. The company contacted both parties and began an online discussion. The participants in the dispute resolution process were the supervisor for the company that produced the racks and a lawyer from the buying company's legal division. The dispute background had been transmitted directly from the business-to-business exchange company's customer service department through an XML connector, so the mediator had a good sense of the primary areas of contention before the discussion began.

Photos provided by the buyer of the sample drying racks were uploaded into the online dispute resolution environment, and the supervisor from the producing company initially argued that there were no obvious problems with them. In caucus, the mediator (who spoke both Mandarin and English) clarified the main issues and discovered the real issues on each side. The lawyer representing the buying company did feel the racks were sellable, but at a reduced price, and he wanted the producer to accept a decreased payment for the racks so that the department store would have essentially the same margin. In turn, the producer did acknowledge that there had been staffing problems at the factory as of late and that the goods being produced were not of the highest quality.

After airing several possible solutions and consulting a database of resolutions to similar conflicts, the parties agreed on a reduced price for the eight thousand drying racks. The business-to-business exchange was notified of the resolution, and the appropriate amount of the money held in escrow was credited to the account of the Chinese producer, with the remainder flowing back into the buyer's account on the site.

Analysis

A popular commercial touting the power of online B2B marketplaces depicts a Japanese boardroom in a panic because their supplier of a key component has just doubled the price. After much yelling and hand wringing, a junior associate in the corner of the room announces he's found a replacement supplier for the component on the Internet who is only charging a third of the original price the company was paying. When asked where the supplier is located, the junior associate looks up at the chairman of the board through his thick glasses and says, "Texas." The commercial ends with a grease-smeared guy with "Earl" stitched over the pocket of his shirt tapping the enter key on his laptop and saying (in a thick Texas accent), "Domo arigato."

This makes for an entertaining commercial, but from a dispute resolution perspective, one can't help but think through the ramifications of that transaction. What if the components arrive and they are the wrong size? What about the complex shipping and tariff arrangements that need to be made to transport the items? What about the language barrier? There is little doubt that Earl's ability to sell in Tokyo is good for Earl and good for the Japanese company, but if something goes wrong, there is no safety net or support system to work out the problem. Earl's one phrase of Japanese will not do him much good if the check doesn't arrive as expected. In addition, Earl's local lawyer in Lubbock or Laredo or wherever will probably not have the Japanese Commercial Code sitting on the shelf of his law office.

Businesses are not naïve enough to ignore these issues. One transaction that goes awry is enough to dissuade future participation in online marketplaces. The buyer of the drying racks may just decide that it isn't worth the hassle to wrestle with international suppliers if the products are going to be inferior. To keep buyers and sellers coming back, the operators of the trading environments must provide the support necessary to assure businesses that anything that does go wrong will be handled efficiently and effectively.

Online exchanges offer unquestionable value to the businesses that participate in them. But businesses will only continue to use the exchanges if they feel that they provide a trustworthy, well-lighted place for buyers and sellers to engage in transactions. If the environments are dark and murky, and buyers and sellers cannot see each other clearly, businesses will stay away. ODR is an important way to keep the marketplace well-lit, reassuring buyers and sellers, and underscoring the trustworthiness of the exchange.

CHAPTER SEVEN

Maximizing Efficiency

How ODR Can Help the Insurance Industry

T he best example of how online dispute resolution is useful in offline disputes is within the insurance industry. From relatively minor insurance claims (such as fender benders) to more serious ones (including medical and legal malpractice cases) to extremely serious cases involving multiple parties (such as environmental claims), insurance claims are big business.

The current claims-handling process utilized by insurance companies is very inefficient and unwieldy. In 1998, the top twenty United States insurance companies paid $34.1 billion in claims administration.[1] Billions of dollars are spent pushing paper back and forth between insurance companies or haggling over relatively small details.

Integrating online dispute resolution into the insurance claims resolution process will save hundreds if not thousands of dollars per claim in administrative costs. This will result in significant savings for insurers and insurance consumers. Insurance companies that successfully integrate ODR throughout their operations will benefit from significant competitive advantages stemming from streamlined operations, faster case resolution times, and enhanced customer service.

THE INSURANCE INDUSTRY

The two main divisions of consumer-focused insurance companies are the property-casualty insurers, which deal with policies like auto or home insurance, and life-health insurers, which deal with medical and life insurance. To give a sense of the size of this industry, the National Association of Insurance Commissioners reported that in 1999 the total assets of life-health insurers in 1999 was approximately $10.2 trillion, while their yearly profits were $694.7 billion. Property-casualty insurers, in contrast, earned $910.7 billion.[2] The average family spent more on insurance in 1995 than they did on clothing or entertainment.[3]

The Cost of Settlements

While an industry this large can seem overwhelmingly complex, the experience of individual customers is often fairly uniform and easy to understand. Once an accident occurs the insurance companies deal first with the involved parties and then with each other. The negotiations between insurance companies to resolve differences over payment obligations, called subrogation, is a complex and costly process. Most insurance customers are insulated from this process, but the subrogation system is paid for by all of the premiums collected from insured customers. The subrogation process involves two savvy parties, the insurance companies, figuring out which side owes what to the other. Sometimes these subrogation issues can be very complex, involving multiple insurers with interwoven liabilities and obligations.

The majority of these negotiations between insurers are successful in reaching resolution; one-third of claims become lawsuits, and only 2 percent of these lawsuits are decided by a court verdict.[4] The rest are settled. That said, settlement usually takes a very long time. According to *Current Trends in Product Liability,* an industry publication, the median time between when an accident occurs and when a settlement is reached is thirty-eight months. The median time to reach settlement in a major metropolitan area is forty-five months.[5] A major Canadian insurance company recently put its average closure rate of casualty losses at 4.42 years. These numbers are just the averages.

Awards in insurance cases brought to court are getting bigger and bigger. Unlike e-commerce disputes, where claim values in the B2C context are usually under $500 and in the B2B context usually under $10,000, insurance disputes are often much higher in value, $100,000 and up. In areas like medical malpractice the awards can reach well into the millions. Often the claimants have experienced something very traumatic as well, which means the amount of a likely jury award can be staggering.

Product liability claims had an average award of $500,000 in 1996. Environmental claims have even higher valuations. The long-term, high-payout nature of the awards from asbestos cases in the 1960s and 1970s raised the bar for the size of payouts, and it hasn't gone back down since. Each court outcome shapes the expectations of future claimants and sets a precedent for the next case. This is another reason why insurers have a strong incentive to resolve these matters early, before they get to a court proceeding.

The industry has also felt enormous pressure due to costs. Some insurers have been able to shrink their costs down as a percentage of premiums to less than 10 percent. Insurers and claims managers are also struggling to combat the impact of rising costs for defense and litigation. Staffs are being cut while expectations of customer service are rising. Pressure is building on adjustors to settle claims quickly and efficiently. Because of the structure of the industry, companies that can contain costs most effectively have a major advantage with consumers, so insurers that successfully compress their costs retain a significant competitive advantage.

Insurance companies lose money every day a case is open. Administrative costs, case monitoring, accrued interest, and legal fees run up the value of open cases. Insurance companies have a strong incentive to resolve their open claims, but they are not willing to do so at the expense of a fair outcome.

A major reason for the escalating cost of settlements in the insurance industry is the problem of fraud. There is a growing group of repeat offenders and professional claimants who play the system to extract settlements. The costs from these types of vulnerabilities are growing for insurers, and the ability to combat them is shrinking with growing consolidation and internationalization. Overburdened claims adjustors are often too swamped with cases to carry out the detailed fact-finding required for a firm fraud determination. The fragmentation and inefficiency in the existing claims handling process aids those who try to profit from fraudulent activity by providing them more cover for their actions.

The Ability to Satisfy Customers

In addition to all of these pressures on the insurance industry, customers are becoming more informed and more demanding. As information is disseminated about how insurance actually works, both through the Internet and through new companies attempting to change the insurance game (such as GEICO, a direct-sale insurance company, and QuoteSmith, an Internet-based insurance reseller), older insurers are being forced to transform their ways of doing business. Also, some customers are feeling comfortable enough to represent themselves in negotiations with insurance companies, which leads to new possibilities for abuse as insurers realize that the individual customers are not as savvy about claim values or insurance industry regulations and standards.

INSURANCE AND ADR

The insurance industry has long been one of the premier consumers of face-to-face dispute resolution services. Many successful mediators subsist entirely on insurance cases. Once a claim is initiated, the insurer has a clear incentive to resolve it as quickly and efficiently as possible, both to contain costs associated with the management of the claim and to prevent further escalation of the matter. Dispute resolution is a perfect fit with these insurance company priorities, and channeling certain cases into mediation and arbitration has become common in claims departments.

In fact, the way the insurance claims system works can be viewed as a huge ADR process. Efficient claims resolution saves money, increasing corporate profits and reducing premiums. There is little controversy over the idea that insurers should make use of mediation whenever possible, and to use arbitration instead of the courts when both sides are unable to craft a mutually acceptable agreement. Because the parties on either side of the dispute are often savvy, repeat players, and because there are strong industry precedents for how claims have been valued in the past, it is often relatively easy for neutrals to move the two sides beyond accusations and fact disputes into a frank discussion of what each side needs to put the matter to bed.

However, from a systems-design perspective, there are some obvious procedural shortcomings to purely face-to-face dispute resolution in the insurance context. While face-to-face ADR is a huge improvement over the status quo system of endless phone calls between claims adjustors and lawyers, online dispute resolution systems can get disputes resolved even more efficiently by eliminating distances between the parties and removing the convening penalty.

When two cars get into a fender bender and the drivers call their insurance companies, a sprawling ADR process is initiated. The two claimants probably go to their mechanics and get their cars repaired relatively quickly, and then their brokers write them a check for the cost. But the claim is not yet resolved. A complicated process of fault determination is initiated between the insurance companies who wrote the checks, one that can take several years.

Insurance companies have many built-in incentives to use ADR. Because their compensation comes through premiums, insurers have strong cost containment pressures, as every dollar they are not forced to pay is held onto as profits. Unlike law firms, who have an economic incentive to continue working on a case because they are paid hourly for the amount of time they work, insurers want to save every dollar they can in managing their claims and payments.

Disputes can break out at every level of insurance. Customers and brokers can argue about the amount of payment deserved as a result of an accident (for example, "Was it really necessary to replace the entire fender?"). Brokers can fight amongst themselves about who should pay what based on whose fault an accident was ("Didn't the Isuzu Trooper you insure cut the light a little close?"). Even reinsurers can fight with underwriters about how much of a claim they should be required to pay based on the nature of the claim and the underwriter's actions in resolving it ("Did you really have to retain outside counsel to gather evidence regarding the tire's wear patterns?").

Many successful mediators and arbitrators make their livings handling these types of insurance cases for brokerages and underwriters. Often insurance companies will have lists of preferred ADR providers whom they use to resolve matters out of court. However, with the staggering number of claims and cases processed by the industry, convening a face-to-face dispute resolution process for each issue is not always a possibility.

There is some controversy about how useful mediation and arbitration actually are in resolving insurance disputes. Some argue that the industry is now so fragmented with middlemen, and loyalty between providers is so hard to come by, that any procedure short of a full court trial is naïve. Also, with new awards in environmental cases reaching unprecedented size, some feel the stakes are too high to take a risk on the decision of a single arbitrator or on the parties themselves in mediation.

The prevalence of actuaries and mathematical calculations makes moving quickly and resolving a dispute with a handshake less likely. Other issues in the process, like choosing a dispute resolution service provider and approving a neutral or panel of neutrals, can create new conflicts that distract from the actual issues surrounding the matter at hand.

Arbitration processes in the insurance field have become more and more drawn out over time, looking a lot like actual court hearings. Some insurance lawyers feel that dispute resolution focuses too much on compromise, so people with weak cases will aim for arbitration or mediation because they are more likely to get something than in a court case where they may walk away with nothing.

Some observers in the insurance field have argued that the ADR process needs to be streamlined with better rules of engagement to make the discussion more focused from its inception. Also, some insurance general counsels may feel that finding a good arbitrator is often harder than finding a good legal team willing to fight it out in court.

There is also some sensitivity to the idea that ADR will make it easier for perpetrators of fraud to get away with their scams. There is a sense, however, that the real forces that enable fraud perpetrators to succeed are lazy adjustors, management that ignores problems, and insurance companies that don't cross their T's and dot their I's.

All of these misgivings notwithstanding, there is willingness to use arbitration in insurance disputes, but the process needs to be improved. Almost all observers agree that mediation and negotiation are better alternatives for resolving insurance disputes than arbitration when the parties are willing to try it in good faith. Increasingly insurance companies are being required to use ADR as a result of court-mandated mediation processes and legislation. In some provinces of Canada, for example, insured motorists and parties to many civil disputes must attempt mediation prior to initiating litigation.

HOW ODR WORKS FOR SETTLING CLAIMS

Almost everyone who works in the insurance industry has an idea for how to make the claims resolution system work more efficiently. A popular suggestion is by improving the efficiency of the settlement process. Online dispute resolution is clearly the most effective way to achieve this. The escalating cost of settlements, combined with the need to satisfy customers, and the existing role for face-to-face ADR all lay a perfect foundation for the integration of online dispute resolution. The complex existing case management process, spread across multiple companies with different platforms, could be standardized on a central data scheme to allow for easy exchange of claim data and rapid resolution through ODR systems. Trumbull Services, the technology wing of The Hartford Financial Services Group and a pioneering organization in adapting technology to insurance, has already drafted a proposed XML standard for such a system. Once those in the industry are educated about how such a system might save them money it will be an easy decision to invest in the changes necessary to join such a system.

Bridging Geographical Distance

While it is true that many initial insurance claims involve parties in the same geographic area (for example, the owners of two cars that were in an accident), that convenience quickly dematerializes. Once a claim is filed with the respective insurance companies the dispute is shifted to their claims departments, which are usually not in the same place. While the dispute rates between larger insurers are very high, claims are rarely aggregated and dealt with in bulk, so disagreements over minute details can still arise.

Often the claims departments for these companies are on different coasts or are in different cities. They may be organized by region or may reside in the head office of the company. Often insurance company headquarters are in major centers, many miles from the risks they insure. As the insurance business becomes more and more international, some of these cases cross oceans. Asia, for instance, is one of the hottest new markets for insurance and reinsurance companies, as countries like the Philippines and Malaysia have opened their doors to foreign involvement in their domestic insurance markets. As larger economies (such as China and India) enter the mainstream of the global economy they too are looking to increase foreign investment by partnering international insurance companies with local insurers. This global spread will generate more disputes where the negotiating representatives are in different countries or even on the other side of the planet.

As a result of cost pressures, geographic spread, and the large volume of claims the average insurance company has to process, the Internet is a logical place to work these cases out. Dozens of industry pundits have observed the inefficiency of the way disputes are currently handled in the insurance industry and have suggested that dispute resolution and online aggregation might be a better way. As a result, several companies have created Web-based claims processing platforms, and online dispute resolution is often a prominent component of these platforms.

THE EMERGENCE OF BLIND BIDDING

The insurance industry is by far the largest user of automated dispute resolution mechanisms. Because so many cases come down to a monetary amount, it is relatively simple to build a technology-administered process that can allow adjustors to resolve large numbers of cases with great efficiency. The largest ODR companies that have emerged so far, such as Cybersettle and ClickNsettle, have focused primarily on this market: providing automated, blind-bidding mechanisms to insurance companies to resolve their outstanding claims. By some estimates this sector alone is worth $15 billion. Most of the discussions in the insurance industry to date have centered on these blind-bidding technologies.

PROVIDER PROFILE: CYBERSETTLE

Cybersettle has been the most prominent company in bringing ODR to the attention of the insurance industry. Most executives will have heard of Cybersettle if they have heard of ODR at all.

Cybersettle was founded by Jim Burchetta and Charles Bronfman, two attorneys with extensive experience in medical liability cases. Burchetta had represented plaintiffs in those cases, often families whose children had been harmed by mistakes at medical facilities. Bronfman had represented the medical facilities. In working against each other in several different cases, the two of them had used a blind-bidding mechanism on paper that allowed them to come up with a compromise settlement value for the case. Once the Internet started to become more popular, Burchetta and Bronfman realized that the same mechanism they were using on paper in a courtroom in front of a judge might translate well online, so they hired some programmers and put the solution together. After showing it around to some people in the insurance community and garnering much excitement, they were able to raise millions of dollars from a reinsurance company in Bermuda that believed in the promise of their technology. (For more information on blind-bidding mechanisms, see Chapter Two.)

Cybersettle initially did not present itself as a dispute resolution company. Their focus was on settlement, so their target market included lawyers and insurance companies, not dispute resolution professionals.

This initial activity spawned dozens of imitators. Though Cybersettle filed the first patent on blind-bidding technology, many smaller companies rushed into the space. The basic blind-bidding code was not very difficult to replicate, and it was created over and over again by other companies who wanted to get a piece of the pie once the application really took off. Cybersettle wrapped its technology in a very compelling package, however, and backed the algorithm up with a sizable call center filled with case managers ready to answer any questions.

The media blitz put on by Cybersettle was dazzling to behold. Cybersettle took out full-page ads in the *Wall Street Journal* proclaiming their tool "The First Tool to Settle Insurance Claims Online." At one point Cybersettle had the full side of a building in New York City painted with their advertisement, as well as the billboards on either side of the entrance into the Lincoln Tunnel. At the 2000 Risk and Insurance Management Society (RIMS) Conference in San Francisco (a major conference for the insurance industry) Cybersettle had dozens of representatives on the conference floor in support of a huge display promoting their settlement tool. Their public relations firm, Porter Novelli, put together a very slick media packet, including copies of the dozens and dozens of articles that had been written about Cybersettle. Through the spring of 2000 Cybersettle got the best exposure money could buy.

One of Cybersettle's early difficulties, however, was their perceived connection to the insurance company side of the industry. Because Cybersettle's earliest investor had been an offshore reinsurance company, perceived to be on the side of the insurers, plaintiffs' lawyers viewed the tool with some skepticism. Would there be a way for insurance companies to game the system, getting the upper hand in negotiations? Insurance claims departments would likely use the system hundreds if not thousands of times a year, whereas the average plaintiff's lawyer would probably settle only a few cases through the tool over the same period. Would the repeated use give the insurance companies some kind of advantage?

Cybersettle was perceived to be the leading ODR company through spring 2000, largely because of the amount of money they had spent promoting their service, the awareness of the company in the minds of many insurance companies, their pending patent, and their case load. At the Federal Trade Commission's June 2000 conference on ODR, Cybersettle was a plenary presenter. Perhaps recognizing the advantage the National Association of Mediators (NAM) had over Cybersettle stemming from their panel of face-to-face mediators, Cybersettle announced that they were going to move into the human-powered ODR space as well, outlining a structure for their procedures and exploring partnerships with some other companies. They closed an investment rumored to be worth more than $30 million that summer involving prestigious Internet venture firms such as Internet Capital Group (ICG). One of their goals in completing the investment round was to dilute the equity holding of the reinsurance company that had given them their first investment, to combat the perception problem that had haunted them.

However, the new investors insisted on a change in priorities at Cybersettle, and Bronfman became the sole CEO. The restructuring reoriented Cybersettle squarely on the insurance market, and their plans to expand involvement with ODR were scrapped. Cybersettle's strategy was to focus on a few major insurance clients and to educate those claims departments as to how to most effectively use the Cybersettle blind-bidding algorithm. They key was to get the "right cases" into the pipeline, meaning cases where the two sides were within the likely settlement range. Cybersettle actually focused down to working with insurance companies to develop "e-claims" departments within larger claims offices where employees could be trained on how to use the blind-bidding tool to best effect.

Cybersettle has sharpened their focus to several in-depth pilots with a select group of insurance companies. Their patent was awarded in the winter of 2001, giving them the intellectual property rights to blind-bidding mechanisms, broadly defined. This has not stopped many of the imitator websites, however. Cybersettle also sealed a partnership with the largest plaintiff's attorney organization in North America, the American Trial Lawyers Association (ATLA), which goes a long way to silencing the old concerns about Cybersettle's possible bias toward insurers.

CRITICISMS OF BLIND BIDDING

The insurance industry is based on relationships, and some feel that these automated negotiation and blind-bidding services are dragging the industry in the wrong direction. However, the countervailing sentiment is that there is nothing wrong with putting these tools in the claims adjustors' toolbox. If online blind-bidding technology is just a way for claims adjustors to interact more efficiently, then that's a positive development. If technology like online blind bidding and settlement can be proven to enhance the speed and productivity of claims adjustors then those benefits will outweigh the costs associated with greater impersonalization.

Hybrids of offline and online technology are also very important. The argument is not that technologies like Cybersettle are going to replace all adjusting, it's just a tool for the adjustor's toolbox. It should be used in circumstances in which it makes sense that it should be used. This will make it easier for insurance companies to integrate the new techniques into their existing ways of doing business.

The human aspect of the claims adjustment business is an important element of the way the insurance field works. No one thinks that some advanced computer armed with artificial intelligence could replace insurance claims adjustors. The goal is to portray ODR technology as a more efficient way to keep track of cases and to communicate with the other side so as to resolve them—it is a communication tool, like the fax or the telephone.

Cybersettle has long argued that the most important thing in appropriately using new claims technology is to make sure that the right cases are driven toward the settlement mechanism. In a blind-bidding situation, if the parties are too far apart in their expectations the mechanism won't do them any good. ODR systems need to help in this case triage process to make sure cases are routed to the most appropriate dispute resolution mechanism.

The risk with technology is that adjustors will hide behind the phone or the Web browser and it will result in less-responsive customer service. Some adjustors who don't have experience doing everything that needs to be done to effectively handle a claim will use technology to cut corners.

Responsible adjusting takes time—time to search through the issues and to get the facts. Much like a reporter for a newspaper, you need to go and get the information yourself to make sure you get the right information. A common aphorism in the insurance industry is that the adjustor's task involves "investigation, evaluation, and negotiation of coverage, liability, and damages," and technology doesn't change that.

ODR AND E-COMMERCE INSURANCE

Some very large insurance companies have begun to integrate ODR into the way they do business. The leading edge for these efforts is in the e-commerce insurance arena. E-commerce insurance policies ensure buyers and sellers that they will get their money back if they are the victims of online fraud. Insurance companies are focusing on ODR in their e-commerce policies first because parties to e-commerce disputes are likely to be:

• Separated by geographic distance, because the involved parties are anywhere on the Internet when they engage in the transaction that generated the dispute

• Tech-savvy, as they have to know something about technology to get involved with an e-commerce transaction in the first place

• Comfortable with the use of the Internet to interact with others, even strangers, and even over a matter where there is disagreement.

For these reasons e-commerce policies are often the preferred place for insurance companies to begin experimenting with online dispute resolution clauses.

E-commerce insurance policies usually operate as transaction protection programs. For instance, one large company is offering a program through which e-commerce companies (like eBay or Amazon.com) can cover any purchase below a certain amount, say $100. If a buyer purchases a good and for some reason is dissatisfied with the item, doesn't receive it, or it is damaged in shipping, then they need to contact the seller to obtain redress for the problem. These types of disputes are discussed in great detail in Chapter Five. If the seller is unwilling to do what is necessary to make the buyer whole, then the buyer may initiate a claim through the site's e-commerce transaction protection program.

The insurance company charges a premium to the e-commerce website based on the projected number of problem transactions. The website probably integrates the cost for the premium into the fees it charges users on the site. So assume for example that twenty-five cents is added on to each transaction to pay for this transaction protection insurance. When a dispute arises that can't be worked out between the parties, then the buyer can go to the insurer and, if they substantiate their claim, they can be refunded for the money that they paid.

Usually these programs have a cap on the amount of money you can get back through the transaction protection program ($100 in our example), and they have some sort of claim validation process where they substantiate that the claim has merit. The insurance company makes money if its estimate of how many claims are going to be made through the program is accurate, because then the premiums it charges will cover the cost of the approved reimbursements. The e-commerce site benefits from increased transactions, because buyers and sellers will transact with confidence knowing that they have redress should something go awry.

Many of these e-commerce sites are experiencing a high level of fraud, however, so the viability of the insurance system depends on the willingness of the users to pay the bump in rates required to cover the premium. In most cases, however, if the damage coverage is minimal and the premium is built into basic operating fees the users will not mind the modest additional cost.

Insurance companies have a strong incentive to integrate ODR into these policies for several reasons. First, if ODR can resolve 70–80 percent of these cases to the buyer and seller's satisfaction, then the insurer doesn't have to pay out those reimbursements. Every dispute resolved through the ODR program is money in the insurer's pocket.

The cost to the insurer for the ODR service is also integrated into the premium, so the ODR provider becomes something of an insurer itself. If the ODR provider receives five cents for every twenty-five cents charged to support the transaction protection program, then the ODR provider agrees to handle every dispute that arises on the site. If the dispute estimates are accurate then the ODR provider can make money. If there is a higher rate of disputes, however, the ODR provider is still on the hook to handle those disputes, even if the earned revenue as a portion of premiums does not cover the full cost for the services rendered.

These mechanisms apply equally well to B2B e-commerce. The premiums paid by the members of the online marketplace and the minimum coverage may be higher because of the increased transaction value, but the rationale for inclusion of the ODR service is the same: greater trust in transactions will result in greater transaction volume, and every dispute resolved puts money into the pocket of the insurer.

Surety Bonds

Another variation on the e-commerce insurance model that is currently being promoted is surety bonds. If you do business with a surety bond holder you can be sure that they will do what they promise to do, because if they don't their insurance company will pay you full compensation. Surety bonds are an excellent way to integrate quality dispute resolution into the e-commerce business process. Surety bonds are not a new idea. They have a long history in industry, stretching back more than a hundred years.

When two parties agree on a contract and one later backs out, the party left in the lurch can have difficulty recouping its investment. For example, suppose a race car driver hired a mechanic to build him a new car. The driver assumes that the mechanic will meet the contractual obligations. However, if the mechanic did not follow through and build the car, the driver would lose projected revenue from the advertising deals, competition winnings, and so on, as well as whatever price he had already paid to the mechanic. By suing the mechanic, the driver might be able to recover the money he had paid but possibly not the money he had projected to earn from the use of the car. Surety bonds exist to remedy this problem.

A third party issues a surety bond to promise that the insured party will perform any contractually agreed-to service for another party. In the example given here, a surety bond provider might offer a bond to guarantee the mechanic's completion of the car. Should the mechanic fail to deliver the agreed-upon car, the bond would cover the driver's expenses and lost revenue. The surety bond does more than merely protect the driver. Since the surety bond issuer is responsible for reimbursing the driver should anything go wrong, making sure the mechanic does the job properly is a priority for the bond issuer. This could involve background checks on the mechanic, status reports on the job as it is being completed, and rules about quality of materials and treatment of labor. The surety bond issuer has an interest in making sure the mechanic is up to the task and will only issue a bond for him if he meets their stringent criteria.

Surety bonds are a well-established concept in offline business. Surety bonds are common in the construction industry, for example.

The U.S. government requires surety bonds on all federal construction projects. The U.S. Small Business Administration issued more than $500 million in surety bonds covering a variety of businesses in 1998.[6] The innovation is in the expansion of the surety bond idea into electronic commerce.

One of the major problems with e-commerce today is its lack of accountability. If a customer orders a product online and she never gets it, she has little recourse. A possible solution is providing surety bonds for online retailers. If the customer doesn't receive the proper product, she would have a method of getting a refund for the amount paid. Surety bond providers would perform the same types of background checks they currently perform when insuring construction contracts. E-tailers would have to prove they were reputable in order to do business.

Surety bonds have other value for e-commerce companies. If a prominent insurer is willing to issue a surety bond to your company, that means potential customers who might not know your reputation have a powerful vote of confidence from the insurer, a name they might already know and be willing to trust. They can take the bond into consideration when they decide whether or not to do business with you. If a prominent brand in one region of the country wants to expand into other regions where it has no brand awareness, for example, a surety bond can help them make the transition.

There are also benefits from surety bonds that extend beyond the customer. If a company covered by a surety bond should go bankrupt, the bond issuer will cover all of that company's obligations, including its obligations to partners or suppliers. The trust in transactions that comes from doing business with a company that has been issued a surety bond extends to strategic partnerships, reseller arrangements, and loans of goods and services.

The surety bond issuer has a stake in the fair dealing of the company it covers. Bond issuers could become monitors for e-commerce companies, ensuring that they are not engaging in fraud and that they're keeping their customer service efficient and effective, as well as vouching for their financial stability.

As a component of that monitoring role, the bond issuers have a strong incentive to require the company to engage in online dispute resolution to resolve any disputes that do arise between the company and its customers and partners. Because ultimate liability for all problems that arise resides with the surety bond issuer, the issuer will put pressure on the covered company to resolve all disputes to the customer's satisfaction. Also, the surety bond provider needs to evaluate the validity of any claim made through the bond program, and online arbitration is an efficient and effective way to do that. Some e-commerce surety bond issuers are writing online dispute resolution directly into the language of the bond agreement.

Risk Pooling

The last model for online insurance is retailer assurance programs. In industries where there is a high risk of transaction problems, businesses are coming together to create a pool of funds from small surcharges that can cover any disputed transactions that arise. For example, an association of online vitamin retailers might agree to put a small surcharge on purchases from all of its members. All the member sites would put a trust seal on their websites promoting the availability of the transaction assurance program. If any purchaser had a dispute over a transaction from one of the association members, then they could file a case with the online dispute resolution program available through the trust seal. Should the neutral agree that the customer deserved their money back, and should the seller refuse to pay it, the customer could be refunded from the association's pool of surcharges.

This transaction assurance model has several benefits. First, it provides a strong incentive for a customer to purchase a good from an association member as opposed to a retailer who was not part of the association. Second, it puts the association into a supervisory role for all of its members, because they want to defend the reputation of the vitamin retailers in the association and they want to prevent excessive payouts from the pooled surcharges. It also gives the customer a powerful ally in their attempts to get satisfactory redress, as opposed to merely being a single voice battling it out with a customer service department.

A model similar to this one could be applied to a wide variety of online retailers, both B2B and B2C. It also could be applied offline, through mail order or direct sales. It has its history in the rural mutual insurance companies, when groups of farmers came together to pool funds to help deal with unpredictable growing seasons. These risk-pooling programs are merely the cyberspace equivalents of traditional mutual insurance arrangements.

Case Study : A Rear-End Collision
(Blind Bid and Settlement of a Subrogated Claim)

One morning in Pittsburgh, three cars were involved in an accident at a major intersection downtown. After the light had turned green the line of traffic had started to move ahead. Once the cars reached a speed of thirty miles per hour, a man driving a truck at the front of the line of traffic stomped on his brakes. The station wagon behind the truck was able to stop before rear-ending the truck, but the sedan behind the station wagon rear-ended the station wagon, and a hatchback behind the sedan rear-ended the sedan. The truck driver, unaware that any accident had occurred, drove away from the accident scene.

Before long the police arrived and they asked the drivers involved if they wanted a police report. The driver of the sedan said yes, so the police started to put one together. The sedan in the middle of the chain of cars was undrivable after the accident so it was towed to a nearby repair shop. The hatchback was severely damaged on the front end, but the driver insisted on driving it away. The station wagon suffered only minor damage. All three of the drivers exchanged insurance information and went on their way.

The driver of the sedan had the owner of the repair shop look at the damaged car and give an estimate for repair costs, which ended up being greater than $5,500. The sedan owner decided the repairs weren't worth the headache, and filed a claim for the value of the car with his insurance company, Allied Insurance. The owner of the hatchback had his brother repair the car, but he obtained an estimate that put the cost of the repairs at $2,700. He filed that claim with his insurance company, Granite. The station wagon owner needed a new bumper at a cost of $800, and she filed with her insurance company, Optimal Insurance.

Allied Insurance sent out a representative to examine the sedan and determined that it was indeed totaled. Based on the book value of the car, the representative determined that the owner should receive a $6,800 payment from Allied. The owner of the hatchback actually began the repairs before the representative from Granite could examine the vehicle, which led to some confusion about the true extent of the damage, though the hatchback owner insisted that the $2,700 estimate was accurate. Optimal Insurance issued a check for the $800 repair to the station wagon's bumper on the spot.

The claims department of Optimal contacted the claims department of Allied three months after the accident. Based on phone calls with the drivers involved and the police report, it was clear that the station wagon driver was not at fault. Even if the truck in front of the station wagon had caused the accident by stopping short, Optimal argued, the fault lies with the rear-ending cars for following too closely. Allied agreed that the station wagon driver was not at fault, but asserted that the damage to the bumper was primarily caused by the hatchback colliding with the back of the sedan, propelling it into the station wagon. The file was left open until Granite could be consulted.

Granite was a smaller, regional insurance company in Pennsylvania, whereas Allied and Optimal were national companies with larger claims departments. Because of their small claims department, Granite took a long time to get around to responding to the calls from Allied. The Optimal adjuster recommended that Allied play the lead with Granite and determine the appropriate split for the payment back to Optimal for the damage to the station wagon.

After multiple calls from Allied, a Granite representative finally responded. The Allied adjustor, somewhat frustrated at Granite's slow response, asserted that the bulk of the $6,800 payment made to the sedan owner should be paid by Granite, because the slight damage to the station wagon showed that the real source of the accident was the driver of the hatchback. Granite, which had not called the drivers of the sedan and station wagon, and which was still in dispute with its own insured, the owner of the hatchback, as to how much should be paid out for the accident, responded aggressively. The damage to the sedan was so extensive, on both ends, that the hatchback could never have caused the full extent of the damage, the adjustor argued. Little progress was made beyond these initial assertions, and eventually the call ended.

Allied continued to call Granite in an attempt to conclude the matter, but Granite's response was infrequent. Optimal began to put pressure on Allied to pay the $800 owed for the damage to the station wagon. Granite eventually decided to pay the hatchback owner $2,000 for the damage to his vehicle ($700 more than the cost of the parts used by the brother to make the repairs). After two months of phone tag and warning letters the dispute between Granite and Allied slipped to the back of the claim files.

Allied and Optimal had many cases that they worked on together, and during a claim review from a supervisor the decision was made to unilaterally pay Optimal the $800 for the damage to the station wagon to preserve relations between the two companies. A note was inserted in the claim file that all $800 should be recouped from Granite when the case was eventually negotiated.

Six months later, during a pilot project with a blind-bidding online dispute resolution company, the Granite-Allied case file involving the hatchback and sedan was automatically selected as a good candidate for resolution through the online mechanism. The adjustor working with the online dispute resolution company looked through the file at the values involved and then logged the case into the Web-based bidding form. For the three bids entered into the system, the adjustor put $7,200 for the first bid, $6,600 for the second bid, and $6,000 for the third bid.

The case administrators at the blind-bidding company contacted the claims department at Granite and informed them that a case had been opened on the system that involved a Granite claim. The ODR case administrator also sent a fax and a letter to Granite explaining the process. One of the three adjustors in Granite's office had heard about these new online claims resolution platforms and was curious, so she logged into the system. After learning how the mechanism worked and agreeing to the terms and conditions, she reviewed the file and entered her bids. For the first bid, she input $4,000, acknowledging that as the rear-most car in the collision the hatchback deserved the majority of the blame. Because the two bids ($7,200 and $4,000) were not within 30 percent of each other, the case did not settle. For the next bid, she input $4,500. Again, the case did not settle (with the other side's bid of $6,600). Finally, she input a bid of $4,800, which she felt was eminently reasonable based on the minor damage to the hatchback. This time the system informed her that the two bids were within range ($6,000 and $4,800), so the case settled for the median, $5,400.

The online system automatically generated the forms cementing the terms of the resolution and faxed, mailed, and emailed them to both sides. Signatures were secured, and Granite mailed the payment check to Allied within 120 days after the signing as specified in the agreement.

Analysis

This type of dispute is very common in insurance subrogation. The bulk of the work is put into contacts between adjustors, disputing fact patterns, and debating responsibility. Then the matter is again lost under piles of other open cases. Fortunately most participants in subrogation disputes are knowledgeable and rational about claim values, and they have an intimate understanding of relevant traffic laws because they deal with so many disputes regarding them.

In this circumstance, the blind-bidding tool was a perfect fit with the needs of the adjustors because everyone was anxious to resolve this matter and the companies were within a reasonable range of each other in terms of their expectations for payment. Because this dispute was not over a lot of money, and because it involved insurers that did not have a history of close communication, it might have sat in the files for years before it was eventually resolved or abandoned. The blind-bidding mechanism provided an easy way for the adjustors to resolve it and get it out of their caseload.

Case Study: A Declaratory Judgment Dispute
(Insurer versus Reinsurer and Online Arbitration)

Barnett International, a public relations firm in Seattle, Washington, had a one-year insurance policy from Apex Insurance in Portland, Oregon. A reinsurance company in Chicago, Illinois, called Hoosier Re issued a policy to Apex that covered the policy that had been sold to Barnett. During the life of the policy, the Equal Employment Opportunity Commission (EEOC) charged Barnett with discrimination in its hiring practices. Barnett then filed a claim with Apex to help cover the cost of defense against the EEOC action, which Apex denied. Barnett then sued Apex, seeking a declaratory judgment stating Apex's obligation to pay for Barnett's defense in the EEOC matter. Apex defended its stance that it had no obligation to pay, and it eventually won the declaratory judgment.

The next year Apex notified Hoosier Re of the declaratory judgment action and billed Hoosier Re for 20 percent of the costs it had incurred defending against the suit from Barnett International, approximately $8,500. Hoosier Re examined the agreement with Apex and concluded that there was no coverage for declaratory judgment expenses, so it denied Apex's request for reimbursement.

Apex examined the low amount of the requested reimbursement and determined that initiating a formal proceeding would be wasteful in this situation. However, even though there had never been another case where payment of declaratory judgment expenses were at issue between Apex and Hoosier Re, Apex believed this was an important issue to work out on principle. So Apex suggested that Hoosier Re join in an online arbitration through a mutually acceptable insurance ODR firm, InsurODR.com, and Hoosier Re agreed.

Apex initiated the case, and Hoosier Re was then contacted by an InsurODR.com case administrator to be brought into the process. A panelist was assigned to the case and an online hearing room was opened. Both Apex and Hoosier Re agreed to the panelist selection and bound themselves to accept the decision of the arbitrator as binding. Both sides also agreed to use a documents-only process to resolve the matter, primarily to keep the process simple and efficient.

Lawyers for both sides logged into an online meeting room configured to support the documents-only process. Apex's submission folder was opened first, so Apex's litigation counsel uploaded their brief for the arbitrator and Hoosier Re to see.

Apex's brief argued that the reason why declaratory judgment expenses were not specifically covered in the agreement with Hoosier Re was the age of the document. When the agreement was originally put into place between the two companies, declaratory judgments were almost unheard of. It wasn't until the asbestos cases in the 1970s that declaratory judgments were systematically applied to insurance matters, so it made sense that there wouldn't be a specific provision in the agreement. However, the contract between Apex and Hoosier Re did specifically cover "expenses incurred in the investigation or settlement of claims," and Apex argued that this was exactly what the declaratory judgment with Barnett fell under. The contract between Apex and Hoosier Re also explicitly covered Apex's "ultimate net loss" in all matters, including "attorney's fees and other costs of investigation." Apex believed that because they had actually paid out the value defending against the claim that their expense in the declaratory judgment should be covered by the agreement with Hoosier Re.

Once Apex's brief was filed, their submission folder was closed and Hoosier Re's submission folder opened. Three days later, Hoosier Re uploaded their brief to the room.

Hoosier Re's lawyers took a different perspective in their brief. The contract between Hoosier Re and Apex dealt only with the risks covered by the reinsurance policy. Therefore, Hoosier Re could not be held accountable for risks not included in the original policy written by Apex for Barnett. Because the declaratory judgment expenses did not come from the original policy, Hoosier Re was not responsible for reimbursing the costs. The agreement spelled out all of the covered cost categories in great detail, but it did not mention declaratory judgments. Hoosier Re's lawyers made it clear that they saw these declaratory judgment expenses as a cost of doing business for Apex, not a portion of the risk taken on by Apex when they wrote the policy for Barnett. This declaratory judgment was much more important to Apex than it was to Hoosier Re, because it set a precedent for Apex's other customers. Hoosier Re got no such benefit out of the judgment.

Apex then was allowed to submit a rebuttal to Hoosier Re's filing, and Hoosier Re responded to the points made by Apex in the final rebuttal. The panelist was given the right to ask questions of the parties through the case manager, but he waived that right and decided to rely only on the documents filed. Two weeks later the arbitrator issued his decision: Hoosier Re was not obligated to pay Apex for the costs incurred in the declaratory judgment because it was not part of the risk covered in Apex's original policy for Barnett Industries. A copy of the decision was emailed to both sides, and a formal paper copy executed by the arbitrator and InsurODR.com arrived in the mail soon after. Apex and Hoosier Re signed their respective copies and agreed that the matter was resolved.

Analysis

Reinsurance is fundamentally about maintaining a good relationship and fair dealing between the reinsurer and the insurance provider. Insurers and their reinsurers are essentially business partners. If a reinsurer loses confidence that a company it supports is dealing fairly or managing its business properly it will terminate the coverage. Relationships are central to the effective operation of the reinsurance system.

Online dispute resolution, when made available at an early stage to handle disputes between insurers and reinsurers, can be very effective in preserving this relationship. A simple, documents-only process to resolve this dispute provided an easy way to resolve this particular matter. The neutral chosen could have been an insurance expert who did not require extensive education about declaratory judgments and reinsurance relationships (as a trial judge might have).

It is also important to note that parties to a reinsurance agreement are usually highly sophisticated. Both Apex and Hoosier Re were savvy players with access to competent counsel. They made the mutual decision to utilize dispute resolution in this matter and were pleased with the efficient outcome.

Conclusion

Several people familiar with the insurance industry have compared it to an aircraft carrier. It is a huge entity, awesome in its scope and power, and when it gets going in one direction it takes a lot of effort to slow it down. Even though those in the captain's nest may have concluded that a change in course is warranted, it takes a lot of time and planning to turn an aircraft carrier around.

It is important to remember that the technology revolution is only about twenty years old. There is little doubt that technology will transform the insurance industry as we know it, and online dispute resolution will be a big part of that transformation. It won't happen overnight, but it is crucial that people who understand the potential for ODR's integration into "the way insurance is done" keep the fires burning so that the momentum can grow. It may be that we won't have fully integrated ODR in claims departments until we've improved audio- and videoconferencing technology. But by reflecting on the facets of the way the business is done right now, identifying the inefficiencies, time delays, inconveniences, duplications, and frustrations that are taxing the industry and causing it to be cumbersome, slow, strained, and expensive, we can begin thinking about better ways of doing it. By thinking through the practice challenges involved in ODR's integration into insurance we can better prepare platforms to support the use of ODR, and ensure that the systems we eventually put in place will meet the needs of customers, underwriters, their service providers, and reinsurers.

CHAPTER EIGHT

ODR and Employment
Resolving Workplace Disputes Online

Workplace disputes are a major concern for businesses. If a company is to operate efficiently its employees need to have productive working relationships. Conflict is often part of a healthy workplace, as ideas are championed and different divisions jostle over control and project priorities. However, if disputes go unresolved, they can lead to resentment or infighting. If the workplace becomes choked with conflict or division, or if the environment is uncomfortable for some of the employees, the productivity of the workplace will be compromised. On a purely cost-benefit analysis level, businesses must effectively manage conflict in their workplace or they will pay a price.

In addition to this economic calculation, businesses also have legal responsibility for workplace disputes. If certain kinds of disputes arise and management does not proactively address them the penalties can be severe. Sexual harassment, worker's compensation, and Equal Employment Opportunity Commission (EEOC) disputes can all result in stiff fines for businesses or even multimillion-dollar jury awards. Often these types of claims are a pattern of unresolved complaints that were ineffectively handled by management.

Gone unresolved, disputes can also escalate to the point of criminality or violence. Many workplaces around the country have had to deal with employees and former employees vandalizing business property, destroying or sabotaging important records, or even threatening co-workers and supervisors. Even if a company abides by the letter of the law there is still the possibility that some employees will feel wronged or vengeful, and will use their insider, trusted status to cause problems.

In acknowledgement of these risks, businesses often rely on their human resources (HR) departments to handle the inevitable issues that arise between employees. In addition to managing compensation, benefits, vacation time, and the like, HR departments are frequently charged with the maintenance of healthy workplace relationships and the resolution of workplace disputes. However, HR departments are not the best channel for resolving all workplace disputes. Some employees are reluctant to take a matter to the HR department because they fear that doing so will impact their working relationships. HR departments are not necessarily neutral players in disputes, as they are divisions of the management of a company. Some employees are reluctant to involve HR in their workplace difficulties for fear that it will affect their advancement, brand them as troublemakers, or make a private situation into a public one.

Once a complaint is lodged it has an impact on an organization, particularly if there is a risk that it will escalate into a more formal claim. If an employee has the beginnings of a sexual harassment or bias claim, some organizations may overreact, entering a defensive posture and becoming very legalistic. In an attempt to protect the business from legal exposure administrators may risk further alienation from the aggrieved employee, adding to the risk that a formal complaint will arise. Also, once word gets out in a company that a certain dispute is happening, the reputations of everyone involved may be sullied. Managers accused of inappropriate behavior may be stigmatized before any facts have emerged, and employees may be branded as troublemakers.

Because of the magnitude of potential exposure connected to workplace disputes there is a lot of sensitivity surrounding the subject. However, that sensitivity does not always translate into an effective response to the problem.

HUMAN RESOURCES AND DISPUTE RESOLUTION

Many HR representatives have extensive experience working confidentially within their organizations to resolve matters that arise between co-workers before they escalate into formal complaints. As a result, there has been a growth in the number of HR representatives receiving training in dispute resolution. Several excellent books have emerged focused on disputes in the workplace, including *The Manager as Negotiator and Dispute Resolver* (1987), and *The Promise of Mediation* (1994).

It is obvious to many observers what shortcomings HR departments have in acting as dispute resolvers in the businesses they service. No matter how sensitive an HR manager may be to the needs of employees, it is often very clear that the HR department has a bias in how disputes are handled. An important component of any dispute resolution process is impartiality, and HR departments are clearly charged with helping to advance the overall goals of the business.

Some workplaces have explored the use of an ombudsperson to represent the interests of employees or even outside clients and partners. Ombuds, a concept originally from Scandinavia, involves the creation of an office inside an organization that has the responsibility to represent the interests of those outside the organization. The theory is that the ombuds office will have the insider status necessary to impact the agenda of the organization while at the same time maintain an awareness of the needs and perspectives of those outside the organization. This model has been deployed effectively in very different businesses, such as hospitals (where ombudspeople may represent the interests of patients and employees) and media outlets such as newspapers (where ombudspeople pay special attention to the criticisms of readers as to how particular stories are covered). This inside-outside role often gives ombudspeople the distance to be able to credibly perform impartial dispute resolution procedures.

Moving a step beyond the ombuds model, some HR departments have relationships with outside ADR experts who they can bring in to deal with specific situations. When a dispute arises and the parties are not comfortable having their HR representative act as a mediator these outside experts can be brought in to help the parties think through the dispute and to craft a mutually agreeable resolution. These outsiders can even play an ongoing role, following up with the parties to ensure that agreements are maintained and progress continues.

Case Study: Postal REDRESS

One of the largest successes in workplace ADR has been the United States Postal Service's REDRESS program. The Postal Service is the largest employer in the United States, with more than 700,000 employees. Faced with escalating complaints from employees and some high-profile acts of workplace violence, the Postal Service instituted a program in the early 1990s that they entitled REDRESS. This program used outside dispute resolvers, trained in a particular style of workplace dispute resolution, to hear and help resolve complaints lodged by postal employees. The model used in the REDRESS process is a transformative one, meaning that the goal is not to resolve individual disputes in isolation, but to work over the long term to build more communicative workplaces that can better handle future disputes.

Since its establishment, the REDRESS program has become one of the most sophisticated and widely used employment ADR programs in the federal government. A recent audit of the program found that 81 percent of cases mediated through REDRESS are eventually closed without a formal complaint being filed. Satisfaction with the structure of the process was also extremely high, with exit surveys completed anonymously by 26,000 participants indicating that 88 percent of employees are highly satisfied or satisfied with the amount of control, respect, and fairness in the REDRESS ADR process.[1] This figure is significant because the satisfaction rate for the Postal Service's traditional adversarial workplace process is only 44 percent. Moreover, both employees and supervisors are equally satisfied with ADR.

Significantly, the REDRESS program is also changing workplace culture at the Postal Service. In the first year after full implementation of the program, the number of complaints dropped by 24 percent as compared to the previous year. Formal complaints continued to drop in 2000, by an additional 20 percent.[2] In an agency as large as the Postal Service, this reduction of several thousand complaints per year leads to huge cost savings. Processing a simple workplace case can cost the government $5,000 in administrative expenses alone, and a more complicated case that reaches a formal adjudication can cost up to $77,000.[3] Thus the Postal Service program saves millions of dollars each year, in addition to improving morale and productivity.

THE VIRTUAL WORKPLACE

Face-to-face dispute resolution has proven very useful in resolving workplace matters and keeping organizations productive and on track. But the workplace is changing. Increasingly the notion of a single office where all a business's employees come in to work everyday is eroding. Some employees find that there is no reason for them to commute into the office everyday to perform the tasks they are assigned, and that they can more efficiently handle those tasks remotely, either working from home or from a branch office. Technology has made working remotely even more powerful, as network hardware and software can make a user's desktop at work appear on their computer screen at home, giving them access to all of the information they would be able to access were they physically in the office.

The expansion of business around the world has also put pressure on the one-building corporate model. Branch offices in locations where projects are underway have led to multi-ethnic, multi-language corporate presences, where the culture of the home office may be very different from the culture at the manufacturing plant. Employees can be in constant contact with project groups around the world, and the employees essential to deliver a particular project may never have met each other face-to-face. Travel also has led to a greater reliance on technology, as sales teams log in to central servers to strategize for market launches from their hotel rooms across the country and across the world. Some organizations, for example, consulting firms, have their employees perpetually in motion, and staffers report to the airport each Monday morning to find out where they are off to instead of meeting in a central office downtown. Technology is the only way to coordinate and deploy such virtual organizations, and technology is the means of getting key information deployed across all the divisions, no matter where the employees may be that day.

These developments make it very difficult to describe the new workplace. Teams are constantly in flux, communicating through email and over the telephone, working jointly on documents and contributing diverse information from wherever they may be. This new arrangement allows organizations to act with greater flexibility and more power to address new challenges. But they also generate new kinds of disputes.

HR departments increasingly need to deal with matters that cross continents and time zones, and perhaps even languages and cultures. Getting the people involved into a room, shutting the door, and working it out may no longer be a viable option. Technology is why these new disputes can arise. It can both exacerbate bad situations and help parties to resolve them, but it must be used effectively.

Virtual Workplaces Lead to Virtual Workplace Disputes

One of the difficulties in finding out about workplace conflict is the stigma that comes from formal involvement in a resolution process. Employees know that if they walk into the HR office and begin talking about a workplace situation that they are initiating a formal process with many moving parts. Some HR representatives have even told me that they often don't want to know about certain office situations, because once they know they have many responsibilities to follow up.

For example, if a supervisor and supervisee have been engaged in a romantic entanglement with each other on the sly for some time, and then difficulties arise in their working relationship after they break up, there can be wide ramifications to HR's knowledge of that information. What if a promotion was offered during the course of the relationship that could be interpreted as inappropriate once word of the relationship is leaked? What if project assignments were perceived as biased during that period? What if the internal performance review process was affected? Other employees, once they find out (or if they were suspicious all along) may feel that they were dealt with unfairly because of that situation. In such circumstances, an HR representative can hardly be blamed when they feel that it might be easier just never to know.

This situation can arise in a virtual workplace as well. Not to put too fine a point on it, but amorous entanglements do not always require physical proximity. It may be that certain members of a project team would be more likely to get into a compromising situation with co-workers with whom they are not geographically near. The difficulties in a working relationship that arise from such a virtual entanglement may in fact be more difficult to work through than those that arise from a face-to-face one.

ODR Best Deals with Virtual Workplace Disputes

ODR opens possibilities for dealing with these situations that do not exist in a purely face-to-face context. For instance, ODR systems can enable the parties to consult a neutral or to even engage in a dispute resolution process wholly anonymously. A dispute resolution service provider can initiate a process between a supervisor and a supervisee without ever knowing their real names, or even what city they work in. Employees could be informed of the availability of such a service in their HR orientation manuals, and there could be signs posted in the workplace advertising the availability of such a service. Should an employee desire some advice on a particular matter, or if she wanted to engage in a dialogue with the other involved party in a neutral forum, she could make use of the ODR resource in such a way that she was certain the information would not make its way back into the overall organization.

Such a process would be highly impractical if not impossible in the real world. Meeting someone face-to-face prevents him from concealing his identity. It also requires that both the neutral and the parties be in the same place.

ODR procedures also can help with disputes that arise between employees of different cultures, or even who speak different languages. Dispute resolution processes can take place in multiple languages through translation, or neutrals can be selected that are either from the culture of the disputants or who have extensive experience working inside their culture. If one or both parties are not comfortable with their language skills an ODR process can put them more at ease by giving them time to craft their responses and to make sure their words accurately represent their feelings in the matter.

ODR environments can also change the communication dynamic between parties. Some disputants get into frustrating or destructive communication patterns, alternately interrupting each other's comments or not really listening to what the other side is saying. Face-to-face mediators can do some things to combat these communication patterns, pointing them out or setting ground rules intended to provide different structures to conversations. However, ODR environments frequently introduce entirely different communication patterns that enable the parties to interact in wholly new ways.

Some computer-mediated communications can also work to combat power differentials between parties. If a supervisee is frequently intimidated or bullied by a supervisor in face-to-face interactions, making it difficult to accurately present his or her thoughts and reactions, online environments may help that supervisee feel comfortable enough to say what he or she needs to say without having to deal with the imposing presence of a supervisor. Many employees are able to be more forthcoming in an email to the CEO of a company than if they were given the opportunity to sit down across from the CEO's desk.

The slight remove provided by online communication can help to even out power differentials and to break out of face-to-face communication patterns that have contributed to the development of the misunderstanding in the first place.

I had a conversation with an HR officer at a high-tech company that employed a large number of engineers from Southeast Asia. She had been trained in dispute resolution and had made clear to everyone in the workplace that she was willing to provide dispute resolution services should any disputes arise. She had very few takers. Then one day, almost by accident, she got into an email exchange with one of the engineers who complained about a dispute he was having with his team leader. The team leader then began interacting with the HR officer as well about the matter, also through email. When she offered a face-to-face meeting to the disputants to discuss the conflict they refused, but they were more than happy to continue writing her long emails about the matter. Finally they came to agreement about how the situation should be resolved, and the resolution was accepted by both parties through email. The matter had never been discussed face-to-face, but a solution was achieved. The theory of the HR officer (who was herself from Southeast Asia) was that the involved engineers were very sensitive about saving face, and neither wanted to confront each other directly about the matter, though they were both very concerned about it. She explained the importance of this in many Southeast Asian cultures. The online communication avenue was removed enough from the face-to-face to enable the two parties to discuss the issue.

GETTING INVOLVED EARLY

One of the truisms in dispute resolution is that the earlier you can attempt to resolve a dispute the better. Once a dispute has gone on for a long time it is extraordinarily difficult to undo the damage that has been done to a relationship. The best (and most effective) course of action is to look for disputes before they boil over so that the underlying issues can be resolved before they contribute further to anger and resentment.

Disputes often start small, with a seemingly minor event, but they escalate when the parties begin a pattern of retaliation and response. For example, a member of a workgroup makes an inappropriate comment in an email sent to all of the members of the workgroup. When one of the recipients replies by sending an email message taking offense, the writer of the original comment counteracts by saying that the respondent is being oversensitive. Then the respondent is angry with the writer's lack of sensitivity, and forwards the message on to a supervisor complaining about the exchange. The supervisor contacts the writer about the original posting, and the writer becomes angry with the respondent for placing a formal complaint, and so on. The matter escalates as each response adds to the conflict.

The best way to prevent these cycles from perpetuating themselves is to create a culture of conflict management in an organization, so that everyone sees themselves as having a role in resolving disputes before they escalate out of control. This is not a matter of deputizing every-one in an organization to act as conflict police, or to expect everyone to walk around with a cloying oversensitivity and a halo hovering over their head. It is merely to instill in a workplace the sense that everyone has a role in resolving misunderstandings as early as possible.

ODR tools can be extremely useful in these efforts, because they can be made available right where the dispute arises. Instead of having to go to the HR department to make a formal complaint, and then having the HR officer find an available third party to meet with the employees involved in the dispute, an ODR mechanism can be deployed right from a company's intranet with the click of a button. A neutral mediator, either from inside the company or outside, can respond in a matter of hours or minutes instead of days. Especially in online interactions, where the dispute arises in electronic communi-cations, ODR can be brought in right at the beginning of a dispute, before the cycle of escalation has begun.

Uncomfortable working environment issues, like those that often precede sexual harassment disputes, can also be addressed much earlier by an ODR mechanism than by a formal ADR process. If a comment can be contributed anonymously by an employee who is uncomfortable then there is a much greater chance that employee will act sooner rather than later in taking action to address the situation. If a neutral experienced in dealing with these types of situations is made available online as an ever-present resource for counsel and advice then inappropriate patterns of behavior can be nipped in the bud before more egregious violations take place. This is better for the business, because it decreases their exposure to full-blown claims, but it is much better for the potential victims of these situations, as they can address matters before they are victimized by them.

TURNING OVER SENSITIVE INTERNAL MATTERS TO OUTSIDERS

It is important to note that many businesses are reluctant to involve outsiders in their workplace disputes. Some businesses repeatedly refer to themselves as a "family," and as with most families, there are some topics that are considered inappropriate for outside ears. Some companies make the strategic decision to sit on certain embarrassing internal developments for fear that they will harm the reputation of the company. Sometimes this strategy backfires, but usually the aggrieved party will just "lump it"* and the situation will disappear.

Online dispute resolution service providers need to build trust with the organizations they work with if they are to combat this tendency. Businesses are unlikely to direct sensitive matters, particularly those with frighteningly large financial implications, to outside organizations that they do not know or trust. One way to do this is to build relationships organically, through word of mouth, so that businesses come to the provider based on recommendations from others they trust. Another way is to make abundantly clear the depth of experience of the panelists providing dispute resolution services and the importance placed on privacy and confidentiality in all cases.

ODR AS AN EMPLOYEE BENEFIT

Many organizations realize that access to online dispute resolution is helpful to employees even outside the workplace. Employees may be affected by disputes in their personal lives and they may not know how best to deal with them. Some businesses provide limited legal services as part of an employee assistance package (EAP), so that if the employee needs to write up a will, or get a divorce, or write a lease, some limited legal services are provided to them, either free or at a reduced cost, as a benefit of their employment. ODR can also be a component of these packages, provided at reduced cost or free as a component of EAP packages. The service benefits employees, because they can resolve disputes quickly, efficiently, and at a low cost. The service also benefits employers because it ensures that employees will be less likely to get entangled in drawn-out legal proceedings or be emotionally and financially impacted by the pressures of a trial.

---

*To give in and take no further action.

IMPORTANT CONSIDERATIONS

While ODR has much to offer in workplace situations, it is not always a good fit. HR departments and neutrals need to assess the particulars of each dispute to determine whether or not ODR makes sense for the needs of the disputants. For example, many workplace disputes are emotionally complex, and they have built up over time. Apologies and effective listening are particularly important in these situations, two things that are not done as effectively in ODR environments. Perhaps hybrid strategies, in which initial meetings take place online and end up in a face-to-face interaction, might make more sense in these circumstances. For some of these matters in which the employee has moved on and is now at a new job (and perhaps even a new city), ODR may be the only option.

Also important is the risk of bias on the part of the dispute resolution service provider. In most workplace ODR models the employer pays all the costs for the services. The HR department, not the employees, probably maintains all ongoing interactions with the neutrals, and HR officials will assign new cases, not employees. All of these factors indicate that ODR neutrals involved with workplace cases need to be cognizant of their biases, because all repeated interactions likely take place with management.

BINDING EMPLOYEE ARBITRATION CLAUSES

One of the hottest topics in dispute resolution is the use of binding arbitration clauses in employee contracts. Long debated by employment law specialists, the Supreme Court recently issued a decision upholding the use of pre-dispute binding arbitration clauses in employee agreements (the Circuit City case, and further in the Waffle House case[4]), so the use of such clauses will undoubtedly continue to increase in the near future.

When an employee is offered a job by a company there may be a clause in his contract that states that any dispute that arises out of the employee's relationship with the company will be resolved by a third-party arbitrator. Often the organization that will provide the arbitrator is specified in the agreement, such as the American Arbitration Association. When the contract is signed, most employees do not think about how the employment agreement might end in a bitter dispute, so there is often little concern expressed by the employee about such clauses. Employees often do not understand that they are signing away their right to a formal hearing in a court of law.

Almost every kind of dispute that can arise between an employee and an employer is covered by these clauses. Sexual harassment, promotion issues, wrongful termination, long-term disability disputes, and injury-oriented compensation, as well as many other dispute types, all fall under these clauses. Some types of federal disputes, such as EEOC matters, may be exempted from these clauses. But they are the exception, and there is normally a high bar of proof required to get out from under any binding arbitration clause.

If a dispute arises, the employee has no option but to submit to a binding arbitration process under the clause. Ideally the arbitration process is efficient and fair, but there are many horror stories about employees forced into these processes against their will who believed the process was biased, the arbitrator incompetent, and the outcome unacceptable. In many respects if the employee feels forced into a process, there is little chance that he or she will accept it, even if it is conducted appropriately.

The main argument against these clauses is that employees are often persuaded into agreeing to them far in advance of any actual dispute. Because employees do not understand the full ramifications of these clauses when they sign, they are caught by surprise when later they realize that they've given up their right to a court date.

Businesses, on the other hand, are often anxious to insert these clauses to insulate themselves from what they perceive to be frivolous or abusive legal actions from former employees. Because damages awarded in employment matters have been rising steadily over the past few decades, arbitration clauses are seen as an effective way to insulate a business from the unpredictable excesses of a jury.

There are unquestionably ways that businesses can make employees more comfortable with binding arbitration clauses. Providing a choice of different arbitration institutions is one way to make the employee feel like he or she has more control over the process. The employee and her lawyer can research the different organizations and choose one that they are most comfortable with. Also, the employer can provide information about the arbitration process in advance of the employee signing the contract. Then the employee can make the choice as to whether the presence of the clause is enough to make her rethink taking the job. There are persuasive arguments that it is in the interest of employees to have arbitration agreements as well, as it may save the employee significant legal expense if a dispute eventually should arise. These strategies will go a long way to making the employee feel more comfortable and informed about the arbitration process, as opposed to feeling surprised and taken advantage of should it be exercised.

Online dispute resolution takes no side in this controversy. ODR platforms can easily be used to administer employment arbitration proceedings, and the lower cost and convenience may be preferable to both businesses and employees. Effective online arbitration proceedings involve procedural fairness, competent arbitrators, clear expectations on the part of lawyers and disputants, and carefully thought-out decisions. Individual ODR providers can make the decision as to whether or not they want to provide services in these contexts.

Case Study: Supervisor-Supervisee Difficulty

Michelle began working at Aeronautic Associates (AA) as a researcher, doing basic economic analysis for a wide variety of partners and departments. Soon after, she was promoted to associate and assigned to the business strategy division, headed by a partner named Richard. Richard was younger than most of the founders of the firm, but through his intense work ethic had emerged as one of the firm's most influential leaders. Richard had joined when AA consisted only of six partners, seven researchers, and a handful of administrative staff. During the six years of his employment at the firm, and largely in response to his aggressive business development, the firm had grown to more than one hundred.

Richard had a reputation for being focused and unforgiving with his staffers. He frequently challenged younger workers to exceed his output or his billable hours. Michelle found this reputation to be equal parts fact and fiction. It was true that Richard was a focused, intense worker. However, he also possessed a biting wit and a sense of adventure. Michelle quickly gave herself up to the projects in the business strategy division, and Richard fed her increasingly challenging assignments. Their work styles meshed well, and Richard started to bring Michelle with him to visit clients.

Suzanne was a human resources manager who was brought into AA when the number of staff increased to more than sixty people. She had been a full-time HR executive at a financial services firm, but when she had kids she decided to switch to her current position at AA, where she spent two days a week in the office and was available by phone on a third day. Suzanne was personal friends with one of the founding partners of AA, and she reported directly to him. Upon her arrival at AA she was dismayed to find the ragged state of human resources in the company—confusing organizational charts and responsibilities, unclear benefit structures, and erratic performance evaluation procedures. Limited by time as she was, Suzanne set about clearing some of these items up.

One of the employee assistance programs Suzanne brought to AA had a counseling and mediation component. In the employee orientation handbooks, Suzanne inserted information about the program's availability to all AA staffers. Though Michelle was already on staff at the time AA joined the program, she received notice about it in her mailbox and she stuck it in her desk. Copies of the notice also appeared around the office on bulletin boards.

Though Michelle's working relationship with Richard was progressing rapidly, and providing her with very interesting work, there was a component to her relationship with Richard that made Michelle uncomfortable. It was inevitable that Michelle would come to learn more about Richard's personal life as they traveled around to different destinations. She soon learned that Richard and his wife had been separated for some time and that they had long been fighting over Richard's devotion to his work at AA. These conversations made Michelle uncomfortable, especially because the tone in her relationship with Richard had become slightly more personal. He would make comments about Michelle's "quirks" or the way she looked at him, and he would say things like "you're so cute," or "I know you too well." None of the comments were explicitly sexual, but they made Michelle uncomfortable around Richard.

After several months of working together, Richard had the responsibility of writing a performance evaluation for Michelle, which he did in glowing terms. Michelle was pleased with the positive performance evaluation, especially because it was tied to her future salary increases. But Richard would refer to the evaluation in his interactions with her, challenging her to "justify that evaluation I gave you" or saying "you'll thank me when the raises come around." None of the comments were outwardly inappropriate, but Michelle was troubled by them. She felt Richard was picking up on some of her hesitancy in the relationship, perhaps questioning why she would turn down some of the opportunities to travel with him. Michelle did not think that Richard would ever approach her intimately without her consent, but she wasn't sure where he was trying to lead things.

Complicating matters was the fact that Richard had a very turbulent relationship with the founding partner who had brought in Suzanne. Michelle felt that if she approached Suzanne about these matters with Richard they would most likely get back to the founding partner and perhaps be used against Richard in some way. Also, Michelle had no real relationship with Suzanne, and was reluctant to trust her with these concerns.

Michelle's eye caught on one of the posters offering counseling and mediation services to AA employees, and she visited the Web address listed on the flyer. After being assured that she could speak with someone anonymously, she filled out a form and got an email a few hours later. After asking a few questions about the service, and learning about the person on the other end of the line (a human resources consultant and lawyer with more than twenty years experience, located on the other side of the country), Michelle explained the situation. The consultant asked some direct questions, explained the legal situation, and offered Michelle some advice about how to deal with the situation. She also offered to serve as a mediator between Michelle and Richard, if Michelle thought that might be helpful. Michelle said that she'd prefer to try out some of the consultant's advice first, and that she might get back to her. She took down the consultant's email and thanked her for the advice.

In her interactions with Richard from then on Michelle tried to set clear boundaries. She wasn't aggressive in rebuffing his intimate communications, but a little more distant. Michelle saw Richard reacting to her new attitude, and he seemed somewhat saddened by it. Over a few weeks, however, the comments came less frequently and Michelle felt that the situation had eased somewhat. However, Michelle didn't dare bring up the issues directly; Richard had a wild temper, and she was reluctant to have it out with him face-to-face, especially as he was her boss.

The next month, Richard brought a new associate into the business strategy group, a young woman who had joined the firm a year after Michelle. Michelle observed Richard doing very similar things with this new associate that he had done with her when she had first joined the group—giving her choice assignments, taking her on travel, and speaking with her in a borderline flirtatious manner. Michelle also came to feel that this new associate was being given responsibilities that should have gone to Michelle, and that Richard was flaunting these interactions at Michelle to punish her for pulling away from him. Michelle grew increasingly upset with the situation, but she remained hesitant to raise the situation with Suzanne. Richard had brought Michelle farther in her few months of working with him than any of the other associates hired at the same time. Michelle was worried that this could be taken away, and she didn't want to further jeopardize her position by involving Suzanne.

Michelle again contacted the consultant she had spoken with a few weeks before and explained the situation to her. She asked for advice, and the consultant outlined the online mediation process for her. Both Michelle and Richard could remain anonymous, as the consultant sent all communications to them through the ODR website hosting the service, so she only knew ID numbers and first names (if Michelle and Richard were comfortable with that level of identification.) They could speak about the situation in total confidence, even using their home computers instead of work computers, if that made them more comfortable. Michelle agreed that mediation would be a good option in this situation, and she asked the consultant to contact Richard to ask if he would participate in the process.

When contacted, Richard acted quite surprised with the consultant. He said he didn't know about any of these feelings, but when he learned about how the communication would work, he agreed to participate. The consultant sent both Michelle and Richard login information to an online meeting room where they could speak about the situation in confidence. Over the next two weeks, Michelle and Richard participated in a dialogue about the situation at work, and Michelle felt comfortable speaking her mind about their interactions for the first time. The consultant did a good job reframing issues and clarifying ways that problem interactions could be avoided in the future. Richard seemed genuinely surprised by Michelle's feelings, and he did acknowledge how Michelle could have perceived the new associate's promotion in the way she did. He also expressed appreciation for the fact that Michelle had chosen to deal with the matter online in order to prevent rumors about the situation in the AA office.

In the office, Michelle and Richard said nothing about the online discussion, but after a week had passed, Richard called Michelle into his office and asked her to sit down. Richard acknowledged Michelle's feelings and apologized for some of the misunderstandings, but also made clear that he appreciated Michelle's intellect and ability and that the new associate did not represent a threat to Michelle's work in the business strategy group. After this discussion, Michelle felt much better about the situation, and the online mediation quickly came to a close.

Analysis

Workplaces have become increasingly dependent on email for communication, and it is inevitable that some dispute resolution would start to take place through that channel. While many mediators would say that the disputants should just sit down together to talk the matter out, that is not always possible. In some circumstances the availability of an online channel can give an employee a chance to get some outside, expert advice without any fear that it will get back to others in the workplace.

In the case study, Richard appreciated Michelle's use of the online channel because it signaled her desire to keep the matter contained, as well as her sensitivity to the office politics that Richard might have fallen victim to had word about the situation become public.

CHAPTER NINE

Electronic Democracy

ODR and Government

─◡◡◡─ It could be argued that the central task of government is to resolve disputes. The democratic system is really a very large, ornate dispute resolution process, through which proposals are brought forth, everyone is given a chance to weigh in, and a decision is made.

Some of the most interesting applications of online dispute resolution tools and technology in this area involve supporting the democratic process. These applications are sometimes termed *participatory* or *deliberative democracy.* Technology is shifting information and decision-making power out of the hands of a few elites sitting in capitol buildings and back into the hands of citizens.

The central task of deliberative democracy is involving people and informing them about what their government is doing. ODR can go a long way toward achieving this goal. By applying ODR tools to the dispute resolution process (online discussions, convening, facilitation, document sharing) much of the promise of deliberative democracy can be achieved.

This chapter focuses primarily on the federal government in the United States. However, many of the observations made here about the value of ODR in the federal context can easily be applied to other national governments around the world, or even state and local governments. Some other national systems, such as Canada, Australia, and several European countries, may be even more favorably predisposed toward the use of these tools in their policy-setting and public consensus-building processes.

THE SCOPE OF GOVERNMENT

Government has the largest client base of all businesses. In the United States the numbers are staggering—more than 250 million customers that need to be tracked and serviced. Conflict inevitably arises in the delivery of government services, such as disputes over tax collection, over benefit payments, or over documents (passports and driver's licenses). Since a wide range of services are offered to each citizen, individuals may interact with the government in several different roles (as tax payers, veterans, social security recipients, and so on).

Every agency in government confronts disputes. Citizens may protest their parking tickets, or they may be angry they couldn't get a White House tour. Veterans may protest that they are not getting the benefits they deserve, or citizens may complain that they were harassed while attempting to renew their passport. Complaint handling is a central function of almost every unit of government.

Because government is involved with the full scope of society, the range of potential disputes is overwhelming, from land use issues to environmental cleanups to arts funding to community disputes. Governments have a vested interest in resolving these disputes, both to keep citizens happy and satisfied and to ensure that federal responsibilities are carried out efficiently and effectively.

Government is not only about service delivery, however. Many governmental institutions are decision-making bodies, issuing rules and regulations that govern the operation of society. In a democracy it is important to conduct these deliberative processes in as inclusive a manner as possible, to ensure that the outcome of the policy-making process has maximum buy-in from those affected.

To a large extent, government is the ideal host for dispute resolution, because government has a strong incentive to resolve disputes to keep society functioning smoothly. Government is also a good host for dispute resolution because it usually has no vested interest in the outcome of most of the matters it is in charge of deciding.

Unique Pressures

The public understands that the rules are different when they interact with the government. Transparency is often required by the law, which puts limits on how confidential federal dispute resolution processes can be. Public data trails may discourage government employees because a record of every communication is available to the public. The digital trail can help governments track what services have and have not been delivered to each citizen.

Many citizens are uncomfortable giving their private information to a corporation or a non-profit that they know nothing about, but they are comfortable with the government having that information.

Government also has an enforcement role to play in society, such as finding and penalizing fraudulent marketers. When government builds ODR systems they can construct them in a manner that maximizes their integration with these criminal systems, so that information can be fed in both directions.

Because there is no profit motivation, government is less likely to create unfair dispute resolution mechanisms that stack the deck in favor of one side or the other. Because of public disclosure requirements, government actions are often made out in the open as well, making the use of confidential, closed dispute resolution mechanisms impossible.

Many government actions are also bound by due process prescribed by legislation, so non-binding dispute resolution mechanisms like mediation are often easier to implement than binding mechanisms like arbitration.

People have a negative view of dealing with government bureaucracy; any interaction with the government is expected to be inefficient and frustrating. This puts many constituents into a combative mindset before the interaction even begins.

GOVERNMENT AND TECHNOLOGY

Many of the functions that the private sector has developed to improve the efficiency of their operations, such as customer relationship management software, have even more utility in the government context. Because there are so many different areas in government it is an enormous task to coordinate all of the federal efforts in one place. Technology can provide this infrastructure.

One common application class used in the business world is enterprise resource planning (ERP) software. Companies like SAP and PeopleSoft have made their reputations providing these software platforms to large businesses. ERP packages are often quite complex to integrate into an organization because they reach into every area of the business, such as accounting, procurement, human resources, and customer relationship management. Often the choice of an ERP package is the choice of an operational model, and companies need to adjust the way they work to match the functionality of their ERP package.

Increasingly this software model is being translated into the government as well. While it may be complicated to introduce an ERP package into a large company, it is much more complicated to roll out such a system through an entire government. Several states have successfully launched statewide technology platforms that coordinate all agency resources, budgets, and personnel from a single interface. Such standardization allows for more effective planning and more efficient resource allocation. It also creates a smoother experience for citizens working with government, as they don't have to deal with each agency in a vacuum.

Governments have been working toward updating their services to utilize advanced technology. Building in online dispute resolution is a natural extension of that process.

ODR filing options can be built right into the websites of government agencies, allowing citizens to file their complaints right where they get information about the services offered. Because most agencies are located in the capital of a state or in Washington, D.C., it is usually impossible or impractical for a citizen with a grievance to be required to file their matter in person.

ADR AND THE GOVERNMENT

Government has great incentive to use ADR. No government official relishes the prospect of legal action against constituents. Resolving disputes efficiently is in the interest of the public, because the public pays the bills for the process.

Since the federal government enacted the Administrative Dispute Resolution Act of 1996, dispute resolution has become a part of the way government does business. Every federal agency is required to have a dispute resolution representative who can educate the agency about opportunities in applying ADR to make things happen more efficiently. The National Performance Review in the early 1990s further underscored the importance of dispute resolution and gave it additional weight.

Government is now using ADR to resolve workplace and contract disputes, and even to inform policy and regulation setting. The government also passed legislation that requires ADR be used to solve problems such as Superfund cleanups and transportation reauthorizations. Sometimes government outsources a particular dispute resolution function to a third party, like the Better Business Bureau's Autoline program for car dealerships around the country.

Regulatory negotiation (or "reg neg") is the use of ADR techniques during the policy-making process to lessen the risk of lawsuits after a rule is adopted. If stakeholders can be brought into the deliberation process on the front end, then they can contribute their perspectives and achieve buy-in on the regulation before it is put in place. Instead of government officials examining matters behind closed doors and issuing rules and regulations, the public is involved in the discussion surrounding what might work best, leading to more effective decision-making. Effort put into regulatory negotiation in advance of adoption has been demonstrated to result in fewer legal challenges and less enforcement problems post-implementation.

There is a clear message being communicated in the federal government that agencies and employees should constantly be on the lookout for opportunities to use dispute resolution to increase efficiency and effectiveness. The report to the president prepared by the Department of Justice in spring 2001 detailed the rapid growth in ADR in the federal sector, in a wide range of agencies and offices. The success of the Postal Service's REDRESS program, the EEOC's workplace dispute resolution efforts, the Community Relations Service of the Department of Justice, and the regulatory negotiation efforts of the Environmental Protection Agency (EPA) are just a few of the programs held up as examples of how ADR can complement the work of government. Many other agencies are beginning pilot dispute resolution programs to complement their work, such as the IRS's fast track mediation program, as well as several projects in the armed services coordinated with the military courts.

The 2001 Federal Dispute Resolution conference in New Orleans had more than one thousand attendees representing the full alphabet soup of government agencies: the DOA, DOD, HHS, BATF, Treasury,

VA, the EEOC, FLRA, FMCS, GAO, the International Broadcasting
Board, MSPB, NSF, NASA, OPM, the Office of Special Counsel, and
the United States Postal Service. Government officials are learning
about dispute resolution techniques more rapidly than other professional areas because there is a clear sense in Washington that dispute
resolution is where government is heading.

HOW ODR CAN ASSIST GOVERNMENT

ODR has many benefits for government agencies above and beyond
face-to-face ADR. Much of the work of government in the past has
focused on information management. Technological advances hold
the promise of streamlining data handling, and it is a relatively simple matter to extend that streamlining to complaint intake and case
management. Many agencies are moving toward a model where
individual citizens handle many of their data management tasks
themselves, such as changing addresses, paying parking tickets, or filing their tax returns. The infrastructure being put in place to handle
these tasks can easily be adapted to providing online dispute resolution as well.

Automated dispute handling can resolve a large number of cases
without requiring citizens to jump through administrative hoops. If
there is a repeated problem with printing veterans' benefit checks that
involves 30,000 veterans, then instead of each one of those veterans
having to call a complaint line they can instead file their complaint
online. If their information matches the information in an internal
database, then the problem can be addressed automatically.

This kind of complaint handling leads to greater citizen satisfaction with government, as it gives a sense that government is more
responsive and flexible. These automated resolution mechanisms cannot be expected to handle every situation, so it is important that a
means to handle exceptions be built into the system so that non-
standard disputes can easily be pulled out and directed to a live person who can best address the matter. But for many problems these
automated systems are efficient and effective resolution options.

The applicability of ODR to government does not stop simply at
constituent services, however. For public participation efforts, the
introduction of ODR can open the door to people who would never
otherwise have had an opportunity to provide input into the deliberations of government agencies. Experts can be involved in regulation

setting processes, information can be exchanged with the broader public, and consensus can be built that results in better governmental decision-making. An experiment in the use of ODR at the EPA in 2001 was analyzed by a prominent environmental consulting firm, Resources for the Future, who concluded that the effort was an unqualified success. More than one thousand people contributed their opinions to the EPA on the issue of public participation over a one-week period. As the study's author concluded, "87 percent thought similar on-line dialogues should be conducted in the future. EPA accomplished its goal of garnering broader input about what it does right and wrong. It also opened up new lines of communication with the public and generated some good will."[1]

Finally, using ODR to improve government's workflow also has great promise. ODR can be used to resolve employment disputes or labor management issues, to facilitate the cooperation of various agencies, and to improve the management of virtual teams. All of the benefits ascribed to the integration of ODR in Chapter Eight can also be realized in its integration into federal workplaces.

PROVIDER PROFILE: FMCS

The Federal Mediation and Conciliation Service (FMCS) was created in 1918 as the U.S. Conciliation Service and renamed in 1947. Its mission has always been to help resolve disputes between labor and management before they escalate. By law, unions and corporations must consult with FMCS before beginning any labor action. As a result, FMCS has 80,000 built-in clients that they need to support and stay in communication with. FMCS neutrals are some of the hardest working people in the federal government, because of the scope of the area that they cover and the complexity of many of the issues they work to help resolve.

Over the past ten years, FMCS has increasingly become the home of ADR in the federal government. In addition to working in the labor management area, FMCS now works on regulatory negotiations, employment grievances, and international disputes.

One of the difficulties for FMCS has been finding enough time for neutrals to meet with all the parties that want to work with them. FMCS neutrals now average more meetings with parties than they have workdays in a year. This challenge is magnified by geography, as FMCS neutrals often have responsibility for a multi-state area in which it is difficult to get from one place to another quickly. Some FMCS neutrals are on the road three weeks a month just getting to all the meetings that they need to attend. Often they live like firefighters, ready to go at a moment's notice whenever things seem to be escalating.

Partially as a result of these pressures FMCS has become an innovator in the application of technology to dispute resolution. In 1999 FMCS introduced TAGS—Technology Assisted Group Systems. Originally TAGS was used primarily for face-to-face meeting facilitation. Based on underlying technology from Facilitate.com, a San Francisco-area company focusing on how technology can best assist face-to-face meetings, TAGS has been used for everything from board meetings to elections for union leadership.

TAGS integrates certain functionalities, like brainstorming and polling, to best support the work of groups of people. FMCS has invested in hundreds of wireless networked laptops that can be set up anywhere. When a group wants to utilize the TAGS platform they file a request with FMCS, and if the hardware is available FMCS comes on-site to set up the network and facilitate the meeting. Each participant is given a laptop that is logged into the TAGS system. Working inside a structure predesigned by the meeting facilitator, parties can brainstorm ideas, rank preferences, make suggestions, and view aggregated data all in real time. Tasks that might have taken hours using a flipchart with a marker (such as brainstorming hot topics and deciding which items are most important) can be handled in just a few minutes.

Teams of FMCS mediators and facilitators working across the country and around the world have used TAGS to help resolve disputes in a wide variety of contexts. In fact, growing demand for TAGS has driven FMCS to purchase more laptops so that several full TAGS systems can be in operation in different areas of the country at the same time.

FMCS is now expanding the TAGS facilitation tools into the realm of mediation, allowing FMCS neutrals to administer cases online. FMCS's new online dispute resolution components (currently dubbed "tRooms") enable neutrals to communicate with parties and to make progress in dispute resolution procedures without requiring them to be in the same room. By addressing the convening penalty (the time required simply to get together with the parties) this use of ODR promises to increase the effectiveness of FMCS neutrals. But beyond that, the integration of TAGS's facilitation component with an online mediation component promises to give the agency a new reach for its services.

Case Study: RuleNet

The Nuclear Regulatory Commission's (NCR) RuleNet process was an innovative attempt in 1996 to open up federal rulemaking procedures to public involvement using electronic communications networks. By designing an online process that allowed the participation of diverse stakeholders in a dialogue on the difficult issue of fire protection, the NRC gathered more useful information about the positions of all of the involved parties.

A major issue under consideration at the NRC was fire protection at nuclear power plants. The topic was a hotly debated one, with strong opinions on both sides. Several staffers at the NRC, responding to calls for the greater use of technology and dispute resolution, decided that an ODR process might be a good way to address the issue of fire protection. They called the project RuleNet.

RuleNet built on principles already held by many at the NRC. Essentially, it was a forum for everyone to be heard. Advertisements for these discussions could be distributed in the same manner as the advertisements for the NRC's public meetings, only these would be billed as "electronic" public meetings.

Technically, the development of the ODR platform offered few surprises. As the technology of RuleNet took shape, a set of tools that could be used by the participants and facilitators to advance the dialogue were built into the software. These tools helped the facilitators focus discussions, summarize information, and identify peripheral issues that should be brought into the center of the discussion. The tools became the primary means by which the moderators and facilitators affected the flow of the dialogue and urged the group closer to consensus.

When a comment was received from a participant, it went through a content filter that checked it for certain words. The ground rules were that there would be no libel, no offensive language, no capitalization (which was construed as shouting), and no anonymous postings. The technical team referred to these as "bozo filters."

If the posting made it through the filters it went to the moderators. Some of these people were engineers and technology people at the Lawrence Livermore Laboratory. If a message needed a technological interpretation they would often provide it. If there was a problem with a proposed posting, the moderator could contact the poster and have a one-on-one dialogue about how the problem might be resolved.

The final line of defense was the facilitators. Their job was to participate in and facilitate the group process. They played the key role in trying to work toward consensus. The facilitators' primary task was to synthesize ideas through rephrasing of the main ideas in the discussion. If a posting was very technical then the facilitators could confer with the fire protection engineer affiliated with the project for clarification. The facilitators attempted, through natural topic aggregations, to focus the technical questions down to manageable topics.

On January 5, 1996, RuleNet began with a videoconference that linked sites around the country. The videoconference was considered important because it put faces to the email addresses of some of the key players in the dialogue. The videoconference was transcribed live over the Internet so that anyone with Web access could read the proceedings and contribute questions.

Each user participated in a different way. Some chose to be "lurkers," who watched the proceedings but did not participate. Many logged in frequently for a certain period and then dropped off. The active participants numbered about twenty, including a handful of NRC staff who were involved throughout the process. Outside of the NRC, most of the active participants were representatives of industry. Two of the active participants were academics.

The NRC staff kept a watchful eye on the participants. If someone was burning out from information overload then the staff could detect it and contact the user directly to work out the problems. In this way the participants were supported and kept as part of the dialogue. Without this attention from the facilitators the number of active posters might have dwindled even further.

The kickoff videoconference was followed by a ten-day period for the public to review the provided background information for clarification questions and issue identification. The moderators and facilitators drafted some specific statements and asked participants to respond to them (using the "consensus evaluation" tool). Some participants chose not to register their opinions, perhaps indicating their desire to wait until further in the dialogue to explain their positions.

After the initial period, another ten-day phase began in which participants were asked to propose solutions to the issues raised in the first phase. The RuleNet facilitators and moderators developed six questions that were designed to get participants to suggest solutions. The number of comments received varied widely. On the questions where participation was low the issues were dropped from the discussion.

At the end of these first two phases, the NRC staff with subject knowledge worked with some staffers from the Lawrence Livermore Laboratory to synthesize the comments and suggested solutions into a set of concrete proposals. These proposals were then posted to the RuleNet site. Then the participants were asked to respond to them. The opportunity to caucus with other members to discuss the proposals was made available, but most responded only with formal statements.

The dialogue among the participants and staff on the three concrete proposals was very focused. In addition, a question dealing with the effectiveness of the RuleNet process itself received the most responses, forty-one comments in all. Overall the participant views were positive, mostly in that they allowed public participation in pre-viously closed governmental decision-making processes. However, it was suggested that a cost analysis should take place before further online processes were integrated into the regulation-setting process.

In the opinion of the NRC, the tools used in the RuleNet process worked well. A survey was sent out to 150 of the RuleNet participants immediately after the end of the project. A small number actually responded. Of those who did respond, many of their assessments were positive, saying that the process had been valuable. Almost all, however, said that such a process was useful only as a supplement to traditional rule-making procedures and not as a replacement.

The NRC staff felt that the process had contributed significant value to the com-mission's deliberations. As the NRC *Policy Issue* concludes, "As the RuleNet process evolved over a period of weeks, a much greater insight into the opinions and attitudes of the participants was derived than could be achieved by written submissions alone."[2] Through the online dialogue, the staff was able to acquire more detailed information about both the substantive issues and the RuleNet process than they would have been able to gain in any other way. However, the staff acknowledged that the process did not yield any major revelations, only a clearer understanding of the participants' concerns.

The NRC concluded that the RuleNet process was useful in several areas. First, it allowed the NRC staff to examine all of the proposals and concerns in a central forum, rather than examining each one sequentially. Second, the effort required for partici-pation in the paper process may silence some of those people who are not motivated enough to submit a comment. The participation of two academics with expertise in the area may reflect the benefits of the lower effort threshold of the electronic process. Third, the feedback from the staff encouraged elaboration and participation, and this may enrich and enhance public participation in the rule-making process.

In this last area, public participation, the NRC concluded that the RuleNet approach was more effective than the traditional paper-based rule-making processes. Addition-ally, the RuleNet process showed benefits in the area of satisfaction for the inter-ested public. While this program was only a beginning, it showed significant promise and it opened new avenues for future federal attempts to involve the public in its deliberations.

MULTIPARTY DISPUTES

The most sophisticated application of ODR may be in multiparty, public disputes. Public disputes are those in which the government is involved, either as a facilitator or as a stakeholder, and in which the public has an interest in the outcome of the matter. Because of the complexity in coordination among many parties and the large quantity of information that needs to be shared, ODR can result in process efficiencies. Handling multiparty cases is very work-intensive for the facilitator, as each participant must feel as if he or she is being heard in the process.

Zoning disputes are excellent examples of public disputes. For example, a development company decided that it wanted to build a new mall on a vacant lot of land in a suburban community. It may be that the matter involves only a few parties directly, such as the developer and the landowner and perhaps a few local merchants. But the public as a whole is indirectly involved as well, because of traffic, environmental, and property value concerns. There might be thousands of individuals who would be affected by the outcome of the zoning process. It would be impossible (or at least highly impractical) to get every one of the stakeholders into a single room to debate the issues. So the way communities often deal with this type of situation is to convene a public process to resolve the matter, usually governed by elected or appointed representatives and open to participation from any interested party.

There are strong incentives to use dispute resolution in multiparty situations, because when more than two or three parties are involved the courts become a very complex way to resolve the matter. Courts are good at determining who is right and who is wrong, but they are not very efficient at sorting out matters where there might be dozens of involved parties. ADR is much more effective in these situations, because mediators can act as convenors and facilitators, working to build consensus behind a particular resolution to a matter as opposed to finding fault.

Much of the work of the mediator in a multiparty process is in this convening role, getting the parties together, drafting and redrafting documents to build party buy-in, and shuttling communications between the different parties. Often the deliberations in multiparty matters are very technical, requiring sophisticated analysis and extensive research.

Dispute resolution techniques have been used to resolve multiparty matters for quite some time. Organizations such as the Center for Dispute Resolution, ADR Associates, the Consensus Building Institute, and CONCUR have focused their efforts on multiparty, public disputes and have built an impressive track record of successes from the last three decades. The environmental conflict resolution (ECR) area has evolved into a well-defined field, and the Association for Conflict Resolution has a section devoted to environmental and public policy disputes.

HOW ODR BENEFITS MULTIPARTY PROCESSES

Public dispute resolution processes have many clear benefits to be reaped from the integration of ODR. Online technology can help with information sharing, deliberation, analysis, and follow-up. In her chapter in the *Consensus Building Handbook* (1999), the definitive guidebook on this topic, Connie Ozawa identified five aspects of consensus building that can be affected by the use of technology:

- Dissemination of and access to written materials
- Discussion, debate, and deliberation
- Analysis
- Decision-making
- The drafting of written documents

Handling multiparty cases face-to-face is work intensive. Many of the tasks that fall to mediators of public dispute resolution processes are administrative in nature, such as circulating agendas and draft revisions, setting up meeting times and places, and tracking contact information for participants. An inordinate amount of time can be spent on minutiae, which is all separate and apart from the actual work of making progress toward a resolution to the dispute.

Document Sharing and Management

Document sharing is a major challenge in and of itself. Every time a change is made it needs to be distributed to and approved by all of the different involved parties. ODR can streamline this information dissemination process by tracking versions of documents, making edits clear to participants, and providing searchable repositories of information to all participants around the clock.

For many multiparty processes the goal is to generate a document at the end of the process that all of the participants are willing to support. The drafting and redrafting that goes into the creation of these documents is often very complex, involving the synthesis of myriad comments from many different participants. Simply keeping track of the suggested changes, much less integrating them into a coherent whole, can be a challenge. Often the deliberative process needs to be cut short because discussions on different points can be so time consuming, so a facilitator simply drafts her own suggested resolution and presents it to the participants for a thumbs-up or thumbs-down decision.

Online technology can help to organize these deliberative exercises so that the parties can make progress on language without relying on the facilitator to shuttle every proposed wording change around to everyone who might be interested. Because the deliberative process itself is text-based it is easier to translate the discussion into one text that satisfies all of the participants.

Scheduling

Another challenge is simply scheduling meetings or including stakeholders who may have a strong interest in the outcome of the process but cannot travel to all the meetings. Often the most important participant in a process is also the person who has the least time in his schedule to spare for a meeting. In an ODR process there is no limit on the number of people who can attend a meeting, and geography is not a limitation. It's not even necessary for all of the participants to schedule a meeting, as asynchronous participation does not require everyone to be available at the same time.

Progress Between Meetings

As ODR enables parties to make progress in an ongoing way, a multiparty process that would require five meetings face-to-face may be doable in two or three face-to-face meetings if progress is made online between the gatherings. Much of the time of each meeting is spent getting participants back up to speed, reminding them what was covered in the last meeting (as there is often several weeks or months between meetings), and filling in participants who were absent from prior gatherings. Because ODR happens in a more continuous way, the flow of the discussion doesn't stop for long periods of time, so it's harder for participants to lose track of the topics under consideration. Also, because the discussions are automatically archived, if an individual does need to be reminded what was discussed before, they can easily fill themselves in. Participants who might have to miss a meeting can consult the online record to update themselves on what was addressed.

Consensus Evaluation

ODR also can facilitate the consensus evaluation process. One of the challenges of multiparty disputes is the degree to which communications between the facilitator and the participants is public. In a large group meeting it is very difficult for the mediator to speak one-on-one with any of the participants because the group as a whole needs to keep moving forward. If the facilitator wants to evaluate where the group is with regard to reaching agreement on a particular point, most likely he will need to go around the room and ask everyone how close they are to agreement.

Online tools make it easy to share large quantities of information, to jointly edit documents, and to take polls of participants. The ability to set up subsections of virtual meeting rooms allows for the simple spin-off of workgroups and caucus discussions. These discussions can happen concurrently with the joint discussion, so workgroup members can continue to participate in the overall dialogue at the same time they work in their smaller group, unlike face-to-face meetings. Facilitators also have the ability to be in multiple conversations and workgroups at once, as they have access to all the electronic conversations going on.

Inclusiveness

It is important to note that online communication can open the door to people who are normally excluded from face-to-face deliberative discussions. Often group discussions are dominated by a handful of participants while others, perhaps even the majority, stay silent. Certain individuals are very comfortable and perhaps even compelled to express their opinions forcefully in public situations, while others are reluctant or even reticent to do so. Online communication options often result in a different group of people expressing their opinions; participants who would not contribute much in a face-to-face meeting discussion have a new medium in which to express themselves. This can result in a much richer process for all involved, in addition to providing important information to the facilitator.

Case Study: Addison Zoning

The Addison Zoning Board was at a standstill. Two consecutive meetings had been shut down by protests from a small but vocal group of residents and community activists. The zoning board had also been receiving pressure behind the scenes to resolve key issues from the city manager's office downtown as well as the lawyers for some major real estate interests in the area. At private meetings, the zoning board members had been expressing their increasing frustration.

The Apollo Company, a major developer in the area, had recently purchased a plot of land at the intersection of Inwood Lane and Midway Road in the northern part of Addison, a primarily residential region of the city. The area of land in question had been zoned for light retail use, but the only occupants had been a small gas station on the corner of the intersection and a major department store that had closed in 1993. The Apollo Company subsequently announced that they were planning to build an eight-screen movie theater on the property.

Several residents in the area formed community groups and immediately registered their displeasure with the plan. At meetings where the theater zoning issue was to be discussed and voted on, community groups had disrupted the proceedings and ignored the appeals from zoning board members to be quiet. Accusations of bribery and cronyism were levied against the zoning board members. Several board members had refused to attend subsequent meetings unless certain residents were refused admittance.

After some discussions, the head of the zoning board, who was appointed by the city manager, decided to call in a panel of mediators from nearby South City. The three mediators sent were from Public Disputes, a non-profit consulting group that works to resolve multiparty public issues such as this one. They suggested the option of an online meeting, with the possibility of a future face-to-face gathering after some of the key issues have been clarified. They contacted each of the participants and everyone agreed to give it a try.

The participants in the online process could be roughly grouped into three categories: government, development opponents, and development proponents.

The first category is governmental interests. The Addison Zoning Board had four representatives that participated in the online dispute resolution process: the head of the zoning board, the secretary, and two delegates. The city manager's office also sent one of its representatives to participate.

In the development opponents category, four local residents participated in the online discussion. Two residents in particular felt very strongly that this movie theater was an abuse of power from the corporations and corrupt politicians downtown. The other two residents were not as angry about the proposed development, but they were concerned. Two community activists had gotten involved after being called in by the particularly angry resident. The environmental concerns also prompted the participation of two local environmental advocates.

In the development proponents category, the Apollo Company provided two representatives for the online discussion: a lawyer and a public relations representative. Another proponent of development involved in the online discussion was a representative from the Real Estate Consortium of Greater Addison. The last proponent of development was a representative of the Greater Addison Chamber of Commerce.

Public Disputes assigned three mediators to handle the matter. Because of the impasse at the last two face-to-face meetings, they thought they might try out this new online tool, which some other public ADR groups had told them about at a conference.

To begin the process, the mediators spoke with all the participants over the telephone. When possible, they arranged face-to-face meetings with key parties, such as the most vocal resident. They got a sense of the major issues and discussed the possibility of using technology for the initial meeting. Because all the parties were amenable to the use of the online technology they decided to move ahead with it. They explained how the process was going to work, and set some ground rules for the parties.

Next the mediators designed the technology and crafted an agenda. At the recommendation of another public dispute resolution firm that had already used the online technology, they first created online caucus spaces for the three groups to interact before they jumped right into a joint discussion. Each category of participants (government, proponents, and opponents) was given access to a special online room where they could interact with the other people in their group, share files, or even engage in a chat session. There was also an animated movie explaining how to use the online environment tools in a simple way. This enabled the parties to become comfortable with the technology before the dispute resolution process began.

For the agenda, the mediators were clear that they wanted to aim the discussion toward a face-to-face meeting. The goal of the online process was to express ideas, form possible proposals, and build a foundation for a face-to-face gathering. They also knew that they wanted to use the consensus evaluation tools of the platform to develop an ongoing assessment of how close or far away the group was from an agreement.

Once the room was set up and all the user accounts for the participants were entered, notification emails were sent out to all the parties, followed up with phone calls. The emails contained login information for every participant, making it as simple as clicking a link in the email and entering a provided username and password. The parties could then enter into the online environment, learn how to move around, and engage in some discussion in their caucus areas.

The mediators crafted three questions that they felt captured the essence of the matters under debate:

- What are the key issues involved with the proposed construction of the theater?
- How can those issues be addressed?
- What would be the ideal outcome for this process?

These questions were entered into each of the caucus areas, and the first task for the participants was to discuss the questions within their groups to come up with a common set of responses agreed to by all the participants within the group.

The mediators agreed that they would split up the different caucus areas so that each mediator would be able to focus on a single group. They also created a mediator caucus space so that they could best communicate among themselves about how the process was evolving and what steps should be taken next.

The parties logged into the system and began their discussions. Once all three groups had drafted their responses to the questions, the mediators put all three in a public document visible to all the participants. There were some striking similarities between the opponent and government answers, and the proponent answers indicated much more flexibility than the opponents had expected. When groups viewed the others' answers, it led to much activity within the caucus area discussions as the groups changed their strategies in response to the new information.

The mediators then drafted a list of issues aggregated from the answers provided by the parties and posted it in a public document. Then they asked each of the caucus groups to select a representative to participate in an initial joint discussion.

A joint discussion was created so that the three group representatives could meet with the mediators to discuss the answers that had been posted by the mediators. The representatives continued to interact with their constituent groups in the caucus areas. Initially the joint discussion was accessible only to the three representatives and the mediators, and several proposed solutions were crafted. Then, after reaching agreement with all three representatives, the mediators opened the joint discussion for observation from all of the online discussion participants.

The three representatives were constantly reality-testing proposals with their constituents, seeing what would work and what concessions were most important to them. The technology allowed for this kind of concurrent caucusing, where the representatives could engage in a discussion with the other representatives at the same time as they were bouncing ideas off of the others in their group. This ongoing checking let the representatives function much more effectively than they might have in a face-to-face process.

Finally the group representatives crafted four proposals dealing with different aspects of the theater construction. The mediators then put these proposals into a consensus evaluation tool, where all the room participants could express their feelings about the proposals in terms of what they did well and where they fell short. This feedback was generated confidentially, so that the participants did not have to make their positions public. This is important because one of the community activists offered feedback suggesting that some of the residents were being unreasonable and that they did not represent the broader neighborhood. The Chamber of Commerce representative also urged the mediators to ask more of Apollo in terms of providing community improvements. Neither of these contributions would have been made if only public feedback was possible.

The mediators crafted this feedback into two proposals, which they summarized and tightened into a single document that they posted for all to see. They also called for a face-to-face meeting between all the participants in three days. They then opened a joint discussion for all of the online participants to use to offer feedback on the document. Input came fast and furious for the three days before the face-to-face meeting, generating more than seventy messages. Many new issues were raised, and the mediators made clear that each issue would be addressed at the face-to-face meeting.

At the meeting, the mediators began the process by summarizing the progress that had been made online. The belligerent resident spoke up early, raising a host of concerns, but he also praised the work that had been done by the representatives and expressed confidence that something could be worked out. The issues raised in the joint discussion over the prior three days were brought up in the meeting and addressed, and the two proposals were refined to encompass the new observations. The process did not overheat or escalate as the participants were focused on the agenda that had been developed online.

The mediators called a break after an hour of discussions and invited everyone out into the lobby to have some refreshments while the mediators summarized the agreed-upon solution on a flipchart. When the parties were brought back in, the proposed solution was presented and final feedback was collected. The mediators confirmed that the parties were happy with the resolution and the meeting adjourned after two hours.

The mediators then posted the text of the resolution online in the meeting space, and each party logged on and formally expressed their support for the proposal.

As a result, the zoning board presented the results of the process at its next public meeting, alongside several of the participants in the online discussion. Once the outcome of the dialogue, and the process that had generated it, were described to the full board, the proposal was accepted unanimously.

Analysis

Complexity in dispute resolution processes increases exponentially with each additional disputant added into the mix. Multiparty processes such as this zoning case illustrate that principle. The tools

ODR provides to neutrals may prove most useful in these large, public cases because there are so many individual communication channels to manage.

Hybrid processes that utilize technology when other communication channels (such as public meetings) break down may be the most appropriate use of ODR in the majority of multiparty matters. Ending a productive series of online sessions with a face-to-face signing ceremony is often a nice way to bring the real and the virtual together into a satisfying whole.

CHAPTER TEN

Confidentiality and Privacy
Health Care and Finance

P rivacy is the next online battlefield. Internet observers have long speculated that the biggest struggles regarding the expansion of the Internet will come over the issue of privacy. Organizations like the American Civil Liberties Union (ACLU) and the Electronic Freedom Forum (EFF) have battled the Department of Justice and the FBI for years over online privacy. In the wake of the terrorist attacks of 2001, the tide has shifted in favor of government curtailments of privacy rights in the name of national security. This has piqued the ire of many activists on the other side of the issue, who believe government is overstepping its bounds and severely curtailing individual rights. Lines are being drawn for a major struggle.

Many people are not so concerned about their loss of privacy. Corporations tout the power that comes with unfettered access to information, such as better-targeted marketing campaigns and greater responsiveness from customer service departments. Some individuals have resigned themselves to the fact that privacy will inevitably be eroded by global networks.

Privacy defenders, though, fear a day when it will be impossible for individuals to keep any secrets. Governments around the world have come to acknowledge the seriousness of this privacy issue, and many have appointed Privacy Czars to help address the problem. Politicians have picked up on the fears the public has about all of these coming privacy violations and have introduced legislation to deal with the issue. Congressional committees have been convened to examine the privacy issue, non-profit organizations have sprung up to advocate on either side of the issue (some pro-business and some pro-consumer). Consumer advocates have raised alarm about the negative effects that could grow out of these developments in the long-term. What this means in a nutshell is that disputes over privacy will become more common and more contentious.

THE NATURE OF PRIVACY VIOLATIONS

Legally there are several different kinds of privacy, such as the right to be left alone. On the Internet the primary type of privacy people are concerned with is personal control of private information. The question is whether or not individuals own certain pieces of information about themselves, or whether others can traffic that information without the consent of the information holder.

One way to protect the privacy of information is through encryption. Mathematical algorithms exist that can prevent others from reading the contents of online exchanges. One battlefield for privacy proponents and opponents is the issue of limits on encryption technology. For a long time the export of certain strong encryption mechanisms was illegal, because law enforcement worried that those tools would enable criminals to communicate with each other in a way in which it would be impossible for the government to listen in. Privacy advocates are comforted by the knowledge that technology can protect private information even if governments are unwilling to protect it.

Privacy disputes respect no boundaries. Massive databases connecting information around the world are a major reason why concerns about privacy are so pressing. As databases are aggregated, information in a variety of places can be combined into a single location. Companies like DoubleClick have progressively acquired information about consumers from a variety of sources and created centralized databases so that information that was previously not connectable can be attached to individuals. This action facilitated the further erosion of barriers hindering access to private information. Eventually these connections will be made in many different areas, and one piece of identifying information will be all that is necessary to find out anything about anyone.

There are other, smaller types of privacy violations as well. Many websites use "cookies" to track information about the people who visit. Cookies are little bits of information that reside on a user's local hard drive but that are accessible to Web pages when they browse the Internet. While the information stored in cookies is usually innocuous, many Web users are hesitant about the practice of tracking cookies because they don't want their information monitored at all. The debate is raging over whether or not information contained in these cookies is owned by the websites that put the information there or whether it's owned by the individuals on whose computer the information resides. Other websites have recently been found to put invisible-to-the-Web "dots" on their pages that serve to track where visitors to the site go after they visit that particular page.

The global nature of the Internet makes privacy regulation very difficult. If a pharmaceutical company puts up a website and starts collecting information, there are no limits on who can visit that website and enter information. Consumers from France, Germany, Asia, or Australia can all access the site and enter information about themselves in order to get more information about the products or services being offered. However, each of those countries may have very different privacy regulations and different limits on how data can be used, particularly medical data. By simply putting up a website, the pharmaceutical company may be exposing itself to dozens of different privacy regulations around the world.

Many websites now display formal privacy policies, extensive documents that lay out what information will be collected by the website, how that information will be used, and who to contact should any complaints about privacy arise. Often websites assure the users that the information will not be shared with others. As marketing over the Web has become more sophisticated, however, this personal information is becoming more and more valuable, and some sites are selling it or using it for unsolicited email campaigns.

NEW PRIVACY LEGISLATION: HIPAA AND THE GRAMM-LEACH-BLILEY ACT (1999)

The two areas where privacy is getting the most attention are in the financial services and health care arenas. In financial services, a 1999 piece of legislation called the Gramm-Leach-Bliley Act has been adopted that deals with the privacy of financial records. These records can include banking information, brokerage information, and information on trusts and estates. All this information is potentially very sensitive, and with the rapid changes in the financial industry and its migration onto the Internet, legislation was introduced to put control over that information back in the hands of the people to whom the information refers.

On the health-care side, a piece of legislation called the Health Insurance Portability and Accountability Act (HIPAA) was enacted in 1996. This legislation is more sweeping than the Gramm-Leach-Bliley Act. HIPAA gives control of private medical information to the people to whom the information refers, and everyone in the medical industry is struggling to come up with ways to abide by HIPAA's requirements before the penalties take effect in 2002. Private medical information is defined extremely broadly in the legislation, so any organization that collects information that could be termed medical information must abide by the strictures of HIPAA.

Every organization that has medical information is covered by this bill, from the doctor's office on the corner to huge HMOs. And it's not just medical services—pharmaceutical companies, medical device companies, even informational websites like WebMD are all covered by the bill. If a user comes to a website and fills out a form inquiring about a particular type of medication, the company operating that website then has a responsibility to handle that information within HIPAA's requirements.

Because medical information is tracked by so many different companies, institutions, and individuals, HIPAA has resulted in a lot of handwringing in the health-care community. One particularly troubling provision is that there are stiff financial penalties attached to the misuse of private medical information, and in certain cases there may even be criminal penalties attached to the intentional mishandling of medical information. Many medical facilities are already stretched in terms of their resources, and they're concerned about their liability in terms of the care decisions made within the facility. Having to reexamine and redesign the way that private medical information is handled is a daunting challenge and an expensive proposition.

Complaint Handling

One of the interesting components of both HIPAA and Gramm-Leach-Bliley is that companies need to provide a mechanism for their customers and users to file complaints should they believe that a violation of their privacy has taken place. Because there are so many different types of organizations that handle this information, filing a complaint in the right place can be a challenge.

For instance, let's say an individual visits the website of a pharmaceutical company because she saw an advertisement on television talking about a new drug that has been developed. When she enters her email address (and maybe even her postal address, to receive a glossy brochure) that pharmaceutical company now must abide by the rules of HIPAA in handling that information. Now presume all of the email addresses of people who visited the pharmaceutical company's website and asked about that particular drug are unintentionally passed along to an insurance company, and the insurance company contacts those individuals with new coverage that may be of interest to the people who expressed interest in the drug over the Internet. Those individuals may suspect their privacy has been violated because their confidential medical information was shared without their knowledge or permission. However, it's not immediately apparent where the information came from, who was responsible for its misuse, and how to get redress.

EUROPE LEADS ON PRIVACY PROTECTION

Europe has led the privacy discussion by instituting some of the most aggressive data protection standards in the world. Other countries, notably in Asia and Australia, have appointed privacy commissioners to examine the issue and to recommend regulation. Because of the transboundary nature of privacy claims on the Internet, privacy is a very difficult thing to regulate, and it is even more difficult to handle privacy-related disputes once they arise. Because of the complexity of these claims, and the range of legal exposure that can be faced by companies collecting electronic information, online dispute resolution makes the most sense as an effective way for companies to abide by these requirements.

In 1998, European countries established a protocol called Safe Harbor that sets baseline data protection standards for non-European companies to meet. Though the Safe Harbor protocol has been heavily promoted in the United States, there have been relatively few companies that have filed the paperwork necessary to participate. One of the requirements of the Safe Harbor protocol is that complaint-handling and dispute-resolution mechanisms must be in place to deal with any privacy claims presented to the company by its users and customers.

WHAT DOES A PRIVACY RESOLUTION LOOK LIKE?

One of the problems with privacy disputes is that resolving a privacy complaint is like un-ringing a bell. When private information is released (a mailing list sold or the confidentiality of medical records compromised) outside eyes have access to that information. Once the complaint is filed it is possible to collect the information that was released and to bring it back, preventing further access to it, but that doesn't solve the problem of the original release of the information.

For instance, if a mailing list is sold, spam email is sent out to hundreds of thousands of users, and a handful of those users complain that their privacy has been violated, it may be possible to get those email addresses back from the originator of the spam, or it may be too late—the email addresses may have already been forwarded to other spam mailers. Aggressive policing is necessary in order to catch these claims early and to take action to get the data back under control after it has been compromised.

This confusion has everything to do with the early stage of the law in this area. The law surrounding privacy cases is still being defined. There is no clear legal precedent about how these matters will be handled, what penalties are appropriate or reasonable, or even what law enforcement efforts are appropriate.

HIPAA has begun to put monetary values on privacy disputes, thereby establishing an evolving understanding of what certain violations are worth. The foundation of clear penalties for specific breaches of privacy will lead to clearer consensus on what types of redress are reasonable for what types of offenses. But because the complaint often comes after the information is already compromised, it's much harder to creatively craft resolutions to privacy disputes. It may be that privacy ODR will look a lot more like an arbitration, primarily because privacy complaint processes may be more fact-finding exercises than integrative, creative dispute resolution procedures.

ODR IS THE BEST WAY TO HANDLE PRIVACY DISPUTES

The necessity of a rapid response in these types of situations is a strong reason to utilize online dispute resolution as opposed to resorting to the courts. If a complainant has to arrange a face-to-face process, and perhaps even wait for a hearing, before they can have their privacy complaint addressed, it may be that the data has been compromised beyond recovery by the time those required steps have taken place. Privacy claims can also arise anywhere the Internet reaches, and the laws regulating these matters are wildly diverse around the world. Waiting for a court-based process to begin makes little sense in these circumstances.

Online dispute resolution promises to create a common complaint-handling mechanism for individuals who suspect that their privacy has been violated. For instance, if hospitals were able to sign up for a service that handled all HIPAA-related disputes, then they could advertise on their website and in their printed material that a trusted third-party organization is available to handle any complaints that patients may have regarding their privacy. On one hand, this clearly demonstrates compliance on the part of the hospitals with HIPAA rules. On the other hand, it signals to the patients that their privacy concerns will be taken seriously, that the hospital wants to do the right thing, and that the hospital puts the concerns of its patients high on the agenda.

Another benefit of using online dispute resolution to resolve privacy cases is the fact that dispute resolution is built around confidentiality. Most likely the complainant would never even have raised a concern in a particular situation if she did not want to protect her private information and she was concerned about who was getting access to her private information. Judicial proceedings are almost always public in the sense that the arguments and relevant information are usually entered into the record of the court. While it is possible to build in some data protection in formal judicial proceedings, it's much more complicated than in dispute-resolution processes, which involve fewer people, are private, and assign a high degree of confidentiality. Privacy is an important issue for ODR providers, because if parties are not confident that their information will be protected they will not agree to participate.

It may be that privacy disputes start out focused on consumers, but very quickly the privacy of businesses and organizations will also come into the picture. Intellectual property disputes, for example, often hinge upon confidential information that certain individuals want to keep private. This type of privacy is very different than individual rights to privacy, but many of the reasons why online dispute resolution is a good fit with disputes over individuals' privacy also apply to disputes concerning the privacy of business secrets or intellectual property.

The financial world has relied on ADR for some time now. The National Association of Securities Dealers (NASD) has a well-developed dispute resolution program for resolving contention between brokers and their customers. If a dispute arises over a particular sale of a stock, for example, a case can be filed through the NASD where a neutral panelist hears the matter and either a) helps the parties work out a resolution as a mediator, or b) renders a decision as an arbitrator. The NASD program has been very successful, resolving thousands of disputes over the past few years. The model could easily be extended to address financial privacy disputes.

The CPR Institute for Dispute Resolution recently issued rules pertaining to privacy violations. These rules could easily be applied to an online dispute resolution process designed to handle privacy complaints. Because the financial value of privacy violations is so difficult to determine it will be hard for individuals to justify paying the convening penalty to attend a face-to-face dispute resolution process to resolve the matter at hand. Because these violations occur online, that may also be the best place to resolve them.

PROVIDER PROFILES: BBB AND TRUSTe

Several organizations have emerged as the primary players in privacy protection online. One of the earliest was the Better Business Bureau's Privacy Dispute Resolution program. Many prominent websites display the BBB seal, part of which refers to that site's privacy practices. One of the earliest features of the BBB's privacy program was an online dispute resolution mechanism. Customers that suspect their privacy has been violated can file a complaint with the BBB, regardless of whether or not the complaint regards a website that displays the BBB privacy seal. A BBB representative will then initiate the case by attempting to determine the facts behind the suspected privacy violation. If the dispute is found to be about more than a misunderstanding, the BBB representative works with the complainant and the complained-about website to resolve the case.

The other most prominent privacy protection organization in the United States is called TRUSTe. This company also offers a seal that can be placed on websites that qualify, based on standards of practice that are issued and maintained by TRUSTe. They have led the way in encouraging websites to display privacy policies. Online dispute resolution is an important capacity to integrate into these privacy statements, so that if an individual website user cannot obtain redress by contacting the owners or customer service departments supporting that site, they can then go to a third-party organization that is willing to work with them in having their claim resolved. This dispute resolution process could reside in a third-party organization focused exclusively on dispute resolution, for it could be hosted by the BBB, TRUSTe, or a similar organization.

Case Study: Privacy Violation

Jennifer visited fuzzysweaters.com, an e-commerce site devoted to wool sweaters. On the home page there was a link to get onto the mailing list for future updates, and Jennifer clicked it. After filling in her name and address to receive fuzzysweaters.com catalogs, Jennifer also checked a box at the bottom of the form that requested that she not be contacted by any site other than fuzzysweaters.com, and that she did not want to have her name passed on to any other e-commerce sites.

One month later, Jennifer started to receive unsolicited spam emails from several other clothing websites she had never visited. Because she had used her middle name on the fuzzysweaters.com sign-up page, something she almost never did, Jennifer knew that the spam-mailers had gotten her address from fuzzysweaters.com. She returned to the site and noticed that they did have a privacy policy posted on their home page, and that they would take any disputes that arose from their use of private information to online dispute resolution. Jennifer sent email to the fuzzysweaters.com customer service department several times regarding the problem but she did not hear back.

Next, she filed a complaint form with the online dispute resolution site mentioned in fuzzysweaters.com's privacy policy. The ODR site contacted fuzzysweaters.com and the manager of the customer service department responded and agreed to participate in the mediation.

At first, the fuzzysweaters.com representative denied that the information had been sold, restating the portion of the privacy policy that said that they did not sell private user information to other companies. However, Jennifer was insistent, because she knew that fuzzysweaters.com201 had been the source of the leak. Finally, after some examination, the customer service manager discovered that the mailing list had been given to a subsidiary of fuzzysweaters.com that had, without authorization, passed it along to another clothing site that had then circulated the database widely. Jennifer received an apology from the president of the company, and they also made an effort to contact the sites that had sent spam to Jennifer and to remove fuzzysweaters.com users from the email distribution lists. The spam emails didn't end, but they were significantly reduced by fuzzysweaters.com's actions in response to the mediation.

CHAPTER ELEVEN

Building a Global Justice System

ODR and Transboundary Disputes

—᠁᠁— T he Internet is creating a new, global online society. This society works by its own rules, and it is not subject to any one particular jurisdiction. These developments pose major challenges to the sovereignty of national governments. Unilateral attempts to regulate the Internet have resulted in some significant failures, such as attempts to control encryption technology and efforts to protect copyrighted materials.

As Stanford University professor Larry Lessig has observed, the real laws of cyberspace may come from the code that underlies the network as opposed to laws issued by governments.[1] Even the United States, who some would say is the sole global superpower, seems helpless to control the spread of the Internet and the activities that take place on it.

Every society needs to have ways to resolve its disputes. In the offline world courts have evolved to play that role. However, in this new online society, the court model does not work. The model that does work is dispute resolution. As some have observed, conflict, and dispute resolution, will grow with the expansion of the Internet society. ODR is the judicial infrastructure of the Internet.

A TRANSBOUNDARY JUSTICE SYSTEM: ICANN'S UDRP

The first robust, transnational online dispute resolution system was adopted by the Internet Corporation for Assigned Names and Numbers in 1997. As many Internet users know, ICANN is the body in charge of domain names. ICANN required all disputes over domain names go through this resolution system, called the Uniform Dispute Resolution Policy (UDRP).

All of the assigned domain names on the Internet are connected with individual addresses (which are numbers, like this: 213.67.23.148) and when an Internet user types a domain name into their browser, the browser consults the ICANN-maintained database to see to which address the user should be sent. It is a very simple system, but because of the reach of the Internet, whoever controls the database holds a lot of power and responsibility.

Domain names are assigned on a first-come, first-served basis. This led to many individual owners buying valuable domain names before offline trademark holders of the terms thought of registering them. Because the system is based on first-come, first-served, there is no assumption that a trademark holder has the absolute right to domain names containing their trademark. As a fictitious example, if an individual registers mcdonalds.com before the fast-food chain McDonald's, McDonald's has no unilateral right to take the domain name away. It may be that the registrant is from the McDonald family, and they want to put up pictures of their family reunion.

In the past, established corporations have paid significant amounts of money to secure domain names that they wanted. If an individual had beaten the company McDonald's to the domain name, McDonald's may have offered the individual $250,000 to transfer the name to them. Then it was up to the individual whether or not it was important enough to them to hold on to the domain, or whether or not they could find another domain that was just as good (McDonaldsfamily.com, for example) and to take the money. Most chose the money, and trademark holders often got the domain names they desired.

Certain individuals and organizations began to see the lucrative potential in registering domain names for $35 a year and selling them for hundreds of thousands of dollars, so they started buying up every domain name of value they could think of. Once domain names were being sold for tens or hundreds of thousands of dollars, or even millions (business.com went for $7 million) a frenzy arose on the Internet of people hoarding valuable names. ICANN saw that the first-come, first-served basis was not able to deal adequately with the conflicts that began to erupt over these name assignments, and that led to the adoption of the UDRP.

The UDRP system works like this. ICANN has approved four domain name dispute resolution service providers around the world. They are the CPR Institute for Dispute Resolution in New York City, the Hong Kong International Arbitration Council (HKIAC), the National Arbitration Forum (NAF) in Minnesota, and the World Intellectual Property Organization (WIPO) in Geneva. For a filing fee in the neighborhood of $1,000 (it's slightly more or slightly less for each of the domain name dispute resolution service providers), a complainant can file a request for a UDRP hearing regarding a domain name.

ICANN adopted rules that delineated when a name was acquired and used fairly and when it was not being used appropriately. For instance, if the registrant of McDonalds.com was posting pictures of family reunions and keeping the site up to date, that is an appropriate usage of the domain name and that registrant could hold onto the name, even if McDonald's the food chain wanted it awarded to them. However, if the registrant has nothing up at the site, and if they are repeatedly goading McDonald's to pay them an extravagant sum for its transfer, then that is probably a case of "cybersquatting," in which a party holds onto a domain name with no intent other than to profit from its eventual sale.

The rules of the UDRP were very clear and structured. Parties would file a complaint with one of the four approved domain name dispute resolution service providers. The complainant would choose whether or not this case would be heard by a single panelist or a group of three panelists. (The UDRP steered away from using legal words like "arbitration" to ensure that the UDRP process would be considered a non-legal, private process.) These panelists were usually experienced international arbitrators or judges who were on the roster of neutrals available through the approved UDRP service provider. The complainant would then file documents with the panelists making his or her case in favor of the domain name swap.

An attempt would then be made to contact the owner of the domain name to inform them of the controversy. If the owner did not respond to multiple inquiries regarding the dispute, then the panelist or panelists hearing the case could award the domain name to the complainant. However, there have been a handful of cases where the respondent did not respond to a UDRP notification and the domain name was still not awarded to the complainant.

Once the respondent did reply, he or she would have an opportunity to make a case as well, using documents only. The UDRP process was designed to be a documents-only process, meaning there was no direct correspondence between panelists and the complainant or the respondent. If any information was exchanged it was usually shuttled by the case administrator between the parties and the panelists. The documents filed were prepared by the counsel of the complainant and respondent and were required to address prescribed topics. The process also took a predetermined time to complete, with various due dates for filings set ahead of time.

Only one of the original UDRP service providers, eResolution, built a purely online process for handling these domain name disputes. The other providers handled most of the correspondence and document sharing through traditional mail and fax. UDRP processes involving three panelists usually would convene a conference call for the panelists to discuss the issues as they were presented by the parties and to talk through the matters involved in the particular dispute.

For example, lawyers representing the actress Julia Roberts filed a complaint with WIPO requesting that the domain juliaroberts.com be transferred from the current holder. The original registrant argued that he was a fan of Roberts, and he had pictures of her posted on the website. After hearing both sides, the WIPO panelist decided that the domain name should be awarded to Roberts.[2]

The panelists handling these cases were distinguished legal personnel from around the world, either experienced arbitrators, retired judges, or intellectual property experts. The panelists were not directly employed by the approved UDRP service providers, and often great pains were taken to ensure that there was no conflict of interest between the panelists assigned to the case and either of the disputants.

Precedent-Based Decisions

Much analysis and research has been put into studying the UDRP system and identifying its strengths and weaknesses. The UDRP design has some particular quirks to it that have generated controversy. First, the system is very legalistic. It is built for lawyers, and many of its operating principles make more sense to lawyers than to non-lawyers. All of the decisions rendered by panelists in UDRP matters are public record, so outsiders can read the decisions and make up their own minds about whether or not the outcome was just. These decisions also become part of a de facto body of "domain name law" as future decisions in UDRP cases are supposed to be based on prior decisions, much like precedent-based legal systems in the face-to-face world. As the number of cases has ballooned, however, the ability of panelists to stay up to date on the latest decisions has been compromised. Leading thinkers in the UDRP system, such as Scott Donahey, a prominent Silicon Valley lawyer who decided the first UDRP case, have attempted to provide a digest of recent UDRP decisions. Donahey writes a periodic column for the website ADRWorld.com in which he discusses recent decisions in UDRP matters. But many decisions have been handed down in which the panelist clearly did not research other UDRP decisions that were relevant to the case at hand, or where the decision actually contradicted other prominent UDRP cases.

Professor Ethan Katsh has recently begun an effort, supported by a prominent foundation, to build a more efficient online infrastructure for going through UDRP decisions. Instead of a simple text-based search algorithm, the plan is to create a system that will allow lawyers to attain access to the decisions relevant to their particular matter and to cite those references simply within the text of their decision. Arbitrators will classify their newly rendered decisions in a simple grid, which will make the identification of relevant cases much easier for future UDRP panelists. Efforts like this may help to increase the quality of UDRP decisions moving ahead, and to ensure the continued viability of precedent-setting online dispute resolution systems.

Forum Shopping

The biggest systemic problem in the UDRP is the problem of forum shopping. In the UDRP system, the complainant gets to unilaterally choose which ADR service provider to file their complaint with. This element of the system, combined with the public disclosure of all decisions, has led to a bias problem that has skewed case allocations. Providers that decide almost equally for the complainant and the respondent are much less likely to be chosen by complainants. Complainants are much more likely to choose UDRP service providers who have a record that strongly favors complainants. As Milton Mueller concluded in "Rough Justice," his important analysis of UDRP decisions, "There is a statistically significant correlation between market share and the tendency to take away domain names from respondents."[3] At the beginning of the UDRP process, cases were reasonably distributed among the four providers, with no one provider having more than 50 percent of the filed UDRP cases. However, over time, WIPO has begun to receive the lion's share of filings, and now more than 80 percent of new UDRP cases are filed with them.

Biased Decisions

Some observers have criticized the UDRP program because they see outcomes heavily stacked in favor of trademark holders. The vast majority of complainants are trademark holders of particular names or terms that want names transferred from smaller organizations or individuals. As Professor Michael Geist observed in his article "Fair.com?," there are lots of subtle ways that UDRP providers can bias processes, such as panelist allocation.[4] NAF and WIPO are both singled out in the Geist article as having questionable panelist allocation procedures. Also, WIPO's status as an international organization created to defend intellectual property rights around the world has led to criticism. How can WIPO be trusted to provide a neutral forum to resolve these disputes, skeptics ask, when their international role is to protect the intellectual property rights of corporations, who are usually the complainants?

WIPO's response is that they are not the ones settling these matters—the panelists they provide are distinguished international legal figures who have no connection to WIPO or its mission. WIPO also argues that the only complainants willing to file the $1,000 or so necessary to initiate a UDRP process are people who are sure that they have a good case for getting the domain name transferred. These are persuasive arguments, but the damage to the credibility of the system may have already been done.

Enforcement

One of the reasons why the UDRP works is because ICANN has absolute power to enforce its decisions. All that is necessary to enforce the outcome of a UDRP process is that ICANN needs to change an entry in its master database. The database is then populated around the world and the domain name is then owned by the specified party. This type of absolute control is difficult to replicate. If the dispute is over a material good that has been shipped from one place to another enforcement is much more difficult. The ODR provider is unlikely to have representatives on the ground in every area that can show up on the doorstep of one of the parties to make them abide by the decision of a panelist. In those cases enforcement is fluid and undefined. In the case of ICANN, however, enforcement is sudden and absolute.

Case Study: Bodacious-tatas.com versus Tata Sons, Ltd.

A recent controversial case involved the website bodacious-tatas.com, which was a site offering pornography. Tata Sons, Ltd., founded in 1907, is India's first integrated steel plant. Searches in popular online Web indexing programs (such as Google or AltaVista) under the name Tata would bring up the aforementioned pornographic site before the Indian company. Tata Sons, also known as House of Tata, contended that its name was a well-known brand in India and that the owner of bodacious-tatas.com had misappropriated the Tata mark with the sole intention of passing off its erotic and pornographic services to users of the Internet.

In a decision that surprised many, the UDRP panelist agreed with the Indian company and transferred the domain name. Observers were shocked by the decision, as it was clear that the bodacious-tatas.com site had absolutely nothing to do with Tata, Ltd. There was some speculation that the cultural differences were to blame for transfer, as the panelist was unaware that "tatas" is a synonym for female breasts. The panelist agreed with the complainant that the registration and "outspoken sexuality, promiscuity and pornography under the heading of bodacious-tatas.com" was bound to affect adversely the value and selling power of the trademark owner, so he transferred the domain name. The case has become a hot-button for opponents of the UDRP, who believe that the UDRP program infringes on free speech at the expense of individuals and to the benefit of corporations. A protest site immediately appeared at the domain name "bodacious-tatas.org" to inform the public about the injustice behind the award.

CULTURE, GEOGRAPHY, AND THE UDRP

Culture is another important variable in the UDRP process. An influential and oft-cited UDRP decision defending freedom of speech was legally radical because freedom of speech is not a right acknowledged in all countries around the world. While freedom of speech may be a hallowed concept in western legal circles, what is the rationale for its role in decisions made in other regions of the globe? Who is to say what concepts are right or wrong in making difficult decisions in domain name disputes? Should the inclinations of individual panelists play a role in making the decisions? Is there any way that such inclinations could be surpressed if it was decided that they shouldn't play a role?

There has been much discussion about the fact that the UDRP providers were clustered in Europe and North America. With the addition of Hong Kong as the newest provider, this complaint has quieted somewhat. However, if the panelists affiliated with the UDRP providers are international, the geographic location of the individual providers may be a moot issue. The rules and structures employed by the various providers, however, may reflect a certain cultural bias. For instance, while most UDRP providers advertise their ability to support multiple languages, character-based languages (such as Korean, Chinese, and Japanese) are not yet fully supported in UDRP ODR platforms.

NEW PRESSURES ON THE DOMAIN NAME SYSTEM

Beyond the ICANN-assigned domain names (with extensions like .com, .org, and .net) there are also country code domain names managed by individual countries, such as .ca for Canada and .fr for France. These domain names are managed individually within each country, and some of them are coming up with different resolution programs for disputes involving that nation's particular extension. There is also pressure from online companies who want to oust ICANN as the sole provider of top-level domain names. A company called New.net has launched more than a dozen new highly desirable extensions (including .xxx, .arts, and .love) and offers a free software patch on their website that reprograms browsers to accept New.net extensions in addition to ICANN extensions. Should efforts like New.net's be successful, ICANN's sole position as the registrar for names on the Internet may be compromised. It is important to note, however, that New.net explicitly specifies that all disputes regarding New.net domain names will also be handled through ICANN's UDRP process.

There is also a push for new domain name extensions from the standard ICANN registry process, with .biz and .info coming online soon. The companies that will be supporting those new names have pledged to use the UDRP process to resolve disputes that may arise. However, the registration process for these new names has generated its own controversies. For instance, the domain names ending in the letters .biz will be assigned on a first-come, first-served basis, but there is a preregistration process in which multiple parties can sign up for a single domain name. If three companies sign up for "apples.biz," for instance, there will be a process through which one of them is assigned the name when the new names come online. These dispute resolution processes are above and beyond the scope of the UDRP, and will probably involve the creation of a whole new dispute resolution system.

ICANN'S FAILINGS AND
THE UDRP'S SUCCESSES

Controversy surrounding the UDRP has been mishandled partly because of the chaos surrounding ICANN. As a governing body, ICANN has been something of a failure, with endless division and arguments hamstringing the organization and preventing it from making decisions or even functioning at all. The election of ICANN delegates over the Web has led to a fractious, divided body filled with people who cannot agree on anything. Recently there has been some discussion about governments taking over for ICANN because the organization has fallen into such disrepair.

The UDRP is the first global online dispute resolution mechanism, and even with its shortcomings, it has experienced impressive success. It has handled more than five thousand cases since its inception, and few cases have been appealed to offline judicial mechanisms. It is the first fundamentally international online legal system, ungoverned by the laws of any one country.

OTHER TRANSNATIONAL ODR SYSTEMS

Treaty-based organizations face many of the same challenges ICANN responded to when they created the UDRP. Determining which law applies to cross-border conflicts is often too complex, so ODR may be the best choice for handling any problems that do arise. The North American Free Trade Agreement has a 2002 ADR Committee composed of dispute resolution experts from the three NAFTA countries. This committee has spent a significant amount of time considering the legal ramifications of NAFTA, and in early 2001 they decided to support a pilot implementation of online dispute resolution to resolve cross-border disputes. Six providers (the British Columbia International Commercial Arbitration Center [BCICAC] and the Quebec Arbitration Center in Canada, the U.S. Mexico Conflict Resolution Institute and Online Resolution in the United States, and the Centro Arbitracion y Mediacion [CAM] and the Mexican Institute for Mediation in Mexico) have teamed up to provide multilingual (French, English, and Spanish) dispute resolution services to businesses involved in cross-border disputes.

In June 2002, the United Nations hosted a conference in Geneva that focused on ODR. This meeting was the first to discuss the adoption of ODR systems in developing and transition economies. A lack of a trustworthy legal infrastructure in many developing countries creates a disincentive for outside investors to get involved in projects there. If a local court in a particular country simply decides in favor of any local business, then international businesses will steer clear of any involvement in that country. Effective and trusted ODR systems, if they could be specified as the avenue for resolution of any disputes that arise during the course of an investment, might remove this disincentive and encourage foreign investment to enter some areas where it previously would not because of the lack of a satisfactory legal infrastructure. In areas where the judicial systems are inefficient or corrupt, businesses might come to rely more on these quasi-public online dispute resolution services than on the in-country judicial systems themselves.

Finally, the Program on Negotiation at Harvard Law School hosts a forward-thinking initiative aimed at the application of ODR to global governance. Based upon the work of William Ury and his book *The Third Side* (2000), and co-sponsored by the international organization Earth Stewards, the e-Parliament initiative aims to convene a global parliamentary body composed of thousands of elected officials from around the world. This organization would convene virtually through the use of online collaborative software to address important transboundary issues, such as environmental challenges and the spread of infectious disease. The working groups tasked with considering these issues would go through a facilitated process aimed at the creation of a consensus policy document that could be introduced in parliamentary bodies around the world. These deliberations would take place in an international forum not burdened by the particular politics of a single country or a single legal code. Such a group would be impossible to convene in the face-to-face world. Only through the power of ODR technology to eliminate distances is such a project even conceivable.

PROVIDER PROFILE: eRESOLUTION

eResolution was one of the grandfathers of the online dispute resolution field. Founded by Karim Benyeklef, a law professor at the University of Montreal, the company was originally called Cyber-Tribunal. Much like the Virtual Magistrate project at Villanova University, CyberTribunal was an early attempt to build an online arbitration resource that could resolve ISP-based disputes.

eResolution made its reputation as one of the four original domain name dispute resolution service providers, along with NAF in Minnesota, the CPR Institute for Dispute Resolution in New York, and WIPO in Geneva. eResolution was the only one of the four approved providers who had created the ODR technology necessary to completely administer UDRP processes online. Aubert Landry, the chief technologist at eResolution, built the company's platform from scratch and ensured that it utilized the most cutting-edge technology available. Computer Sciences Corporation, a prominent IT consulting firm, also played a major role in the development of the platform.

eResolution began its life as a domain name service provider and arbitration-oriented site, but soon it expanded to offer mediation services as well. Because of eResolution's location in Montreal and Professor Benyeklef's roots in Europe, eResolution had some very strong relationships with European institutions. Fabien Gelinas, one of eResolution's hires in 2000, had been general counsel at the International Chamber of Commerce in Paris. Robert Cassius de Linval and Joelle Thibault, two other principals at eResolution, were both lawyers fluent in French. eResolution also provided the technology behind the ECODIR initiative, which is a European Union-funded B2C dispute resolution platform that launched in October 2001.

The panel eResolution put together had a reputation for fairness and reflection, as it contained more academics than the panels created by WIPO, NAF, or CPR. While NAF and WIPO routinely found for complainants more than 80 percent of the time, eResolution found for complainants approximately 60 percent of the time. Because of the forum shopping issue, where complainants chose the provider unilaterally, this reputation began to shift UDRP cases away from eResolution. In spite of the many international complaints about unfairness in UDRP decisions, eResolution steadfastly maintained their process because they felt it was appropriate, even though it resulted in cases flowing elsewhere. The last straw was when the Canadian government, faced with several domain name disputes, decided to utilize WIPO in Geneva to resolve them as opposed to eResolution, the Canadian provider. eResolution had long been subsidizing the cost of handling UDRP cases, as the money paid by disputants was not enough to cover the costs of administering the process, so the decision was made to stop handling domain name cases.

Unfortunately, due to the sagging economy, eResolution was forced to shut its doors a few months later in late 2001. The cutting-edge ODR technology eResolution had created was purchased by NAF for use in their domain name processes.

As a pioneer in the ODR space, eResolution laid the groundwork for how ODR could work and provided the first proof of concept for how technology could efficiently resolve disputes. All future development in the ODR space will build upon the foundation of eResoution's history.

CHAPTER TWELVE

Other Applications of ODR

—◉◉◉—

Online dispute resolution is applicable in a wide variety of areas. As the field has learned with traditional face-to-face dispute resolution, the potential applications are almost limitless. This book presents some of the major application areas for online dispute resolution, but there are many other areas not mentioned in which the tools of ODR can be applied to positive effect. This section presents a variety of promising application areas for ODR that we do not have enough space to analyze more in depth in a separate chapter. There are certainly many more possible application areas for ODR that this book overlooks, and many of them may be as reasonable and promising as the ones listed here. That leaves plenty of topics to address in future volumes.

CLASS ACTIONS

One application area for online dispute resolution that is getting a lot of attention is class actions, which are civil suits brought on behalf of a large group of complainants who share a common grievance. Class actions are frequently filed against large corporations that interact with many different customers. For example, say a telephone company mischarges for a particular type of call for one month. Once the incorrect charges are discovered, there may be tens of thousands of people who were inappropriately charged. A single lawyer can file a class action on behalf of all of the affected customers and receive a bulk settlement on behalf of the entire class. Corporations are frequently fearful of class action litigation because the potential awards can be very large.

Corporations are not the only institutions that have exposure to class-action litigation. Class action lawyers have targeted the federal government in situations in which large numbers of citizens have been adversely affected by governmental error. A recent example was a class action filed against the Department of Agriculture for improper loan-granting procedures to African American farmers in the American South in the early part of the twentieth century. In that class action suit, the government was ordered to pay tens of millions of dollars to the families of farmers who had been improperly denied loans. Once the decision was filed, however, the process was not over. The bulk settlement had to be divided among all of the members of the class. There were thousands of claimants who felt that they were owed some of the money that the government had been ordered to pay, but there was no mechanism in place to evaluate each of the claims to determine its merits. Dispute resolution was used to examine documents provided by each claimant in the class action and to determine how much of the settlement was due to that particular claimant.

Class actions are increasingly common in the United States, and the size of the class can be huge. As the customer bases of corporations continue to grow, such as telephone companies, cable companies, and Internet companies, a small mistake can quickly affect hundreds of thousands of customers. Much of the time these customers are not located in a single geographic area, and it may be very difficult and expensive to convene large groups of these customers in any one place. While class actions may be decided in a single courtroom, and the judge may decide on the amount for a single award, the process of dividing up the award appropriately among all of the members of the class can be very complicated.

Online dispute resolution provides a neat solution to many of the challenges associated with managing class action outcomes. The technology can manage thousands if not tens of thousands of individual cases, and a team of expert neutrals and evaluators can consider the merits of each case and render a decision. The online dispute resolution platform can facilitate the dissemination of information to all of the class participants, enable them to submit relevant documentation, and allow them to engage in question and answer with the evaluator considering their case.

Judicial Arbitration and Mediation Services, one of the top face-to-face dispute resolution firms in the United States, recently teamed with Poorman-Douglas, one of the largest class action administration firms, to build the new e-JAMS service. Poorman-Douglas is not a well-known company in the United States, but it is the number-one advertiser in the *Wall Street Journal* because it administers so many class action processes that require public notification. JAMS has created its e-JAMS service to focus on this particular niche of dispute resolution practice, as it is such a promising application area for online dispute resolution.

INTELLECTUAL PROPERTY

In an information economy, intellectual property protection becomes more important than ever. Businesses are based on ideas, which are frequently translated into software programs, which can be easily copied and duplicated in the blink of an eye at no cost. The information economy moves very quickly, and market opportunities come and go with great speed. A common sentiment in Silicon Valley is that once a high-tech idea makes it to Washington, D.C. and New York the window of opportunity has passed.

Disputes over intellectual property are becoming more and more common. The court system has proven insufficient to address these disputes because it is so slow-moving and because it inadequately protects commercially sensitive secrets. Internet, software, and biotechnology companies are increasingly utilizing alternative dispute resolution to resolve intellectual property disputes because ADR can move quickly and protect the confidentiality of the items under dispute. Because the commercial potential of intellectual property is so time sensitive, the rapidity of the resolution process is often paramount.

Additionally, intellectual property disputes are often very complicated affairs that require a great deal of technical expertise to understand. In a court of law, the judge assigned to hear a particular matter probably will have little or no experience in the science or research that undergirds the dispute. Significant amounts of time are devoted to educating judges and juries about the subtleties and science that underlie intellectual property if the disputants decide to go into the courthouse. In a dispute resolution process, it is easy for both sides to agree on a neutral, possibly even an expert evaluator, who has the substantive knowledge to understand the matter under dispute without requiring extensive education from the parties. This baseline understanding can save significant amounts of time in reaching a resolution.

Online dispute resolution delivers these benefits and more. Because the parties in an intellectual property dispute are likely to be technologically savvy, they may be predisposed to using technology in an innovative way to resolve their claim. Second, because geography is not a constraint on an online dispute resolution process, it may be possible to select a neutral with valuable expertise who has no conflicts of interest or ongoing relationships with any of the parties involved. If the dispute is over a biotechnology patent, for example, the parties can select the best neutral in the world to work with them to resolve the matter, as opposed to only considering experts in their immediate proximity.

ADVERTISING

Advertising is a huge and influential industry in the United States. For many products there is no meaningful distinction for the consumer aside from various advertising campaigns. A friend of mine who worked at a shoe company told me that market research conducted in the sneaker industry had revealed that the only meaningful distinction in the mind of a sneaker-buying consumer between the various major brands was the advertising campaigns that represented the various shoe models. All sneakers, he told me, were essentially rubber pads with fabric on top. The difference between a multimillion-dollar shoe company and a failing shoe company was often the effectiveness of their respective advertising campaigns and the prominence of their various spokespeople.

Because advertising is so important in these markets, companies can become very sensitive about the truth of claims made in the advertisements of their competitiors. If one brand of detergent releases a commercial that makes a statement about another brand of detergent, millions of dollars in revenue may ride upon the veracity of that claim. As a result, national advertising organizations along with the Better Business Bureau have created a dispute resolution mechanism to evaluate the veracity of claims made in advertising campaigns. If an advertisement is released that makes a claim that another company questions, that company can bring the case to the National Advertising Division, which will initiate a dispute resolution process and give the two sides an opportunity to dispute or bolster the claim. If the board decides an advertisement is untrue, they ask for the ad to be pulled. Enforcement rates for this national truth-in-advertising dispute resolution program are very impressive, with more than 97 percent of decisions being honored by the disputants.

In advertising they say timing is everything, and often advertisements are released in a barrage of categories: print ads in magazines and newspapers, television advertisements, radio, and Internet. When a complaint arises surrounding the veracity of a particular campaign, time is of the essence in getting that claim resolved so that the campaign is not finished and the damage done before the complainant has an opportunity to state its case. An online document-based ODR process would allow for very rapid complaint filing and deliberation by the neutrals chosen by the National Advertising Division, which might result in a more effective mechanism for guaranteeing truth in advertising.

CONSTRUCTION

When people tell me that ODR technology is too complicated for people in non-technical industries to grasp, or they suggest that alternative dispute resolution is too idealistic to work in competitive, traditional businesses, I often point towards the construction industry. Construction defect dispute resolution has been one of the fastest-growing areas of dispute resolution for the last decade. Construction projects are often very complicated affairs involving millions of dollars, dozens of involved businesses and subcontractors, complex financing arrangements, and expensive technical expertise. Many large construction contracts are awarded through a bidding process in which a variety of bidders submit their estimates for how much the project would cost to complete. Often the contract is awarded to one of the lower bidders, who then executes an agreement saying that the company will complete the project for the stated bid. A common problem as of late in construction, and particularly in large public construction contracts, is that immediately after receiving the bid and signing an agreement that says they will perform the work, the bidder drafts a new document stating that the costs to complete the project will be higher than they originally estimated and insisting that more money be provided. Often this results in immediate litigation. But as the litigation begins, the construction continues, so as the court case winds its way toward a hearing the building continues.

Many in the industry came to realize this process was untenable. The disputes between the contractor putting the building together, the subcontractors providing important support services to the main contractor such as plumbing and electricity, the architects who designed the building, and the financial backers paying for the building's construction often become huge obstacles to the project's completion. Attempting to resolve disputes over material costs, design flaws, and defects concurrent with the actual construction can be a messy and divisive process. Dispute resolution has proven to be a much more reasonable and effective way to address these conflicts, while at the same time preserving the relationships between all of the partners on the project to ensure that the building is completed as efficiently and effectively as possible.

Dispute resolution in the construction area often comes to look more like project management as it happens alongside the actual construction process. New issues are constantly rising, old issues are being resolved, and new information is being provided, so the disagreements become something of a moving target. Online dispute resolution can complement this type of dispute resolution effectively by providing all of the participants in the construction project with systems that allow them to address existing issues, share information relevant to the resolution, and raise new matters in the most efficient and expedient way possible. In large public construction contracts, which often involve multiple project partners in different countries, online dispute resolution can help minimize the convening penalty and provide ongoing support so that these projects are not derailed by disputes that arise in the course of their completion.

REAL ESTATE

For many families the purchase of a home is the largest financial transaction they will take part in throughout their lives. Buying a home is a complicated exercise, with many different variables and unknowns. State and local agencies govern the real estate process closely as it can be difficult for home buyers and sellers to grasp all of the relevant issues surrounding the transaction. Real estate brokers play an important role in walking buyers and sellers through all of the relevant issues. However, disputes inevitably arise as representations of real estate properties prove to be misleading or untrue, sometimes with no malevolent intentions on the part of the seller.

A couple I know purchased a home in the suburbs outside Boston, Massachusetts, that was in an area that did not have access to sewer mains. Instead the house used a septic tank, which was something the couple knew very little about. In the process of buying the house the seller needed to provide a document that attested to the proper operation of the septic tank, and the couple received a letter from the seller that they believed met this legal requirement. However, before they had closed the transaction, they arranged for a septic company to empty the tank. Once the septic company representative arrived, he informed them that their tank had a problem and would probably need to be replaced. When the buyers confronted the seller with this information, the seller disagreed and refused to pay any money to fix the septic tank. As a result, the couple canceled the purchase of the house. Later, when they purchased another house with a different septic tank, they learned that the problem would likely not have been very complicated to address. They were frustrated at the several months they had wasted negotiating the purchase of the first house, and they wished that they could have gotten some assistance in resolving the dispute with the seller so that they could have completed the transaction. A real estate mediation program may have helped them resolve the matter so that the transaction could have gone through.

Many standard real estate contracts contain clauses urging or obligating the parties to utilize dispute resolution to resolve any claims that arise in the course of the transaction. Though these clauses are very common in real estate agreements, in many areas of the country they are underutilized and ignored. Real estate dispute resolution is often the exception rather than the rule. Because regulation of real estate often happens on a state-by-state basis, dispute resolution programs targeting real estate transactions often are located either only in the state capitol or in major cities around the state.

Recently SquareTrade, the San Francisco online dispute resolution company that works with eBay, started to handle disputes through the California Board of Realtors. Using SquareTrade's online dispute resolution platform, disputants involved in real estate transactions can work with a mediator knowledgeable about real estate law to resolve their disagreement so that the transaction can go through. Online dispute resolution programs like this one, targeted at the real estate industry, can be built into the standard homebuyer education process to increase satisfaction among buyers and sellers, complement the work of real estate professionals, and prevent disputes from going to court.

FAMILY

One of the largest areas of dispute resolution in the United States is family mediation. In a divorce situation, courtroom proceedings often make disputes much worse. A court may be very effective at determining right from wrong, but in a marital dispute many of the issues cannot be effectively resolved by a simple right-or-wrong determination. Particularly when it comes to the custody of children, the courts have a great many shortcomings as an effective dispute resolution mechanism. As a result of this realization the family mediation field has been growing steadily for the last two decades. The Academy of Family Mediators, which recently merged into the Association for Conflict Resolution, was for quite some time the largest professional mediation organization in the world.

When we first started Online Resolution, many of the disputes that we received on our website were family disputes between people who were looking to get a divorce. At the beginning we turned all of these disputes away, referring them to face-to-face family mediators in their immediate geographic area who might be able to sit down with them to resolve the disputes. Over time, however, some of the people that we urged to contact face-to-face mediators argued back that they wanted to deal with the matter online. Our family dispute caseload at Online Resolution never grew very large, but many in the family mediation field have begun to utilize technology in working with divorce and couples. Jim Melamed, former executive director of the Academy of Family Mediators and one of the co-founders of Online Resolution, has led the way in integrating technology into the family mediation process. Many family mediations are hybrids, utilizing technology for some of the discussion but not all of it. Sometimes technology is used only in drafting the final agreement, or to facilitate information sharing between the parties. Technology is also utilized in family disputes to more accurately work with complex financial numbers and valuations and to help find optimal resource allocations in the division of property. Technology can be of assistance in planning for visitation arrangements, analyzing calendars, and following up with agreements reached in mediation.

Many family disputes arise after the terms of the divorce have already been agreed upon. Confusion emerges once an attempt to put the arrangements into place is made. Many times in these situations the former husband and wife no longer live in the same area and do not have much of a desire to get together face to face to clarify the implementation issues in the agreement. In these types of follow-up disputes, online dispute resolution may be a much more practical and desirable choice for dealing with disagreements and may help to ensure smooth implementation of previously crafted agreements.

EDUCATION

My first involvement in the dispute resolution field was in the education field. I got involved mediating roommate disputes at my college and ended up writing my thesis on dispute resolution and higher education. There are a wide variety of disputes that can arise on a college or university campus, as Bill Warters has pointed out in his impressive work on the subject.[1] Faculty can have disputes with administration, students can have disputes with both faculty and the administration, and staff can have disputes with all of the above. Disputes between roommates or dormmates happen all the time, as well as disputes between professors and their students over academic issues. College campuses are often rife with disputes, as students and faculty clash over a variety of issues both internal and external to the campus community.

At first glance, it may seem silly to suggest that disputants make use of an online dispute resolution mechanism when they are likely on the same campus and not too far away from each other. But one of the aspects of the modern collegiate experience is that much of the life of the students, faculty, and administration happens online. While there is undoubtedly a place for peer mediation programs, administration-sponsored mediation resources either through the housing office, the dean's office, or the combatant person's office, and face-to-face counseling services, online dispute resolution tools can also play a valuable role in helping campus communities deal with difficult conflicts. In fact, there are often many people on college campuses who prefer to deal with conflict in an online environment, either in conjunction with a face-to-face meeting or on its own.

Many of the tools being built to allow people to resolve their disputes online are applicable in a wide variety of situations. At the February 2002 Cyberweek conference, the most active discussion area focused on the issue of ODR and peer mediation in schools. A recent cover story in the *New York Times Magazine* dealt with the topic of disputes between teenage girls, and the work of a woman trying to help girls resolve their problems through communication. The article told a story of the woman advising a teenage girl to sit down with her friend, to tell her how much her friendship meant, and to ask her why problems had arisen in their relationship. When the writer later cornered the girl who was given the advice, she asked the girl if it was realistic. Not really, replied the girl, we'd probably just go home after school and resolve it over the Internet.

Many elementary and middle school students leave school at the end of the day and go home to log on to AOL to communicate with each other through instant messaging. Many of the difficult playground disputes or friendly spats that escalate in the hallways at school can be more effectively addressed online, with a little cooling distance between the immediacy of schoolyard interaction and the comfort of home. Peer mediation has been a hugely successful model for dispute resolution in secondary education, and the tools of online dispute resolution could be a powerful complement to peer mediation programs. Kids today are extremely comfortable with textual communications, either through email or instant messaging, and they can often figure out online collaborative applications and put them to effective use in a fraction of the time required by adults.

I frequently conduct demonstrations of online dispute resolution technology at both schools and law firms. In the schools I have gotten into the habit of putting every student at a computer, loading up the Web page, and saying, "Go." The students immediately educate themselves as to how the tools work and how they can be useful. In law firms I am frequently forced to spend hours explaining the basic functionality of the tools, and even then many of the attorneys (peering over the tops of their glasses at the screen) simply throw their hands up in frustration with the conclusion that the tools are too complicated to understand. Merely providing these resources to students and giving them an opportunity to customize them as they see fit will likely generate impressive progress in resolving disputes in educational environments.

Case Study: Peer Mediation

One day at recess, Susan and Ashley got into a fight over the previous weekend's happenings. They had long been close friends, but recently their friendship had gone on the skids as Ashley had started to hang out with Marilyn, who Susan couldn't stand. Earlier in the school year Susan and Ashley had spent every weekend together, sleeping over at each other's houses. This fight threatened to end it all, though.

Susan had found out through the grapevine that Ashley's parents had given her tickets to see a singer that they both knew was their favorite; all through the fall semester, the two of them had sung along to the record and followed the fan sites for the singer on the Internet. Then Susan heard that Ashley had invited Marilyn to the concert, without even telling Susan that she had tickets.

At recess, Ashley came up to Susan and started speaking to her like nothing was up, and Susan became increasingly angry. Finally she boiled over and confronted Ashley with the information about the concert. Ashley was initially shocked that Susan knew about the concert, but after a moment she fired back, accusing Susan of telling nasty secrets about Ashley behind her back to some other girls. The two of them began yelling at each other, and eventually Ashley stormed away.

Rebecca, a mutual friend of Ashley and Susan, witnessed the blow-up. She spoke to the two of them separately later that day. Susan was angrier than Ashley, and she made it sound like the friendship might be over. Susan was even talking about Ashley as if she was an enemy, threatening to reveal more of her secrets. For the next two days, Susan and Ashley refused to speak with each other. Rebecca decided it was time to intervene.

Rebecca had been trained as part of the peer mediator program to help kids resolve their disputes, so she approached Susan to ask if she could sit the two of them down. Susan said she wouldn't be in the same room as Ashley, so that was a no go. However, Rebecca knew that half of the students at her school logged on to America Online in the afternoon to chat with friends, and she had both Ashley and Susan's screen names in her buddy list. When she got home from school that day she checked and, sure enough, both of them were online. Rebecca approached Ashley first.

"Do you still want to be Susan's friend?" Rebecca asked. "After today and yesterday, I'm not so sure," came back the response. Rebecca talked with Ashley about the blow-up, worked through the anger from their confrontation, and eventually Ashley admitted that not being invited to the concert must have been pretty hurtful for Susan. Ashley then admitted that she did want Susan to forgive her, and that she wanted Susan as a friend. Rebecca asked if she could share that with Susan, and Ashley said yes.

Susan was harder to bring around. She was still pretty angry. "How could she do that to me?" Susan asked. Rebecca didn't even have time to type a response before the next message came in from Susan. "All over that stupid Marilyn! I hate her!" Rebecca told Susan that Ashley had said that she wanted to still be friends, and Susan said she would have to have an apology first. Rebecca took that to Ashley. "Not unless she apologizes for telling my secrets behind my back." Rebecca passed the messages back and forth. Finally, Ashley said she'd apologize. Rebecca's buddy list was finally quiet. Susan and Ashley were passing messages between the two of them.

The next day at school Ashley brought Susan a card she had made for her, and the two of them made up. Susan thanked Rebecca for helping out with the fight, and eventually the two of them became close friends. They would have a sleepover when Ashley slept over at Marilyn's (who Susan still hated.)

PART III

Designing Effective ODR for Business

Envisioning the Fourth Party

CHAPTER THIRTEEN

Key Considerations
Designing ODR for People, Not Machines

W hen envisioning the fourth party, the key components to consider fall into three categories: people, process, and technology. Not all of the issues under these broad categories are relevant to every online dispute resolution project. Websites that provide only automated mechanisms may not be concerned with building a panel, for instance, and ODR providers that offer only people-powered solutions may not have to worry about sophisticated exception-handling technology. Overall, however, any successful ODR site will need to think long and hard about these three elements if they are to be successful.

The first consideration, and the most important, is people. People power websites. People power ODR. No matter how whiz-bang the technology is behind your site, you're going to have people using it and people supporting it. The people are the guts of any ODR service, and they are where successful ODR programs begin and end.

DISPUTANTS

The users of your site are going to be people, not machines. The cutting-edge code under the hood of a site means little if the users can't use the site to do what they need to do. Some ODR platforms devote most of their effort toward building complex tools that exist behind the scenes. Neutrals and case administrators, particularly the ones who love technology, like to have complex control panels at their disposal, enabling them to handle any eventuality with a couple clicks of their mouse. Much of this energy is misdirected. The success or failure of any ODR platform will be determined by the response from the disputants who come to the site to get their matter resolved, not by the bells and whistles that make up the case administrator's behind-the-scenes interface.

Listen to the Users

The most important thing any ODR system designer should do is to listen to the people who will use, are using, and have used the system. It has become a buzzword as of late, but being "customer-centric" is essential to effective dispute resolution. Teams of high-paid consultants and interface designers will probably provide less insight than diverse groups of users "off the street" who can give their honest reactions to the interface, process, and services offered by the site.

In early 2001, Anne Marie Hammond and Michael Lang convened several user focus groups to get their reaction to the Online Resolution ODR process and technology. Conducted at Royal Roads University in British Columbia, their study asked some very specific questions about how ODR processes should be structured, how neutrals could best assist the parties, and how to make technology intuitive and useful. The surveys they conducted were extensive, consisting of more than 100 questions, many of which required narrative answers. Their research on the topic of user experiences with ODR remains the most comprehensive to date. The feedback from those focus groups played a central role in shaping the development of the Online Resolution platform, and many of the results from that study are cited in this chapter.

The participants in the Royal Roads focus groups were a fairly diverse group. They ranged in age from thirty-one to fifty, and their substantive expertise varied widely, including government, education, business, finance, law, accounting, and architecture. A third of the participants described themselves as "minimally comfortable with computers," another third "comfortable," and the last third "very comfortable," so the participants were not all computer geeks with a high tolerance for esoteric computer lingo.

The focus group process began with a hands-on tour of the ODR platform. The users who would be participating in the simulations as mediators received extra training that allowed them to customize their online "meeting rooms" as they saw fit before the online dispute resolution process was to begin. Eight different simulation fact patterns were used in the simulations, which lasted for two weeks. The participants then completed a comprehensive online survey and were given an opportunity to provide additional feedback in an online discussion environment set up for that purpose.

The primary lessons gleaned from these focus groups are presented here. Much of the specific information gathered about the strengths and weaknesses of our particular technology platform would not be helpful to present here, so that specificity has been removed. However, such specific technical feedback is essential, so conducting a similar focus-group process to gather it for your specific ODR platform is highly recommended.

Orient and Introduce Users to the Technology

Many websites and software programs seem to use the "throw them in the water and they'll learn to swim" strategy when introducing users to new technology. Often users are expected to manage their own learning curve, with only cursory materials provided to help them become oriented. Some people enjoy learning this way (often the people who build new technology, ironically) so this strategy may work for them, but many other people are threatened and overwhelmed by such a strategy.

Devoting time and resources to easing the learning curve of new users is essential to successful ODR implementations. Provide an animated Flash movie, narrated by a human voice, that explains how to use the ODR tools made available to users. Provide extensive documentation and context-sensitive help files, so that users can always get a quick answer to questions that may arise. As one of the focus group participants put it, "The instructions, tour, and attention to detail were all helpful. For me, it was the 'fear of the unknown' and the . . . belief that [the platform] would be difficult."

It is the job of the designers of ODR technology to proactively address this fear and to ease new users into an understanding of how new tools will benefit them. Don't keep users in the dark or shield them from the ability to truly contribute in the online system, but don't drown them with inadequately explained tools and esoteric interface designs. Providing a simple and friendly introduction to the ODR platform should be a core design priority.

Let Users Learn at Their Own Pace

Learning new technology is an investment. I have visited dozens of offices where there are people desperately holding on to their anti-quated word processing programs because they are terrified of hav-ing to learn a new platform. People fear change, and they fear that learning something new is going to require them to work in a wholly different way. Usually this latter fear is well founded. The only reason to learn a new technology is so that it can help you do things better. It's just difficult on the front end to be sure that the time invested in a new technology will result in a real improvement.

The key question is, when does it make sense to introduce new technologies? Some people like to wait until there is a new project to introduce technology, so as to bring technological change along with workplace change. Others don't want the new technology to detract from the work, so they prefer to introduce change in down periods when there aren't a lot of pressing projects. Because technology does take commitment to learn, and because people are often skeptical of change, it is important to allow for individual users to come to the tools on their own schedule. ODR tools, in particular, should never be forced upon users. Much like mediation itself, if the parties aren't ready or seem resistant to use the technology, respect their lead.

The KISS Principle

Many people have heard of the KISS principle: Keep It Simple, Stupid. Or, alternatively, Keep It Simple, Silly (should one be sensitive to pejo-rative language). The users in the Royal Roads focus group made this point loud and clear. Providing users powerful tools is not a bad thing, but if the tools lead to confusion and clutter they are not worth the effort. The simpler the ODR platform, the better.

Anyone who has designed a complicated website or a computer program will tell you that designing a simple user interface can be very hard. Most people have become savvy consumers of technology over the past two decades. They may not know how to build an effective graphical user interface, but they sure know a bad one when they see it. If the design of a website is a little sloppy, or if the navigation is con-fusing, users have very little patience and they will log off and never come back.

One programmer who built some key ODR technology in the Online Resolution platform explained that his key word was "instinctive." Good technology should be instinctive in that a user should always be able to look at a screen and have an intuitive sense about what it is they are supposed to do. If users don't get that intuitive sense from the program they're working with or the website they're using they will become frustrated.

Focus on Customer Service

Most websites have only one type of customer. E-commerce sites attract people looking to buy products. Whether they are small (individual or home users) or big (corporate or bulk purchasers) their needs and expectations are similar: quality products, efficient shipping turnarounds, and responsive customer service.

ODR platforms usually target several different types of customers. The most obvious are the disputants. The users who come to the site to get their dispute resolved may come in many different sizes (individuals, corporations) with many different types of issues (for example, divorce, buyers and sellers, workplace, insurance, privacy) and many different levels of ODR expertise and experience (first-time user or repeat player), but they all interact with the ODR platform in roughly the same way.

The panelists that provide services are also customers of the ODR program. They may be choosing among a variety of different ODR providers, and they may be referring their own disputants to the platform. They have a different set of needs, as their credibility and livelihood is connected to the ODR programs they work for and recommend to others.

The third type of customer is the institutional referrer. The best referrals for ODR cases are often from non-party infrastructure providers, like online marketplaces, seal providers, government agencies, or trade associations. These bodies have an interest in seeing disputes resolved, because they have a stake in the efficient operation of the system they coordinate, free of disputes and insulated from liability. But they are not parties to the dispute in the purest sense. They do not have any stake in one or the other side getting its way. In this regard, these institutional players are the ideal partners for ODR services. These bodies have their own needs. They are investing their credibility in the promise of efficient and effective ODR services. They are also trusting their customer relationships to a third party. They may have used their influence with one of their customers or clients to get them to try ODR, so they are on the line as well. ODR providers must remain cognizant of this exposure on the part of their referral partners, and work to live up to their expectations.

Customer service is particularly important in ODR, even more important than it is in other Web businesses. Disputants in e-commerce matters often end up in an ODR process because they feel let down by the customer service offered to them by the other party in the dispute. Disputants in workplace or family matters may be quite distraught and emotionally vulnerable as a result of their situation. Inconveniences acceptable in other online businesses, like long waits for customer service representatives, are not appropriate in most ODR programs. Customer service for ODR efforts must exceed the standards set in other circumstances because of the nature of the work being performed.

Customer service representatives must also meet a higher standard. I have called the customer support lines for some online businesses and have been routed to a call center on the other side of the country, speaking to a person who doesn't even know the city where the headquarters for the business is located. These outsourced customer service representatives may be cheaper, but they do not have as intimate an understanding of the products or the company. Customer service representatives in ODR efforts need to be experienced with dispute resolution, as every communication with the ODR provider is part of the dispute resolution process. Even if the disputant calls in before a case is formally filed, the customer service representatives need to treat him or her with respect, and to help to reframe the dispute into resolution-focused categories: What do you really want to achieve in this dispute? What do you and the other party already agree upon?

Customer service needs to work hand-in-hand with the neutrals to support the work they are doing in their dispute resolution proceedings. Responsiveness, respect, and an appropriate understanding of ODR is essential for quality customer service in the ODR context.

Educating Parties

There is significant value in educating everyone about the tools and techniques of ODR. Managers of virtual teams, customer service representatives, and online discussion forum managers can all benefit from the techniques of ODR's core skill groups: active listening online, constant response techniques, affirmative communications, and concurrent caucusing. But receiving this training does not make them ODR practitioners. It may help them to deal with conflict in their particular communities and constituencies, but it does not make them capable of working with parties in a formal process to resolve complex disputes.

One of the things every neutral needs to do at the beginning of an ODR process is to orient the parties and to educate them about how to effectively use the tools being set in front of them. Neutrals need to set expectations for their parties so that there are no unpleasant surprises that can undermine a party's buy-in to the process, or to make them think that they committed to something they didn't fully understand.

Understanding the technology is a big part of that. While in a face-to-face process a neutral often needs to establish ground rules about what types of communication between the parties is off-limits, usually the parties don't require instruction about how to speak to each other or how to ask to interact privately with the neutral. Online there is more of a basic education that needs to happen, to make sure that the parties know how to get around the technology being used and where to get answers to any technical questions they may have.

Neutrals need to have a detailed knowledge of the technology so that they can serve as the first line of technical support. Having to rely on outsiders to answer technical questions can make the ODR process feel less focused and less personal. Encourage neutrals to ask for answers to their parties' technical questions, so that they can provide the answers back to the parties. This keeps the process focused on the neutral and removes the impression of reliance on uninvolved case managers and other outsiders.

For many people involved in a dispute resolution process it is in fact a learning experience, and as they move toward resolution they get a clearer sense of their own needs and interests as well as a sense of what is really motivating the other side. The neutral needs to encourage this learning, but not in a direct way. Ideally the parties will take themselves into this new understanding, with the help and guidance of the neutral. In this sense, the ODR technology is merely a means to an end.

Cultural Differences

Many face-to-face mediators and arbitrators have to struggle with cultural differences. Diverse societies lead to people with different backgrounds frequently interacting in stressful circumstances. Many times cultural baggage plays a role in misunderstanding the intentions of the other party and contributes to the escalation of a dispute.

Online, this phenomenon is magnified. Because disputants can come from anywhere on the Internet the possibilities for cultural misunderstandings are compounded. Most disputes in a face-to-face context happen in the same geographic area, so even if the disputants are from different cultures they are likely to have some understanding of the other side's cultural perspective from prior interaction. Over the Internet, though, it is not safe to assume that both parties will have even a rough understanding of the other side's cultural norms. In fact, the remove provided by online interaction may contribute to stereotyping or mistaken assumptions about the other side's cultural background.

The best work done in cultural differences in ODR has been conducted by Nora Femenia, an Argentine-American in Miami who heads up Inter-Mediacion.com, a Spanish-English dispute resolution consulting firm. In a paper presented to the ODR conference in The Hague in 2000, Dr. Femenia described several different cultural types and discussed how they might use ODR differently. Some cultures can be broadly characterized as "high context," meaning they put a lot of emphasis on community, family, and social good, while others can be characterized as "low context," where the emphasis is on the individual, ambition, competition, and freedom. Members of these cultures view both themselves and others in fundamentally different ways. Their expectations of what is reasonable and appropriate behavior are also different. A low-context person may enter a negotiation from a competitive perspective, oriented around getting as much as possible from an outcome, assuming the other side will act the same way. A high-context person may enter a negotiation from a collaborative perspective, with the goal of achieving a fair resolution, not expecting to maximize her outcome. Once the process begins and the two sides find their expectations inaccurate they may accuse the other party of being irrational or immoral.

ODR case managers and neutrals need to be aware of these cultural differences and to attempt to build awareness of differences on both sides of the dispute. The goal, as in any dispute resolution process, is to build empathy between the two sides ("I understand how you could feel or think that way") as opposed to sympathy ("I feel and think the same way you do"). Helping parties develop this empathy for the other side's cultural perspective is essential to making progress toward a resolution.

The cultural question needs to play a role not only in the actual dispute resolution process as administered by the neutral, but also in the design of the technology. From an access perspective, multiple-language capacity, the availability of the site in different languages, and multilingual customer support can help open up the process to other regions and cultures. Literal translation is not enough, however. ODR concepts and tools may need to be presented in different ways to different cultures. If a blind-bidding tool is completely oriented toward maximizing one side's outcome at the expense of the other side it may be less attractive to disputants from high-context cultures, for example.

Neutral assignment should also focus on these questions. If a neutral who speaks the first languages of the parties and has an appropriate understanding of their respective cultures can be assigned to a dispute, then that is ideal. If no neutral exists that has that joint understanding, perhaps a panel or team of neutrals could be assigned that brings together those capacities.

Empower Participants

Many of the powers in online dispute resolution environments reside with the mediator or arbitrator. Password-protected areas of the website accessible only to the neutral and case managers control almost every aspect of the online environment. Neutrals can move comments around, edit and delete any submission on the site, or even shut down lines of communication.

The best online processes do not showcase these power differentials. Ideally the parties will feel like they are the ones in control of the technology, not the other way around. ODR platforms can be very prescriptive, leading parties through a sequential series of steps that requires them to acquiesce to a predefined process. But even in these processes the parties must feel like they are the ones who are assenting to each step. Remember, ODR platforms must make the participants feel like they are having their due process rights respected by the platform they are using. If parties feel victimized by either the technology or the neutral they will turn on the process, either by walking away or by becoming hostile.

Participants need to feel ownership of the ODR process they are involved in, even in an adjudicatory process in which they have surrendered their decision-making power. If users feel they are being pushed into a process like a treadmill they can't get off of, they will walk away, never to return. Disputants need to feel that they are the ones who are in control, that they are never surprised by a part of the process, and that their role and time is being respected by the process, the technology, and the neutral.

Constant Communication

Because it is easy for participants to walk away from an online process, keeping them engaged takes on the utmost importance. As one online mediator put it, "The process itself is effective and the mediator's greatest gift may be attentiveness." Parties rely on the neutral for a sense of progress. If they don't feel that any movement is happening then their commitment to the online dispute resolution process may atrophy. Then when progress does begin again they may have already emotionally distanced themselves.

In online interactions, silence is often interpreted aggressively. If someone registers a concern, or contributes a comment in an online dispute resolution environment that they feel is important, and that contribution is greeted with silence, it is very easy for the contributor to feel that they are being ignored. This sense of stonewalling from the other side can be wholly inaccurate. It may be that the recipient of that contribution is closely considering the matter, discussing it with the neutral, or composing a thoughtful response. However, this is unknown to the contributor until the response is posted. In an online dispute resolution process the neutral has the responsibility of acknowledging new postings and communicating activity in both directions, so that the parties know they are being heard, that their points are being taken seriously, and that they are not being stonewalled.

It is vital for neutrals to always share progress with disputants. Neutrals must resist the temptation to keep parties in the dark, hoping to bring major progress and concessions later on. Even if the message is that nothing has happened, neutrals should send the message. Parties can't see any progress without communication.

This discipline of constant communication needs to be strongly emphasized in trainings for new neutrals. A message a day to the parties should be considered the bare minimum. Ideally the neutral will be continually engaged with progress in the ODR process and will respond to every new posting within a few hours. The best online neutrals are often those people who are logged in and sitting at their computer for the bulk of their workday. Those neutrals who are using dial-up connections, and who log in once a day or once every other day to check their messages, have a huge hill to climb if they are going to be able to sustain constant communication with their parties.

In this sense, ODR is a "high-touch" process, in large part because the possibility of physical touch is removed. Even if no progress is being made the neutral should communicate with the parties, ask some clarifying questions, or just attempt to move the ball forward. The neutral's job is to communicate to the participants that someone is interested in, focused on, and engaged with the dispute, even if they are not. If two or three days pass in which the parties check the ODR platform and find nothing new, that may be enough to effectively end the process.

NEUTRALS

Dispute resolution is not an easy thing to do. In fact, many of the people who choose it as a career do so because it is highly challenging. While there are lots of people who call themselves mediators and arbitrators, the reality is that truly great dispute resolution service providers are rare. Finding good people is the first challenge of any ODR organization, be they dispute resolvers, customer support representatives, or programmers.

Some people seem to gravitate to online dispute resolution because they think it will be easier than face-to-face practice. This is a myth. The hard work of reaching agreement is the same offline as it is online. In fact, the online processes usually take more time and effort because so much of what is communicated naturally in a face-to-face process (active listening, clear attentiveness on the part of the parties, commitment to the process) must be communicated intentionally in an online process. This takes time, and not every neutral is ready to commit the energy and resources necessary to perform this work.

It is difficult to pick great neutrals out of a lineup, or out of a stack of resumés, but once you are engaged with a truly skilled dispute resolver (or a truly bad dispute resolver) you will know it instantly. And the users of your ODR system will know it, too.

Building a Panel

The first concern of any online dispute resolution service is recruiting quality neutrals to serve as panelists. If you build a really elegant and intuitive ODR system, and you allow mediocre neutrals to use it to work with parties, your effort put into building the system was a waste.

One thing that cannot be compensated for is experience. It is true that there are some individuals who have a natural gift for working with people embroiled in a dispute. Some personalities and communication styles naturally fit into the role of mediator or arbitrator. But natural ability must be combined with learned skill and acquired wisdom to make a truly effective dispute resolution service provider.

The best way to evaluate a neutral is to speak to the parties he or she has worked with. Even better, meet with the neutral and talk with him yourself. Examine her communication skills first-hand. Look for how well he listens more than how well he talks. If possible, observe her in the way she works directly with parties. For mediators, see how prescriptive they are when they work with the disputants. Do they let the parties lead the process themselves, or do they push them in a particular direction?

There have been many efforts to "credential" neutrals, either through a professional exam (like accountants and lawyers) or through the establishment of certain educational requirements. None of these efforts have yet come to fruition, for good reason. It is very difficult to determine the skill of a neutral from a paper exam. It is almost impossible to say what coursework would be required to become a good mediator or arbitrator. Some of the best neutrals have never taken a formal course, and some who have Ph.D.s in dispute resolution couldn't get two disputants to agree on what to have for lunch.

Arbitration is slightly different because in most cases the role requires an in-depth knowledge of the law. Most if not all prominent arbitrators are attorneys and many have experience working as judges. This is not to say that the best arbitrators are the ones who most closely recreate a courtroom environment. Sometimes the parties to an arbitration want essentially a private court, and the ability to faithfully recreate that type of process is valuable. But what really distinguishes an arbitrator is a keen mind, the ability to grasp facts quickly, and the skills to really listen to what the disputants, attorneys, and witnesses are saying.

Mediation is a much harder skill to put one's finger on. Good mediators can come from law, from psychology, from counseling, from social work, or from any of a dozen other fields. There are many types of mediators, from relationship-focused, transformative mediators to very distributive, issue-focused mediators. There is no one kind of mediator that is right for all situations.

The best mediators are focused on the needs of the disputants with whom they are working. They should be able to adjust to the personalities and expectations of their parties. They have a deep self-awareness, and they know when to step in and when to step away. The best mediators aren't pushovers who let the parties walk all over the process, nor are they drill sergeants issuing orders to the parties. The best mediators also have a deep commitment to building understanding and reaching resolution, and it's something the parties can sense when they interact with them.

Whenever I speak to a mediator and he offers me his "record" I am instantly suspicious. "I am thirty and five in my successful resolutions," one might say. Any experienced mediator knows that this statistic is almost meaningless. Working as a mediator I have had disputants come in, sit down, and resolve the matter before I even lay out the ground rules. I've also had disputants come in ready to throw punches at each other, completely unable to communicate. Resolutions have much more to do with the parties and the status of their relationship than they have to do with the skills of the mediator. A good mediator can make or break the process if it comes down to abilities, but more than half of the time it doesn't come down to abilities.

Some of the earliest ODR initiatives argued that because ODR changed the delivery of dispute resolution services so significantly it was not necessary to hire experienced neutrals to deliver ODR services. It was more than adequate, they argued, to find individuals with only a basic knowledge of offline dispute resolution and to train them to become ODR providers. Many of the companies that made that argument are no longer around. Once a party has a negative experience with a neutral who doesn't know how to run a process effectively, that party is very unlikely to use dispute resolution again.

There is no substitute for proven dispute resolution skills. If anything, delivering quality ODR services is more challenging than administering effective face-to-face dispute resolution. As people in the ADR field are fond of pointing out, dispute resolution is part art and part science. The best and perhaps the only real foundation for developing online dispute resolution skills is meaningful offline experience. Perhaps one day ODR will mature to the point where the knowledge and wisdom necessary to be an effective dispute resolver can be acquired through online practice alone. But we're not there yet.

As of today, the people who really understand how to move parties toward resolution are the ones who have sat down at the negotiating table many times and worked out agreements. One of the participants in the Royal Roads focus groups put it succinctly: "This program is good if the mediator is good." Any ODR system that starts with something else is building on sand.

Training

Skilled neutrals are extremely important, but they are not enough. The practice of ODR is qualitatively different than the practice of ADR.

There are some neutrals who are highly skilled in face-to-face ADR who simply will not be able to make it work in an online environment. There are also some good offline neutrals who will emerge as truly great ODR practitioners.

Just as effective offline practitioners must match innate abilities with the acquisition of concrete skills, ODR practitioners must learn some very specific skills before they can handle difficult dispute resolution procedures online. If a neutral doesn't know how to manage the platform she is using to work with the parties, or if she can't effectively multitask between multiple caucus spaces and the joint discussion, or if she doesn't get online and respond to the parties enough, it doesn't matter how well she can engage in face-to-face active listening.

It is the responsibility of each ODR administrative body to invest in its panel and to give its neutrals a chance to acquire the skills they need to be effective practitioners. Neutrals should have the ability to run through in-depth simulations in the ODR platform before they are thrown into a live case. They should be encouraged to interact with other neutrals, and to be mentored by those practitioners who are more experienced. They should try out the language they are using for opening statements and ground rules with other neutrals, and they should be encouraged to discuss difficult ethical and practice issues with an online community of providers wrestling with the same issues.

Online Resolution's training is a sixty-hour program involving extensive self-paced content and three case simulations. The simulations allow each neutral to lead an online process at least once before they are expected to manage a real dispute. OR also has a forty-hour face-to-face training that is intended to introduce experienced ADR practitioners to ODR. None of our trainings are intended for dispute resolution novices. All of our training materials are geared toward introducing experienced practitioners to the technology and challenges of online practice and helping them transition their ADR skills into ODR skills.

Putting the Right Neutral with the Right Dispute

One of the most important powers of ODR program administrators is their ability to choose which neutrals from the panel will handle which dispute. Some ADR programs allow the parties to select their neutral, perhaps by having each side choose a slate of acceptable neutrals and then looking for common selections. Other programs insist on random assignment of neutrals to prevent possible bias or conflict of interest. What is important is that the capabilities of the neutral assigned to the case match the needs of the disputants. Panel selections should ideally respond to a variety of disputant characteristics, including cultural differences, language, gender, ethnicity, income, and education.

At the CPR Institute for Dispute Resolution Annual Meeting in the summer of 2001 I saw a presentation from two lawyers who had been opposing counsel on a case involving the death of a college student during a hazing ritual. One lawyer had represented the parents of the student and the other represented the college. After discussing the matter with the parties, the decision was made to take the dispute into mediation. The parents were understandably emotionally distraught and angry, and the president of the college insisted on sitting across the table from them in the mediation. The parents of the student were almost unable to go through with the session, but the mediator brought in to help with the process credibly professed his understanding of their feelings, because his daughter had committed suicide soon after her arrival at college years before. This life experience of the mediator helped the parents trust his ability to empathize with their situation, and the mediator was able to keep the parents involved despite their anger and frustration. Eventually the matter was settled to the satisfaction of both parties, and as part of the resolution a scholarship fund was set up in the name of the student who had passed away.

Sometimes choosing the right neutral for a dispute is the most important element in helping the parties come to agreement. ODR programs must learn the strengths and weaknesses of their panelists if they are to be able to make the right selections.

Empowering Neutrals

It is very important in ODR processes for the neutral to have firm control when the online process begins. The neutral should be the primary point of contact for the parties, answering questions about technology and providing a clear vision about how the process will be administered and where the process will go. Training is very important in communicating clear authority. The neutrals need to understand the technology backward and forward, and they need to have an articulated strategy in their heads for how they want to direct the process. As one of the mediators from the Royal Roads focus groups put it, "The online medium empowers all players equally—a good thing—so establishing roles and guidelines at the beginning becomes imperative." A disputant from the groups expressed this idea even more forcefully: "The mediator must, as is the case in conventional mediation, take the reins."

Part of this challenge is technological. The neutrals need to have access to the tools they require to manage the process. They need to be able to open and close new discussion areas, to move, delete, and edit messages, and to indicate to participants when new items are waiting for their input or approval. Neutrals need to be empowered by both the technology and the design of the ODR process, so that they can make the choices that best meet the needs of their disputants.

That said, neutrals also need to be careful that they don't abuse their power and become overbearing and domineering. It is easy to get drunk with the power online interaction gives you as a coordinator, and to act hastily in shutting down certain lines of communication or too aggressively rephrasing a user's posting. These misuses of online power can backfire in powerful and surprising ways.

In one of the simulations I conducted at Southern Methodist University I had a mediator who was faced with two very angry parties who began slinging insults in the joint discussion area of the online meeting room. Faced with this breakdown in communication, the mediator then used his rights as a coordinator of the room to shut the two parties out of the joint discussion, preventing them from posting new content and instructing them to come back into the caucus spaces. Instantly the two parties turned on the mediator, who they felt was being too controlling in his management of the discussion. Some degree of unity came from their joint trashing of the mediator's skills in handling the process, but I don't think it was really what the mediator had hoped to achieve.

It is not a simple thing to wield this much power as a neutral. That's why mediators and arbitrators need to learn how to be effective online practitioners. Neutrals must be cognizant of these risks, and they must walk the fine line between firm leadership of ODR processes and prudent use of management tools.

CHAPTER FOURTEEN

Designing the Platform

Technology

—◁◅▻▷—

M any online dispute resolution service providers make the mistake of thinking that they are technology companies first and foremost. This may be true for optical networking and wireless switch-building companies, but it is not true for ODR. In ODR, technology is the medium, not the message. The power of dispute resolution comes from its flexibility, so ODR platforms usually need to support the overall process and stay out of the way. Technology, like stage lighting for a play, shouldn't be the focus—if people walk out of a play talking about the stage lighting then odds are either the play or the lighting wasn't a success. ODR technology should be the same way. The technology is a means to an end, not an end in and of itself. Putting technology in for technology's sake is self-defeating. Some websites get so caught up in their whiz-bang features that they quickly lose sight of the user's core need, the need that brought them to the site in the first place: they want to resolve their dispute.

STRENGTHS AND WEAKNESSES OF ONLINE COMMUNICATION OPTIONS

In Chapter Two, the basic online communication options were presented as examples of some of the choices that need to be made by those designing or administering ODR processes. Existing ODR platforms put varying emphasis on each of these options. In this chapter we present an assessment of the strengths and weaknesses of each option, though the final decision is dependent on the types of disputes and the needs of the disputants in each ODR implementation.

Email

Email is the most common online communication option. Almost everyone has an email address these days, which makes its use easy to introduce to disputants. Using email for scheduling, brief contacts, or short questions may be appropriate and convenient. However, email is usually not adequate for supporting the substantive communications in ODR processes for several reasons.

1. Email is not secure. It is a relatively simple matter for someone to intercept the text of an email message that is sent unencrypted, as 99.5 percent of emails are. It is also extremely easy for email messages to be forwarded to others.

2. Email makes for a very disjointed conversation. It is unclear which parties have seen what messages, and it is difficult for a reasoned, measured conversation to take place in the chaos of people's inboxes.

3. Email may be adequate for sending short messages back and forth, but it is very difficult to effectively exchange documents. One side may have a word processing program the other doesn't have, or messages will cross and neither side will know which copy of the document is up to date.

Email definitely has its place, as it is the preferred means for person-to-person communication on the Internet. There is an immediacy and even an intimacy to email that people appreciate. Many people log on to the Internet every day to check mail, only bringing up their Web browser occasionally (maybe once or twice a week) if they are looking for a specific piece of information. Email's reach into people's lives makes it an indispensable tool for online interaction. But it is usually not rich enough or secure enough in and of itself to support more complex dispute resolution processes.

Chat

As we described in Chapter Two, chat is a Web tool that allows users to send messages to each other in real time. In chat you can see the other person type each character as they bang on their keys. This often leads to something of a race, as most people want the other side to be impressed with their typing speed (or at least not derisive about it).

The early ODR demonstrations at ADR Cyberweek were all chat demonstrations, and all of them were very confusing. It was unclear who was talking when, as everyone was typing all the time. Chat has some significant disadvantages:

- The person who types faster has the upper hand. If one party types at seventy-five words a minute and the other types at twenty-five words a minute, it's the equivalent of one side getting three words to every one word of their opponent. As a mediator, you are at a significant disadvantage if you type slower than one of your parties.

- People don't wait for responses. If a point is made, and you start responding to it with a long, carefully considered thought, the other party will send another message, and then another, while they're waiting for you to respond. By the time you're ready to click "send" to get your response back to them, it probably isn't relevant in light of the newer comments they've made. This creates an incentive to send lots of short messages in order to stay timely.

- Synchronous communication speeds up over time. People have more and more things they want to say, and the interface encourages them to make shorter and shorter comments, so they speed up. It is very difficult for mediators to combat this aspect of the technology.

- Chat encourages escalation. People are removed from the face-to-face, which already lowers their resistance to expressing anger and frustration. But when messages are coming fast and furious, and an off-handed comment is made that one side doesn't like the tone of, the chat interface encourages them to respond aggressively. It is easier to express an angry response in a short, clipped tone than to communicate that you've heard someone and that you understand what they're saying.

Like email, chat has its place, but it cannot be the basis for a full and satisfying dispute resolution process in most circumstances. Occasionally, however, when the mediator wants to caucus with one of the parties, or there is a discrete issue that all sides want to address in a timely fashion, chat can be very helpful. Chat is also useful when the parties are using the technology in real time, such as in a training or as a part of a face-to-face facilitation.

Instant Messaging

One of the hottest online applications these days is instant messaging. Programs like MSN and AOL's Instant Messenger have millions of users, and what was once used almost exclusively by teenagers and computer nerds is now increasingly used for business communications. Some even speculate that once the current standards war is resolved that IM has the potential to displace email as the most popular use of the Internet.

As discussed in Chapter Two, instant messaging is a cross between chat programs and email. Instead of writing a full message and sending it like a letter, as users of email do, IM encourages shorter messages. When the sender opens her instant messaging program and types a message, she specifies who she wants the message to reach and hits "send." Almost instantly a pop-up message appears on the target user's system informing him that he has an instant message, or the message might even pop right up on his screen. It is a simple matter to type a reply and send it, and the reply is seen instantly by the other side.

Instead of email's delayed communication, which encourages each side to draft longer messages, instant messaging is more like a conversation. The exchange is back-and-forth, so it's easy to ask questions and receive answers in the course of a communication.

Users of instant messaging programs have full control over how they want their messages displayed. They can inform their IM program that they are unavailable, and all of the other users on the Internet who have that user listed in their "buddy lists" will see an icon describing the user as unavailable. Some instant messaging programs actually track inactivity at the keyboard, like a screen saver. When there has been no activity for several minutes the user's status is updated to "away from the desk." You can easily see on your buddy list who is logged in at a particular time, who is actively working on their machine, and who is ready to receive an IM.

The good thing about IM programs is that they are not as invasive as the phone. Instead of having to stop doing whatever you're doing to respond to an IM you can ignore it for a few minutes and get around to answering when it is convenient. When the phone rings, especially in the workplace, you almost always have to stop working on what's in front of you to answer the phone call. Email also has a tendency to back up, as people send large quantities of information expecting that the recipient will get through it all. Anyone who has missed their email for a few days knows this phenomenon. Sometimes I feel as if my job is to respond to emails all day. Instant messaging provides a strong incentive for the sender to be brief, and there is no stigma about not responding to an instant messaging request.

While I was working for mediate.com we were all located in different areas of the country. However, we chatted with each other all day through ICQ, another popular instant messaging platform. It was as if we had a virtual water cooler where all of us could gather to discuss different items. Whenever we needed the answer to a particular question we could see who was available over ICQ and fire the query off to them. Usually we'd get an answer back in a matter of seconds, saving the cost of the phone call and allowing us to continue working on whatever we were focused on.

In experimentation with different IM platforms it became obvious that minor features often made big differences in sensitive communications like the ones that take place in a dispute resolution process. In ICQ there is no indication of the status of the message once it was sent. After the text was entered and the "send" button pushed the program simply disappeared down to the toolbar. The user was left waiting for something to happen, unsure if the message was received. The next thing that happened was the arrival of the reply.

The MSN platform has a different post-send process. Once the message is sent off there is an icon displaying the status of the message. It tells you if the message is still in the process of getting to the other user, when it was received, when it was opened (and presumably read), and when the other side is typing a reply.

This little feature, as innocuous as it may seem, makes a big difference in a sensitive communication process. Instead of feeling uneasy about the other side's reaction to a particular message, or maybe feeling stonewalled if a reply takes a long time, this feature gives some crucial information about what is happening with the other party. Similar attention to detail needs to be put into the design of ODR tools, as relatively minor features such as this one can mean a lot in keeping parties engaged, making them feel heard, and making them feel like progress is being made. Humans are hardwired to be very sensitive in face-to-face communication, looking for every detail and nuance so that they can understand what's really going on. In ODR the technology needs to account for that aspect of human interaction and provide information to fill that need of the disputants.

Discussion Forums

The vast majority of quality interaction that takes place in ODR processes happens in threaded discussions. Coming into a threaded discussion that is already full of contributions is like reading the transcription of a face-to-face dialogue. Issues are addressed, ideas traded, clarification requested, and everything is organized logically into separate threads and ideas. Discussion forums maximize the "cooling distance" of online interaction and encourage participants to express themselves in wholly formed ideas.

That said, some discussion forums can be confusing to users as message threads expand and reply is appended to reply. Parties often insist on using asynchronous discussion forums like chat environments, which can be very frustrating due to the delays in the back-and-forth message posting. For asynchronous, substantive communications discussion forums are the best fit, but for shorter conversations or synchronous interactions, chat or IM work better.

ODR TECHNOLOGY BEST PRACTICES

There are many things to take into consideration when putting together the technology for an ODR platform. Some of the best practices are given here and ordered chronologically based on when the suggestion would be relevant (for example, site-building options are first, supporting-user options are in the middle, and follow-up options are last).

Outsourcing versus Building It Yourself

Building ODR technology can be very expensive. Many people have had the experience of starting a technology project (for example, a website, spreadsheet, PowerPoint presentation, or even a company-wide database or intranet) only to find it balloon to the point where it's taking up far more time than was originally intended. Every user has one or two features that they'd really like to see integrated, and in attempting to make everyone happy the project becomes a full-time job. Many organizations seem convinced that the best choice would be to build a platform from the ground up to their personal specifications. They don't realize that the cost of building the technology is less than half of the total cost of managing it. Having your own technological platform is like owning an elephant; yes, you own it, but you still have to feed it every day and find a place for it to sleep at night. And every day the elephant gets a little older.

As ODR platforms evolve to the next level of their growth, including audio- and videoconferencing, ODR providers may be well-advised to not reinvent the wheel by writing these technologies from scratch. Leave that to the companies with hundreds of engineers and millions of dollars to burn through. In many cases outsourcing technology makes more financial sense, and it makes more sense in terms of what ODR providers really want to spend their time doing. That said, outsourcing doesn't generate any intellectual property rights, so there are compelling arguments for both models.

Accessibility Concerns

A key concern in the design of any ODR platform is bandwidth considerations. Many designers make the mistake of building their website on a machine with a fast connection to the Internet and they never test it on a machine that is using a 56k modem. Once they do test the platform, they realize that the delay in downloading complex graphics, images, and the like makes it almost unusable. Other designers go to the opposite extreme, relying only on text to get their message across, ignoring the power of a graphical user interface (GUI). ODR designers should aim to achieve the best of both worlds. Images should be used sparingly, as relying on a series of small icons is often as visually satisfying even though it takes less time to load. Use color extensively, particularly calming colors (like cool greens and blues) but use them as backgrounds instead of in large images. No website can skirt the bandwidth controversy in its entirety. You will always have users on fast connections asking for videoconferencing, and users on slow connections asking to cut down on the graphics. But being cognizant of the challenges can go a long way toward retaining users and resolving disputes.

Interface Design

The goal of any interface is to be intuitive and to empower the user to achieve what he or she wants to achieve. Over time interface design has come to have a technological meaning, implying computers and Web pages and the like, but interface design is all around us. It's in the dashboard of your car, the buttons on your clock radio, and the adjustments on your fancy desk chair. There is a newfangled microwave at my office in Cambridge that has a terrible interface design. I know it can do some amazing things, like cook a whole chicken in fifteen minutes, but for the life of me I can't figure out how to make the thing heat up a mug of water.

As explained in the previous chapter, making an interface that is really easy is often very hard. Good interfaces enable most people to instantly have a sense of what they need to do in order to make happen what they want to happen. It is easy to build an intuitive interface to do one or two things. The complexity comes when you want to build an interface that does dozens of sophisticated things but that still retains that intuitive quality.

Another goal of a good interface is that it is consistent. When a user puts the time into figuring out how to solve a problem in one context, ideally the problem will be solved in the same way in other contexts. GUIs such as those of the Macintosh and Windows operating systems are very strong in this regard. Once you learn how to cut and paste the text in your word processor you can use that skill in your email program, spreadsheet, and graphics editor.

Undoubtedly interfaces will continue to evolve, with speech recognition and other advances in computer-human interactivity. ODR platforms should put high priority on keeping up with these improvements, as intuitive and effective interface design is essential to effective ODR. The goal of interface designers for ODR platforms should be to get the technology out of the way quickly so that the parties and the neutral can focus on the issues in the dispute.

Data Security

A top priority in any dispute resolution process is confidentiality. The participants need to have absolute confidentiality from both the online dispute resolution service provider and whatever case managers may have access to their private information. In face-to-face processes, confidentiality concerns reside almost totally with the actions of the dispute resolution service provider. But in online processes confidentiality goes hand-in-hand with data security. Whatever technological platforms are provided for the parties to use in working out their disagreement need to be well protected against those who might try to compromise the data they contain. If a participant in a dispute resolution process suspects that his confidential information will not be adequately protected by the technology utilized by the online dispute resolution service provider, he will refuse to participate just as quickly as if he suspected the neutral was untrustworthy. State-of-the-art data protection, including encryption, secure servers, and strict password protocols are all important components of any effective online dispute resolution platform. Custodians of servers hosting online dispute resolution procedures must also commit themselves to consistent software updates and patches, as well as ongoing revenue expenditures devoted to the upgrade and maintenance of their site's security infrastructure.

Many users feel that security mechanisms are an annoyance until they are suspicious that their data has been compromised. Once that happens, they inevitably complain loudly about why security was not more robust. Many convenient technologies, such as email, instant messaging, and peer-to-peer programs are currently utilized for a wide variety of online applications. However, the security of these mechanisms is not always certain. Email in particular is extremely vulnerable to interception. Designers of online dispute resolution platforms must weigh the convenience factors against the need for security. One security violation in an online dispute resolution platform may be all it takes to undermine the users' confidence in that particular platform. Because of the often sensitive nature of the information shared in online dispute resolution procedures, system administrators must put the highest priority on top-level security and data protection.

Don't Just Replicate Face-to-Face Interaction

When designing or choosing on online dispute resolution platform, it is important to think outside the box so that the tools selected are not merely copying offline practice. Understanding the subtleties of asynchronous communication and having experience supporting disputants who are interacting asynchronously are essential to the effective operation of any online dispute resolution service or service provider. While it is fine to aim to integrate audio- and videoconferencing into the platform eventually, don't expect that the technology is robust enough to displace face-to-face meetings. The real benefits from ODR come from the new capabilities of the environment, and if designers simply mimic face-to-face processes online they will miss out on many of the benefits ODR can offer parties and neutrals.

Promoting ODR on a Website

In designing the website that will host the ODR service, it is important to follow a few design suggestions. First, make sure that the informational component of the website provides full disclosure about the tools, the neutrals, and the service provider as a whole. If at any point later in the process the disputants feel they weren't told something that was important, they will walk. Second, for e-commerce websites looking to integrate ODR into their services, don't hide this assurance on a page three clicks away from the homepage. The benefits won't be reaped if the notification of the availability of ODR is not announced on the top levels. Put a sidebar on the customer service page, put it in the privacy policy, or even put a little news item on the homepage. Choose the Web seals you subscribe to and display carefully. Sign up for a seal that has a broader trust-in-transactions connotation, as opposed to one that is focused on ODR only.

The Importance of Graphic Design

Strong graphic design is an important element of building Web confidence. Whether or not they know it, parties will evaluate the legitimacy of an ODR provider (or any website, for that matter) based on some very subtle elements in design. Web users are much like savvy television consumers, who can sense badly edited content or unprofessional photography in a heartbeat though they couldn't film or edit a video segment themselves. It is obvious when the designers of a website have put the money, work, and time into building a quality design, and users will put more trust into sites that fit that profile. Much like courthouses with marble columns out front and oak panels in the courtrooms, ODR websites need to communicate credibility and care. If a site is shoddy (badly designed, littered with misspellings, or seems awkward) users will lack confidence in the services provided there.

Maximize Ease of Use

Interfaces need to be intuitive. There's no way that a trainer can take a neutral through every step of every situation they will ever confront when using an ODR platform. The best thing to do is to put together a consistent user interface that always works in roughly the same way, so that when users get into new situations they can figure them out themselves by applying the understanding they've learned in other contexts. The temptation to cut corners in back-end technology is difficult to resist, especially when you have a tolerant user community anxious to get their hands on the latest features. Putting the time into creating context-sensitive help, consistent menus and buttons, and intuitive icons is important in building a platform that people will come to rely on over the long term. If the neutrals start spending all their time explaining to users how to delete this item or how to upload this document then the technology becomes self-defeating.

Build Systems Focused on Specific Dispute Types

The key to building an effective ODR environment is making "forums that fit the fusses." Each dispute has its own needs, and it's optimal to have different ODR processes that focus on those specific needs. Companies like SquareTrade are dealing with a particular kind of dispute, so they could ask very specific questions (such as, "What is your eBay case number?"). This also enables them to suggest particular solutions to users, with the knowledge that their suggestions will be relevant.

ODR platforms can leverage this specialization to increase efficiency. If you know you're going to be taking in family cases you should ask very different questions than if you're dealing with environmental disputes. Designing ODR systems that focus around particular dispute types leads to targeted information and satisfied parties.

Create a "Resolution-Focused" Mindset

ODR platforms should put the parties into a "resolution-focused" mindset. Normally complainants enter ODR processes very frustrated, at their wit's end about the dispute. Their orientation is usually win-lose, they are angry that they have been stonewalled, and they are anxious to have a third party take their side to force the other party into action. The ODR platform, beginning with the dispute intake form, should encourage the parties to think more holistically about the matter, to focus on the core problem under consideration, and to think about what they want to achieve through the dispute resolution process. Often a mediator needs to speak directly with a party to help them to go through this process, but technology can help to frame the matter by requiring the parties to consider some thought-provoking questions. These prenegotiation efforts often prove to be very important to the eventual successful resolution of a case because they set the tone for the discussion from the beginning.

The Use of Icons and the Desktop Metaphor

It is often very helpful to choose a familiar metaphor for website navigation. When parties visit a new site and see menu structures that they understand or graphics used in other programs it gives them a degree of comfort. Effective use of icons and faithful implementation of well-known desktop metaphors can shorten learning curves and make people comfortable with new technology in less time. For instance, the file metaphor used by most operating systems (Windows, Mac, UNIX) is readily intelligible to most users. Creating folders, putting items within folders, and throwing things out in the trash can have become very common and easy for users, even though that has very little to do with the way the underlying technology is working. Choosing established metaphors like these can save time by leveraging knowledge that most potential users already have.

Keep Track of New Content

One of the difficulties with online interaction is the rate at which content starts to grow. If you just have two people posting messages back and forth it's usually a fairly simple matter to stay on top of new messages on a daily or weekly basis, especially as the other side will likely not go on and on unless you respond to some of what they've posted. However, as anyone who's ever been part of an active listserv or newsgroup discussion can tell you, online discussions can sometimes get out of control. In face-to-face brainstorming sessions, where all of the participants have wireless networked laptops that they can use to submit ideas, I've seen two or three hundred ideas submitted from a group of twenty or thirty in less than five minutes. You could spend a full day going through that many ideas.

Online discussions work the same way. Because people can submit as many ideas as they care to, of whatever length, the amount of content can increase very quickly. That's why it's very important for the neutral to stay involved and manage the flow of the conversation. If a hot topic breaks out in the middle of a document, or in a file submission area, the neutral should move it to a more appropriate place quickly or it will immediately get beyond control.

Keeping users engaged with the online dispute resolution process is a challenge, because the ODR process has to compete with all of the other noise on the Internet and clutter in people's inboxes. Making the technology easy to get in and out of, and keeping track of what the user has read and what they haven't, helps to keep the ball rolling so that progress doesn't stall.

Daily Updates

Technology can assist in the achievement of constant communication. Daily notifications of new developments in the dispute resolution process, either by email or by IM, can help. Announcements displayed when the parties log into the ODR meeting space, perhaps triggered by different dates, can also give an impression that an ODR process is alive and making progress. To-do lists with daily, automated email reminders can also give incentive to the disputants by providing a gentle reminder that they have action items due.

Provide Tools to Support Textual Communication

Because so much communication in online dispute resolution is textual, it is very important to provide tools to help users of the system feel comfortable communicating only through words. Encourage users to take their time, to draft their comments and contributions carefully, and to be reflective in their communications.

Spell checking is important in online dispute resolution because it helps to level the playing field between the parties. Textual communication is dependent on words, and people's ability to spell varies wildly. I have had some professors over the years who were brilliant but they could barely put together a sentence, and their spelling would have failed them on most sixth-grade vocabulary tests. In a face-to-face, spoken context, spelling is almost irrelevant, but online spelling can make a big difference. Because there are no visual cues as to the person sitting across the (virtual) table from you it is easy to overemphasize the bits of information you do receive. If a posting from the other side is riddled with misspellings, even one or two, it is easy to jump to conclusions about that person's intelligence or problem-solving ability.

When the temptation is already high to dismiss the other side as unreasonable or uninformed, misspellings can easily tip the balance.

Spell checking tools are also very helpful to people not operating in their first language. Tools like spell checking functionality can often help those less comfortable with their spelling and grammar, and potentially avoid embarrassing situations where important communications are undermined by simple spelling, grammatical, or typing errors.

Caucus Spaces

One of the most powerful aspects of online interaction is the flexibility of caucusing. Caucuses enable neutrals to hold confidential conferences with each side in a dispute. Neutrals can be much more frank in a caucus than they might be in a joint session, pushing harder on particular points or reality-testing proposed resolutions. Caucuses can be effective tools for neutrals to get to the heart of the matters at hand because the other party is less concerned about saving face when the opposing side isn't present.

Many neutrals are conflicted about the appropriateness of caucusing. Some mediators I speak with say that they never caucus, because they fear that interacting with one party while the other isn't around will introduce some sense of bias or preference in favor of one side or the other. Others swear by the caucus, but always insisting that they give equal time to both sides.

A face-to-face caucus usually goes something like this. The mediator gets the sense that the discussion is running slightly off the rails and suggests that the process break into a caucus. If the parties agree, one party goes outside and stands in the hallway while the mediator and the other party chat inside. Once the mediator has finished raising the issues he or she wants to raise, or asking questions that can only be asked out of the presence of the other party, the parties switch places. The party in the hallway comes into the room for a chat, even if the mediator doesn't have any pressing issues to air with them, while the other party goes out into the hallway. Once they're done, usually with the same amount of time being devoted to each side to avoid the perception of bias, the parties reconvene. The mediator has to make clear to both sides that no confidential information from the caucus will ever be shared in the joint session without the owner's permission. Once the parties come back together the mediator needs to get things moving again, usually by asking if the parties had thought of anything new during the caucus.

The process is unwieldy, but it can occasionally yield a crucial breakthrough. Most mediators only use caucuses when things seem to be going badly, such as when the parties move backward into accusatory language and blaming. A caucus is a way to deescalate the rhetoric by giving people time to cool off.

Online caucusing works in a fundamentally different way. Because interaction in an ODR process is asynchronous, the caucuses can progress concurrently with the joint discussion. Such interaction is impossible in a face-to-face ADR process.

This concurrent caucusing ability is very powerful, because it lets the neutral caucus with both parties throughout the ODR process, instead of just when things go off the rails. Most neutrals don't have the experience of caucusing when things are going well in the dispute res-olution process. Usually there is a need to caucus with one party more than the other, which is made very complex by the requirement of equal time allotted to both parties. In an ODR process, because one party has no sense of how much time is being spent with the other party, a neu-tral can spend as much time as he or she likes working with the party that might require more confidential attention from the neutral. One party might not share more than five words in caucus with the neutral, whereas the other party may spend hours discussing items and strate-gizing the most effective way to communicate.

Technology needs to support this concurrent caucusing capacity in a seamless way. Neutrals and disputants should be able to easily keep track of which discussion area they are in, so that they don't acci-dentally post a message intended for a private caucus into a joint dis-cussion, and vice versa. Navigating between the caucus and the joint sessions should be a one-click affair, as too complex a navigation scheme will discourage participants. Also, the parity in the availabil-ity of caucus spaces should be played up, so that both sides are aware of their ability to communicate privately with the neutral, and so that later there are no accusations of unfairness because one side or the other did not know about the existence of the caucus.

Version Tracking

Many lawyers currently use Microsoft Word's version tracking fea-ture for sending documents back and forth with other counsel. This feature enables users to see the language of prior drafts of a document, usually crossed out with a line and displayed in a different color, alongside the new language being suggested by the other side.

In a negotiation this process is particularly important, as it is almost impossible to keep track of all of the different discussion points currently at play in any given agreement. Word makes this process easier, but by no means foolproof. For instance, it's not always clear which document on a user's hard drive is the most updated copy. A Word document might indicate the changes from one iteration to the next, but it can't keep track of the changes through six or seven iterations. It's also a little frightening to think through what changes are being tracked in your document even though you may not have version tracking turned on. We received a non-disclosure agreement (NDA) from a potential partner about a year ago and turned on "track changes" just for curiosity, and we saw all of the ways they had strengthened their NDA just for our partnership. We also saw some of the terms they had offered to their other partners.

Version tracking is particularly useful in document-based, single-text negotiation procedures. Some companies like Beachfire have built extremely sophisticated version tracking programs that can be used by teams of lawyers in contract development. While a tool of that magnitude may be overkill, simple version tracking can often be very helpful to disputants. It is a good example of how technology can simplify tasks that can be very complicated and aggravating offline.

Using an Online Calendar

Another aspect of online communication is the different interpretations of silence. In a face-to-face interaction, if someone isn't responding to you, you can look at their expression to see if you're being ignored or if they're simply thinking about what you've said. There are no such cues online. If someone doesn't respond to your message, most people interpret that silence as stonewalling. Silence is usually taken in the worst way, so a lack of responsiveness feels passive aggressive to the person waiting for the next communication.

A calendar helps to address this dynamic by allowing parties to specify when they'll be available and unavailable at the beginning of a process. If one party makes it clear that they're going to be out of town on vacation over a particular weekend then the delay in their responses through that period is much easier for the other party to accept.

Neutrals can do the same, helping to set party expectations for what days or even hours may turn into crunch times. If the neutral wants to set up a time for a synchronous discussion, either through chat or over the phone, the calendar makes setting a time and date much easier.

Outside Links

An important difference between synchronous and asynchronous communication is the ability for the parties to access outside information. In a face-to-face dispute resolution process it is very difficult to put the process on hold so that you can conduct some research. Many mediators repeatedly state through the process that the parties are not there to debate about facts as much as to come up with a resolution that both sides can accept. But facts are inevitably part of building sustainable agreements, and if information accepted in a face-to-face dispute resolution process turns out to be false then the viability of the agreement can be threatened.

Asynchronous interaction makes fact-checking much easier. Because a response is not expected immediately, and because all of the resources on the Web are available to online dispute resolution parties, it is a simple matter to verify facts or statistics presented by the other side. For example, if the other party asserts that the book value of a car was $5,000, it is a simple matter to log into a car valuation website (such as Kelly's Blue Book) to get an unbiased, third-party assessment of what the car's actual book value might be.

As an example, UDRP domain name dispute resolution decisions are required to take prior UDRP decisions into account. There are several resources on the Internet that enable UDRP panelists to conduct full-text searches on all the prior decisions. In a domain name dispute resolution process, links to those websites can be dropped directly into the online environment, enabling all of the parties to consult prior decisions. In a face-to-face process this type of instant access to information can be difficult to provide.

Full-Text Search and Document Management

Once a dispute resolution process gets going it starts to generate content immediately. Even experienced Internet surfers can forget where they saw a particular comment or which document contains the reference that they need. Full-text search capability is often invaluable to participants. This is especially useful in multiparty disputes that involve lots of documents. The rate at which a room fills up is in direct proportion to the number of users it contains, and multiparty disputes produce content very quickly. If users do not log into the room at least once a day it is easy to get behind in the discussion.

At later stages of a dispute this function is also valuable because parties frequently want to refer to prior elements of the discussion. Once several dozen messages have been posted, finding a particular element can be very challenging. Full-text search puts all of the information that has been gathered in the dispute at the fingertips of the parties so that they can use it most effectively to move the discussion forward.

Many hybrid dispute resolution processes utilize the online component exclusively for document management. Because online file folders can ensure that every participant always is using the most updated version of the document, they can generate significant efficiencies for dispute resolution processes where the parties meet face-to-face for every discussion. Full-text search capabilities are an essential component of effective document management environments.

Building Feedback Loops

Feedback is one of those things that is often paid a lot of lip service but is usually overlooked and taken for granted (much like effective conflict management). Of the dozens and dozens of websites I have put together over the years more than half have put a "feedback" button somewhere in the navigation tree. Usually the button is connected to a Web form that just kicks out an email with the feedback to some pre-defined address. When the user clicks "submit," she gets a nice page thanking her for the feedback and then she gets dumped back at the homepage. If she's lucky, maybe someone will read her feedback before it is deleted. If she's unlucky, she may never hear anything or see any action in response to her comment.

Feedback in the ODR context is much more important than in other online contexts, like e-commerce or entertainment. The ability to systematically gather and aggregate feedback from users is a major advantage ODR has over face-to-face ADR.

The reputation of individual neutrals in the face-to-face dispute resolution field is compiled in a remarkably haphazard way. There are no official ratings guides to mediators and arbitrators where prospective parties can examine other users' opinions of the services they received. Often when someone remarks that they've heard that a particular neutral is skilled, they can't remember precisely who told them that or what the opinion was based upon. This isn't to say that the conventional wisdom isn't accurate, just that it's developed in a fairly random and unplanned way.

The technological focus of ODR enables systemic feedback collection and aggregation in a much more effective and efficient manner. At the close of a process, regardless of whether it was successful or not, the neutral and the parties should all be given an opportunity to provide feedback on the specific dispute process, the performance of the neutral, and the overall platform. This information can be gathered textually, in open-ended forms that allow for specific comments and suggestions, but ideally there will also be ranges the parties can choose from, such as:

How responsive was the mediator in this dispute?
(1) unacceptable (2) unsatisfactory (3) adequate (4) good (5) excellent

How satisfied were you with this process?
(1) very dissatisfied (2) dissatisfied (3) neutral (4) satisfied (5) very satisfied

With this information, the technology can aggregate this feedback into useful statistics. For instance, neutral feedback on a variety of different performance measurements (such as politeness, responsiveness, effectiveness) can be aggregated from all the disputes that neutral has administered. This rating information can be posted on the disclosure pages of all the panelists. This information helps future parties choose effective neutrals and provides a strong incentive for neutrals to maintain parties' satisfaction with their performance.

This feedback can also enable the ODR platform designers to engage in continuous improvements in its service offerings. Gathering suggestions and responses from users provides the platform designers with information from the audience's perspective. It doesn't matter how well a site works for an administrator if the site is difficult for the users, because very soon the administrator will be managing a site no one is visiting. User feedback processes that are given resources and attention can help ODR providers keep their focus in the right place, on the experience of their users, which will result in better customer loyalty and satisfaction over the long term.

Data Archiving

Information archiving is one of the key advantages of online interaction. Instead of having to mail copies of documents to several different parties, or constantly having to fax updates and changes to agreements, ODR can enable parties to have access to all of their most updated information in one convenient location.

Once an ODR process ends, however, there is a question as to what to do with all of the accumulated information. Some of it will likely be of a sensitive nature, and the parties might want to ensure that it can no longer be accessed by anyone. In that case, it is a simple matter to close the room and to permanently delete all of the information contained in it. If the parties request that option, it is easily carried out. Permanent deletion at the end of a process should be the default option in ODR procedures.

However, if the parties wish to keep the data available for future consultation, they can jointly request that the information be saved on the ODR platform's servers. The data is probably not accessible once it is archived, but upon request, the service provider should be able to reopen it and make it available to the parties. Service providers should also think about the liability exposure that could come from such a data retention strategy.

Conclusion

Technology plays a central role in ODR procedures and processes. It can get in the way or it can help parties reach agreement. The technology utilized by dispute resolution professionals should not be an afterthought, cobbled together in an unplanned way. Ineffective technology is much worse than no technology at all, and neutrals need to understand the strengths and weaknesses of whatever technology platform they introduce to their parties. For ODR technology to be worth the effort, it needs to have been well designed by the platform builder, well utilized by the dispute resolution service provider, and well understood by the parties. If those standards are met the contribution of the technology can be invaluable.

CHAPTER FIFTEEN

Defining the Process
Setting Standards of Practice

‑‑‑‑‑‑

I n offline dispute resolution processes, parties sometimes ask what concrete skills and tools a third-party neutral brings
to a negotiation to help reach an agreement. The most concrete tool
a third party brings is a process for resolving the dispute. A map of an
overall ADR process may be what is necessary to focus the discussion
so that a resolution is possible. The neutral is often the custodian of
the process, bringing parties back onto the agenda if they start to slip
away. Designing an effective process and presenting it clearly to the
parties at the beginning is often the most important contribution a
dispute resolution service provider can make. What happens within
the process is up to the participants, but the overall process is the
responsibility of the neutral.

A well-designed process is equally important in online dispute resolution. Understanding the people issues (Chapter Thirteen) is vital,
and designing and deploying effective technology (Chapter Fourteen)
is also crucial to effective ODR. But articulating a fair, clear process is
often the most significant contribution a dispute resolution program
or neutral can make toward helping disputants reach agreement.

Standards of practice lay out the key concerns in developing effective and fair online dispute resolution processes. Standard-setting bodies rarely focus on people issues or technology issues. Their recommendations almost always focus on process concerns. Any designer of an ODR program should be cognizant of the different standards that have been issued around the world so that they can ensure their program meets or exceeds any guidelines that might be used to evaluate it. This chapter goes through some of the major process concerns faced by ODR system designers and then details the major standards of practice recommendations that have been issued for ODR.

ELEMENTS OF ODR PROCESSES

It is of utmost importance that ODR processes be clear to both the neutrals and the disputants if they are to be effective. If the neutral has not done his or her homework and is uncomfortable with the dispute resolution process, moving the parties toward a successful resolution will be difficult. Disputants often look to the neutral for guidance in following a particular process, so the neutral must be able to demonstrate confidence in the process if the parties are to focus on the goal.

In face-to-face dispute resolution it is relatively easy to change the process midstream, because everything rests in the hands of the neutral. In online dispute resolution this is not always the case. Because the process is often built into the technology ahead of time it is often much harder to be innovative and spontaneous in changing a process in the middle of a session. This can be an advantage as well, because parties may agree to a particular technology-driven process at the outset and may not have as much of an ability to sidetrack the discussion. If the process is "hard wired" into the system then it's harder to derail.

Opening Statements and Ground Rules

In a face-to-face dispute resolution process most of the information about how the process will progress is presented during the neutral's opening statement. These opening statements are usually prepared ahead of time and memorized, and they cover lots of points that need to be discussed before the dispute resolution process is begun. For instance, many neutrals inform their parties that if they learn of any criminal activity during the dispute resolution process they will be compelled to report that activity to the authorities. Putting this up front, no matter how unlikely a discussion of criminal activity may appear to be in a particular matter, insulates the neutral should such information be presented. The neutral is better protected because a clear warning was expressed in the ground rules before the process even began. Many of the other elements of ground rules are less legalistic, such as the unacceptability of insulting language, the confidentiality of the process, and information about caucusing. Usually these rules are presented, the parties are given an opportunity to ask questions about them, and then the parties agree to abide by them.

In an ODR, much of this information can be gleaned from the ODR provider's website before a dispute is ever initiated. There may be ground rule language that is injected automatically into an ODR process at the beginning of the online discussion. Also, parties can be asked to specifically check a box saying that they agree to the ground rules, which may be useful later should there be a dispute about what the ground rules said and did not say.

Ground rules also play an important role in setting the expectations of the disputants and creating a sense of due process. Neutrals must make their role very clear and lay out the process in detail at the outset. Parties expect that they will be treated fairly and with respect. They come into an ODR process with certain expectations, usually based on information they received from the neutral, from the case manager, and things that they read on the ODR service provider's website or in the bio for the neutral. If they feel that they agreed to a certain type of process and then are surprised about something that arises midstream they may feel betrayed and decide to abandon the discussion or invalidate their commitment to abide by the outcome. This tendency to walk can be further magnified if they sense they are not going to have a favorable outcome from the ADR process. Clear, well thought-out ground rules that delineate the process in detail can help to address these concerns so that problems do not arise later.

Participant Responsibilities

Not all of the responsibilities in an ODR process fall on the neutral. The parties must also be aware of their obligations should they agree to participate in an ODR process. They have an obligation to log on to the Internet frequently, and they must inform the neutral and the other side should they become unable to log on. They must participate in good faith, exerting their best effort to reach agreement. They should also understand that the neutral is not going to be able to give them personal legal advice during the course of the process and that they need to get that advice from another source.

Making the details of the particular dispute resolution process clear to participants at the outset is also an important disclosure obligation. Parties need to understand that their mediator does not have decision-making power or that they are bound by the decision of their arbitrator. The process should make sure that all of these particulars are clearly understood by the participants before the process begins. Participants should also be informed of the protocol for withdrawing from a process or requesting a new neutral from the case administrator.

Many mediators have their parties sign an Agreement to Mediate or Arbitrate, which lays out many of the responsibilities of participants and requires a firm commitment from the parties to abide by them. It is easy for such an agreement to be implemented online and for the parties to be required to affirmatively represent that they understand and agree to all of their obligations in the process.

Privacy and Confidentiality

The process must build in assurances that private information will be kept private. Explaining how data is protected during the process, and how it will be treated after the process is finished, is an essential component of putting the parties at ease. The confidentiality of the process should be emphasized, along with assurances about the mediator's insulation from being subpoenaed to testify in a court proceeding (presuming the relevant law is clear, based on the locations of the participants—if the law is unclear in this regard it may be worthwhile to explain that to the parties as well).

There is also the option of having the parties sign a confidentiality agreement at the beginning of the process. In particularly sensitive matters a step like this can put the parties more at ease and increase the chance that the substantive issues will be addressed.

Public Disclosure versus Private Disclosure

One of the earliest process decisions any ODR provider needs to make is whether they plan to keep the resolutions achieved through their program private or public. On one hand, keeping all resolutions private maximizes the confidentiality the ODR provider can offer its clients. It encourages parties to bring sensitive and timely matters into ODR, because they can be sure their secrets will not make it into the public. On the other hand, there is arguably a "public good" consideration involved with keeping decisions confidential. If decisions are not released then it is much harder for outside organizations to determine whether or not an ODR system is providing a level playing field for the resolution of disputes. Bias can go undetected and uncorrected if there is no possibility of outside involvement.

Arbitration systems have traditionally been more open with decisions than non-binding systems like mediation, because of the legal precedent and because concerns about bias and conflict of interest are much more pronounced. Blind-bidding systems have kept outcomes private across the board, mostly because the industry is seen as an extension of traditional negotiation.

Orna Rabinovich-Einy has argued that the transparency inherent in the Internet will likely lead to more mediation outcomes becoming public over time.[1] The consumer advocacy groups subscribe to this perspective, because they are very concerned about the potential closed ODR programs have to systematically create disadvantages for individual consumers. Businesses have shown a clear affinity for the other side, as confidential outcomes to disputes help to mitigate copycat claims that arise from one or two complaints getting a sizable settlement.

There are other options that may assuage the concerns of both sides. Resolutions can be made public, but with the identities of the parties concealed. This allows observers to monitor the decisions in attempt to root out any bias, while still preserving the confidentiality of the parties. However, this solution opens up many new practice challenges for the provider. The identities need to be changed enough so that the case can never be traced back to the participants, but the transcript needs to have enough accurate information in it to allow readers to get a sense of what the real issues were in the case.

STANDARDS FOR ODR

Any ODR process should take into account the many standards recommendations that have been issued regarding quality ODR since 1999. With the prospect of rapid expansion of ODR, many governments, multinational organizations, and advocacy groups have expressed a concern that ODR services will be shoddy, biased, and ineffective. As a result, these organizations have issued standards for ODR service provision in droves.

Some of the organizations that have compiled standards for ODR service providers include: the Organization for Economic Cooperation and Development; the G-8; the European Union; agencies in the United States government, as well as those of Australia, Canada, Japan, and New Zealand; the International Chamber of Commerce; the Better Business Bureau; the Global Business Dialogue on e-Commerce; and the Trans-Atlantic Consumer Dialogue (TACD). The international consensus that ODR is an important part of the future of the Web is very well established, as so many international organizations and agencies have weighed in on its behalf. But it appears that most cannot resist detailing their sense of how ODR providers should operate.

As discussed in Chapter Five, almost all of these standard-setting efforts in ODR have focused on B2C e-commerce. This is largely because:

- There is a clear need for redress in B2C e-commerce transactions.

- Existing legal infrastructure does not adapt well to cover these types of transactions.

- There is a major power disparity between the parties.

- ODR often encroaches on legal rights, such as due process and right to trial.

- It is difficult for consumers to get accurate information about ODR and ODR providers.

- There is the potential for abuse of ODR systems by repeat players.

Some of the standard-setting efforts have extended their purview beyond B2C e-commerce, such as the CPR e-commerce initiative or the American Arbitration Association's protocol. The intensive analysis surrounding the ICANN process has also looked beyond B2C e-commerce, concerning itself with other important issues such as free speech and rule of law. Most governmental and non-profit efforts have come back to B2C e-commerce, though, as that seems to be the primary concern of businesses, consumer groups, and legislatures.

One of the ironies of many of these ODR standard-setting initiatives is that the dispute resolution field has largely been absent from the development of these standards. The ADR field has been slow to get off the mark. The Association for Conflict Resolution has convened an online section, and the American Arbitration Association and CPR Institute for Dispute Resolution have issued statements on e-commerce ADR, but no organization has made a strong push into the ODR area. The existing initiatives have been started and run by entrepreneurs, large non-profit organizations, and international organizations. The dispute resolution field has been largely absent from the discussions held by these organizations and institutions around how these new ODR systems should work.

It is easy to get lost in all of these different standards documents, or to start arguing about which wordings are more accurate. Often the concepts in the different standards documents are the same, even if they are slanted slightly differently based on the issuer's constituency.

Focusing on ODR Providers Instead of Individual Panelists

The interesting thing about the current standards discussion for ODR service provision is that it focuses on the administrative organizations instead of the individual mediators and arbitrators. The main face-to-face ADR administrative organizations like the American Arbitration Association, JAMS, and NAF aren't the focus of dozens of global standard-setting bodies putting requirements and constraints on how dispute resolution services should be offered. The real power rests in the hands of the individual neutrals, so there isn't much call for strict regulation and accreditation of the administrative bodies.

ICANN's Uniform Domain Name Dispute Resolution Program is an excellent example of this. All the debate about UDRP reform focuses on the ICANN system, the approved service providers, and the forum shopping problem. Rarely does anyone talk about panelist education, quality standards for all UDRP neutrals, or standards for UDRP practice for neutrals.

The real reason for the focus on the administrators is that in ODR it's much harder to pin down all of the individual neutrals. Panelists could be anywhere in the world, subject to a wide variety of different laws and jurisdictions. In response, the real press for regulation and standards in the online context has focused on the ODR service providers. They usually have a single office, with a single management structure, and they can be held accountable should things go awry. They also have a single Web page where they make representations about policies and procedures. A standard-setting body might be able to examine all of the major ODR service providers in the world, but they have no hope of examining all the possible panelists around the world.

Examining International ODR Standard-Setting Efforts

The best analysis of existing ODR standard-setting efforts was performed by Alan Wiener in 2001. His primer for policymakers and stakeholders, entitled "Regulations and Standards for Online Dispute Resolution," was the first synthesis of all the worldwide standard-setting efforts into a single document. Much of the analysis and compilation he conducted for that document informs this chapter.

Overall, governments have largely come out in favor of online dispute resolution in the B2C context. Governments overall tend to prefer dispute resolution, as it helps to ensure continued stability for societies without the expense of time and resources required by litigation. Statements by the United States government, for instance, are clear on their support for ODR. The Justice Department's report to the president in winter 2001 sang the praises of ODR efforts being conducted by groups like the Better Business Bureau and encouraged further deployment. The Federal Trade Commission and Department of Commerce issued a variety of statements in the wake of their June 2000 conference indicating that online dispute resolution should be the default means of providing redress in B2C e-commerce. However, the government has stopped short of referring cases to ODR providers or endorsing any one provider because of bias concerns.

Self-Regulation versus Government Oversight

The regulatory approach to the deployment of ODR has been very hands-off. Both in Europe and the United States, government agencies seem to be content with "self-regulation," in which industry is encouraged to build ODR into business processes but is not required to do so. Programs promoting this type of self-regulation (such as codes of conduct, trustmarks, reliability programs, and so on) have grown slowly but steadily over the past few years.

This self-regulation approach is preferred by business, for obvious reasons. Most businesses are anxious to avoid additional regulations.

Taking a cue from the government, many businesses have been very proactive in promoting ODR. An understanding has grown within the business world that the only way e-commerce will be successful is if it is trusted by consumers, and this has led to a variety of efforts to build confidence. Trade associations and industry groups have repeatedly issued standards for e-commerce companies that urge the adoption of trust-building measures like ODR.

Businesses often support the application of ODR to B2C disputes, but they want government to avoid getting involved. The attitude in the business world is that the market will provide adequate incentive to put these programs in place and to make sure that they are efficient and effective. Businesses mostly want to implement ODR programs to shield them from liability and court proceedings. As has been discussed previously in this book, many businesses are interested in binding arbitration with their consumers and business partners for exactly this reason. The fear of financial exposure in court is a formidable one. The fear of class action lawsuits is also formidable.

Consumer groups usually assert that consumers should have at least the same amount of protection in online transactions that they enjoy in offline transactions. They point out the significant potential for abuse of ODR processes by business and industry in the absence of strict supervision. Consumer advocacy groups are much more willing to entertain the possibility of government intervention in setting and enforcing ODR standards. Most consumer groups are steadfast in their demand that consumers must retain access to court.

Even if ODR programs are not binding, many businesses want them to be a mandatory stage in any escalating dispute. Consumer groups argue that the reason why businesses want ODR to be a mandatory step is that it provides an additional step in the process that might dissuade some consumers from escalating their complaint.

Transparency

A common baseline standard that appears in almost every discussion of ODR is transparency. One of the reasons why government, judiciaries, and consumer groups are frightened by the possibility of widespread ODR is the power that ODR processes will come to yield. If consumers lose their ability to obtain redress in a public forum like a court, and they are forced instead to have a hearing in a private dispute resolution process, there is significant vulnerability. If the private process is influenced by systemic fraud (or just by incompetent service providers), or if the door is kept shut and outsiders are not allowed to see what resolutions were made (and how they were achieved), then there is potential for abuse.

Transparency enters into dispute resolution in two different ways. On the front end, parties need to understand what they're getting involved in. The process needs to be completely transparent so that the disputants don't feel that they've been pushed into a process that they didn't fully understand. Due process is a crucial component of effective dispute resolution, and if a party ever feels surprised by an element of the process there is a risk that they will feel they were inadequately informed and lose confidence in the system.

On the back end, it is also important to have transparency in ODR processes for outside observers. While the parties may want confidentiality in their matter, it is nevertheless important to allow outsiders to get a sense of several things:

- What types of disputes are being handled by the ODR service?
- What mechanisms are being used to handle them?
- Who is acting as a neutral in these cases?
- What resolutions are being reached (either in mediations, during which the parties craft the outcomes, or in arbitrations, in which the neutrals decide the outcomes)?

Having this information will increase the confidence of outside organizations that the ODR process is functioning smoothly and ethically. If the process is operated as a black box, where outsiders see matters come in and see resolutions come out, parties and observers will increasingly become skeptical about the program, assuming that it has something to hide. This lost credibility will translate into a decreasing caseload over time.

Some standards, like the TACD guidelines, go as far as to require that ODR providers report their cases to a publicly accessible central clearinghouse. Many dispute resolution service providers are reluctant to go that far, as they are concerned about the confidentiality of their parties and they don't want to cede control of their data to a central clearinghouse. If confidentiality is removed, they reason, a major benefit of online and offline dispute resolution processes is gone.

Additionally, some providers are very confident that their process is fair, while outsiders might misinterpret the process outcomes. For some categories of disputes, fairness does not mean that the decisions are split fifty-fifty between complainants and respondents. The National Arbitration Forum was the focus of a story in the *Washington Post* in 1999 that revealed that the forum's decisions went more than 70 percent of the time in favor of the business interest.[2] Many critics took that statistic to mean that the process was biased in favor of the businesses. However, many of the cases taken on by NAF dealt with unpaid credit card bills. These cases are not "pure" disputes, meaning a genuine misunderstanding between two well-intentioned parties. Many of these cases were essentially collections matters. No observer would argue that of all the cases of unpaid bills, 50 percent of cases should result in a win for the credit card company and 50 percent should result in a win for the credit card owner. Many dispute categories are subjective in this way. What should the "correct" resolution percentage be? The confusion over this number is one of the reasons why ODR and ADR providers are often reluctant to provide this type of full disclosure.

Accessibility

The Better Business Bureau supports a dispute resolution program called Autoline, which is intended to help resolve disputes that arise over the sales of cars. It is required by law that every auto dealer in the country put up a public notice advertising the availability of this service. The next time you're in a car dealership, walk around and look for the notice. Often it's hidden in an area where customers rarely go, or listed at the bottom of a brochure that consumers rarely read. Auto dealers don't want to advertise the availability of the program because they worry it will put their customers into the wrong mindset (problem-focused as opposed to optimistic) and that it will lead consumers to think that disputes are more likely.

As Marc Galanter has observed, the vast majority of disputes in the United States are essentially just given up.[3] The parties with the grievance often just decide it makes more sense for them to just "lump it" and take the loss in the dispute rather than hassle with the work necessary to resolve the dispute. Because our society doesn't have many resolution options for low-level disputes, consumers frequently decide that their claim isn't that important because they have no place to voice it. Once a forum is provided, however, the ephemeral grievance becomes a real dispute. One of the ways parties are encouraged to give up is through the institution of a series of hoops a consumer has to jump through in order to obtain redress. If ODR becomes a mandatory step in obtaining redress, for instance, a certain number of parties will look at the work required to get through the ODR process and just decide to give up.

Accessibility is about providing an easy-to-utilize venue for customers and disputants to initiate should a dispute arise. Convenience is a major component of accessibility, as is cost of the service. If a company requires its customers to utilize a third-party dispute resolution mechanism should they have a complaint, and the rules and requirements for that mechanism are ornate and obtuse, that ODR process will not be very accessible.

It is also important to note that ODR has many accessibility benefits that face-to-face ADR cannot match. Convening penalties (geographic distance, cost to travel, and so on) are probably the largest obstacles to accessibility. The IRS just began several fast-track mediation programs around the country to resolve tax-based disputes. However, they are located in only sixteen places, so many taxpayers have a long drive if they want to make use of the program. ODR removes this geographic barrier, which may result in individuals deciding to pursue their complaint whereas before they didn't think it would be worth the effort.

Cost to Consumers

There is a great debate in dispute resolution about who should bear the price for the service. On one hand, parties should have as low a barrier to entry with the dispute resolution process as possible, to give them an incentive to participate. Too low a barrier, though, encourages frivolous claims and can end up wasting money on a few squeaky-wheel customers who complain constantly about minor matters. On the other hand, charging a party money to make a claim can make them feel like they have a stake in the outcome of the process, so they will take the process more seriously. If all the costs are borne by one side in a dispute (such as a merchant) then there might be an implication of bias in that process. The neutral (and, by extension, the ODR provider) will have an incentive to take care of the business interest because that is where the case referrals are coming from.

Ideally the cost for a dispute resolution process should be enough that each party feels some ownership of the matter, and it should be split evenly between the two sides. It should also be low enough that it does not become a barrier to participation. What is reasonable or unreasonable depends on the monetary value of the dispute, the parties involved, and the cost of the process to the provider.

Quick Decisions

Many disputants come to an ODR or ADR provider because they want to get a quick resolution to their dispute. Speed is often the first thing new parties will mention when asked why they decided to use dispute resolution. Unfortunately, some dispute resolution procedures have become so laden with procedure that they aren't much quicker than a traditional redress process. When a system designer is primarily concerned with procedural fairness, or is scrupulous about doing everything with maximum transparency, the dispute resolution process can slow to a crawl. In fact, some dispute resolution service providers use slow processes to urge their parties to reach resolution.

Standard-setting bodies often try to combat these tendencies by putting in time limits to keep the process moving forward. For example, one Canadian ODR service provider guarantees an outcome in forty days. By programming time limits into the operation of the system parties can be well informed on the front end of a process how long the matter will take to resolve. Otherwise parties can become frustrated by slow-moving procedures that don't appear to be making much progress.

Independence

Dispute resolution service providers need to set their own rules. If an ODR provider is too closely tied to a particular organization or constituency there is a risk that their impartiality will be questioned. The procedural decisions on both a system design level and on a case-by-case level need to be made with the needs of the parties as the sole motivation. If an ODR provider begins to enter too close a relationship with any one organization then they are not truly independent. ODR providers should stay focused on the needs of their customers, but they should not get so close to their customers that it shifts their focus from ethical dispute resolution. If a dispute resolution service is funded by an organization that may have a particular preference to outcome, for example, that can lead to an impression of bias. If a service is physically hosted in office space adjacent to organizations that might have a preference as to outcomes, then that can lead to perceived bias as well. To a large degree perception is reality in establishing the independence of an ODR service provider.

Neutrality and Impartiality

While independence refers to the decision-making of the overall ODR service provider, these two terms usually refer to the individual panelists assigned by the service provider to work one-on-one with the parties. *Impartiality* and *neutrality* are often used interchangeably, but they have very specific meanings in the context of dispute resolution. Neutrality is regarded by many in the ADR field as unattainable. No person is truly neutral. One can aspire to be neutral, but it is inevitable that once any information is exchanged neutrality is impossible. Humans always form opinions, and that is important to acknowledge honestly.

Impartiality is a more attainable goal. Even if the person acting as the third party forms an opinion about a matter it should not make her partial to one party or the other. Partiality implies an inappropriate bias toward one side or the other. Third parties should always avoid this type of bias, as it can affect their ability to work effectively with the parties to resolve the dispute.

ODR providers should work to ensure that the panelists they assign to work with the parties are impartial in the services they deliver. This involves more obvious inappropriate connections between the panelist and the dispute (say if the husband of an arbitrator assigned to a dispute used to work for a company that is involved in the matter) as well as less obvious partiality (a mediator assigned to a dispute believes that one of the parties is representing a shoddy company that frequently defrauds its customers). Striving to maintain impartiality in the services delivered to parties is an ongoing challenge, requiring introspection and constant internal evaluation. Such an effort is central to the task of providing quality dispute resolution services.

In this book I have used the word "neutral" to describe the role of an individual who is playing the dispute resolution role in a particular dispute. That term best describes the role of a mediator, arbitrator, evaluator, facilitator, or any other dispute resolver. However, it should not imply that the person playing that role is not allowed to have an opinion, or that he must remain a blank slate without any opinions. Ideally the person in this role will come to the process without any preconceptions that might impede his ability to function as an effective third party in a dispute. During the dispute resolution process he should strive to avoid inappropriate bias toward either side. I use the word "neutral" not as an implication that the person playing the role of the third party is to be a Zen master free from any opinion or thought on the matters at hand. (For more information, see Chapter Thirteen.)

Qualifications of ADR Panelists

One of the best ways to ensure that the services provided by your ODR platform remain impartial is to get top quality ADR practitioners on your panel. Parties are more comfortable participating in a dispute resolution process that is headed up by someone with obvious experience and qualifications. Hiring top-quality panelists with extensive experience is usually the most important factor in building a successful ODR platform.

One prominent ODR company considered having its neutrals deliver services anonymously. Instead of having real names presented on the system the parties would see "neutral0164" or some such identification. This company wanted to displace the "star system" in which certain high-profile neutrals were asked for again and again by disputants. They thought the credibility of the overall platform would be enough to move the parties toward resolution.

It is very hard to see how such a system would work. So much of the dispute resolution process comes from the connection between the neutral and the parties that if there was an attempt to hide the identity of the neutral third party behind a generic ID it would make it even harder to achieve the connection necessary to really make progress in a dispute.

The exact opposite makes more sense. Provide full bios on all panelists, publicly available to parties and observers, and as soon as a case is begun a link to the background information on the assigned panelist is available to the parties. Beginning a case from the standpoint of established, proven experience is often the best way to start the resolution process off on the right foot.

Voluntariness

Dispute resolution is a voluntary process. In non-binding processes like mediation and negotiation the only reason that a party is participating is because she wants to participate and sees it as being in her best interest. If ever she feels that the process is not what she expected, or if she doesn't see things going the way she wants them to go, she has the right to quit. The voluntary nature of dispute resolution is essential to getting parties involved in the process and obtaining their buy-in to any resolution that is reached.

Everyone acknowledges that dispute resolution must be voluntary, but this standard is subject to some debate among the different standard-setting bodies. There are differences of opinion about where voluntariness enters into the process. Some standard-setting bodies might argue that binding arbitration is voluntary at the time the initial contract is signed, but it's just not voluntary after that initial point. Others might argue that participation in an ODR process can be mandatory, even if the participants ultimately have veto power over the outcome.

ODR service providers need to understand that every time they force their parties into a process they do not feel they have chosen voluntarily, the service provider risks a backlash. Effective dispute resolution depends on the good faith participation of the disputants, and if ODR mechanisms are coercive in any way, even with good intentions, there is a risk that the parties will react negatively. Also, because dispute resolution techniques often do not rely on stringent enforcement mechanisms, it is important to maintain strong participant buy-in so that resolutions will be followed. If a dispute resolution process forces the hand of a disputant at any point along the way there is a risk that the disputant will write off the resolution as illegitimate and will not abide by it.

Representation

Even as dispute resolution outcomes do not rely on legal statutes and precedent to the degree a court decision might, legal rights and obligations inevitably enter into dispute resolution processes. Parties constantly are making decisions that relate to the law, and it is important that they be making informed decisions. One important way to make sure that parties are informed about the legal issues surrounding their dispute is to connect disputants with competent legal counsel.

Mediators and arbitrators, who are often lawyers themselves, cannot play this role for the parties. Once a dispute is in progress a neutral panelist cannot offer legal counsel to one side or the other. The role of an advocate is to be on the side of his client, to make sure the client is informed about the legal ramifications of the situation she is in, and to help the client make her case in the most effective way possible. Lawyers take on certain ethical obligations when they agree to represent a client, and many of those obligations clash with the role of an impartial dispute resolution service provider.

ODR platforms need to allow for the participation of counsel should the parties request it. They should also make clear the responsibilities of the parties in advance of the dispute resolution process, and to explain the role of the neutral so that the parties do not enter the process under the assumption that the mediator or arbitrator is going to give them legal advice or help them formulate their cases.

Enforcing ODR Standards

There are a variety of mechanisms proposed to ensure that ODR service providers meet these criteria:

CLEARINGHOUSE This proposal, growing out of the work of the ICC and Consumers International, would drive all B2C e-commerce disputes through a single organization. The disputes would then be referred to ODR service providers who met standards issued and policed by the clearinghouse. Should any providers fail to meet or maintain these standards, they would not receive any dispute referrals from the clearinghouse.

ODR PROVIDER SEALS This suggestion grows out of the work of the ABA eADR Task Force. In this solution, ODR providers would be awarded a seal that they could put on the top of their site demonstrating that they had met certain standards for ODR practice. Should the provider slip from meeting these standards, the seal would be pulled. It may be that the seal would be backed up by some government authority, which would prevent an ODR provider from offering services once the seal was removed.

INTERNATIONAL B2C NETWORK This proposal stems from the network being built by major consumer complaint-handling bodies around the world, such as the Better Business Bureau, Eurochambres, and FEDMA. In this proposal, only the top organization in each country would be admitted to the B2C ODR network. All of the members of the network would sell a trustmark in their home countries to e-commerce businesses, and the trustmark would have a common logo or identity around the world. Consumers would be assured of high-quality ODR services by the position and reputation of the network members.

Conclusion

Designing an effective ODR process is not a one-shot activity, where the process is set in stone at the beginning. Processes evolve, improve, and sometimes multiply into different variations for different types of disputes. ODR systems designers should know that the choices they make in designing their processes will be closely scrutinized by standard-setting bodies around the world. Ideally, ODR programs should endeavor to meet or exceed existing standards, so as to ensure that they do not later encounter resistance or opposition from standard-setting bodies that question their processes.

CHAPTER SIXTEEN

Frequently Asked Questions (FAQs)

F AQs have a long history on the Internet. They can be a little cloyingly Socratic, but they serve a useful purpose. Many questions are asked over and over again about ODR that don't easily fit into the categories addressed in the chapters of this book. It makes sense to address several of the questions commonly asked by customers, neutrals, and businesses here.

WHAT TYPES OF DISPUTES BEST UTILIZE ODR?

Many of the most effective online dispute resolution implementations have focused on disputes over quantifiable issues. The blind-bidding systems, such as Cybersettle and ClickNsettle, focus on a particular monetary evaluation for an insurance claim. SquareTrade has also devoted much of its time to resolving auction disputes, which usually focus on monetary values. Online dispute proceedings that focus on less quantifiable issues, such as relationships or apologies, have had less success. Some types of communications are better suited for face-to-face interaction. Emotional communications, apologies, or conversations about ongoing relationships may be better dealt with offline than online. However, quantifiable or transaction-based disputes may be even more effectively handled online because it is harder for the matters to be personalized.

Online dispute resolution mechanisms can be crafted in a way that focuses the party on the resolution of a specific issue, possibly avoiding emotional issues altogether. In some disputes this can be a boon to the process, moving parties toward a resolution more effectively and resulting in greater satisfaction, while in other disputes it can be a serious problem. Only the neutral can best determine the needs of a particular dispute and craft appropriate responses.

Sometimes the parties have the best sense about whether or not ODR is appropriate for their dispute. At Online Resolution we referred a good number of disputes to face-to-face mediators at the beginning, along with the reasons why we thought a "real" mediator would be a better choice than a "virtual" one in each situation. But in some cases the parties pushed back, insisting that ODR was what they wanted. Just because the parties want to do something doesn't mean it's appropriate for an ADR process, but in some of these cases the strong disputant preference to use ODR may have been a sign that ODR was a good fit with the dispute.

It is important to remember as well that online versus offline is not an either/or proposition. In "hybrid" ODR processes, face-to-face meetings are combined with online tools to create a more efficient and effective overall process. For example, a mediator could meet face-to-face with two geographically separated disputants for an initial meeting, then move the discussion into an online environment for joint problem-solving and agreement-drafting, then reconvene face-to-face to obtain final buy-in. ODR can be introduced on a trial basis in these hybrid proceedings, and if the online interaction doesn't prove productive, or if one party or the other isn't comfortable with the online interaction, the process can convert to a face-to-face only process.

WHAT TYPES OF DISPUTES SHOULD AVOID ODR?

Online dispute resolution, and dispute resolution in general, are not compatible with disputes in which one side is not participating in a good-faith effort to reach a resolution. This includes all fraud and criminal cases. It is not appropriate to use dispute resolution to determine whether or not a party is guilty of a crime. However, dispute resolution has been used successfully in criminal cases after guilt has already been established, where the aggrieved party and the guilty party can confront the crime and determine an appropriate punishment or resolution. These processes can help victims deal with the crime where they were involved, and also help the criminals understand the true ramifications of their actions.

Online dispute resolution is also a poor fit with disputes between two people in the same geographic area who might resort to violence. In a related vein, online dispute resolution is not a good option for working with people who might hurt themselves. When the pressure on participants in a dispute resolution process gets so intense that there is a risk of physical harm, the online mediator is often unable to get involved. For example, in a divorce case in which the parties are in the same area, and there is a risk or a history of domestic violence, it is better to err on the side of caution and urge the parties to work with a face-to-face mediator who can intervene or involve the authorities should the conflict escalate. In such situations the inability of an online mediator to physically intervene in the process could become a major problem.

ODR is also a bad idea when one or both of the parties are uncomfortable or threatened by technology. Often one party is very excited about the notion of using technology to resolve a dispute because he is comfortable with online communication. If the other party is less sure about the use of technology, or seems hesitant about the idea, then ODR may not be the best option. Case administrators and neutrals should make sure to have a face-to-face interaction or a telephone conversation with the parties before an online process begins so that the enthusiasm for the use of technology on the part of all the participants can be determined.

CAN ONLINE COMMUNICATION BE RICH ENOUGH TO RESOLVE DISPUTES?

Some observers (notably Joel Eisen) have questioned whether textual communication is rich enough to support a dispute resolution process.[1] The lack of non-verbal cues, real-time responses, and subtlety of meaning removes elements essential to successful dispute resolution, they argue.

Leading thinkers about online community, including Howard Rheingold and John Perry Barlow, have argued for the sophisticated interaction that can happen in technology-mediated environments. In his book *The Virtual Community* (1994), Rheingold tells the emotional story of a poster in the legendary Bay Area virtual community called The Well. This poster had been an active contributor to the flow of messages on The Well for years, and based on an argument with some of the other members of the community, he used The Well's software to delete all of his old postings from the archived discussion flow. This was damaging to the records of the community, in many respects, because the old message flow was considered a joint product of the community. Once all of this poster's messages had been deleted the flow of discussion was very disjointed and often referred to non-existent ideas and points. Soon after this poster deleted all of his messages he committed suicide. As a community, The Well had to react to and heal from this event, and many people who had never met each other face-to-face, who in fact lived in very different parts of the world, came together to make sense of the loss. Many people who had never met face-to-face came together to comfort each other, much like they would in the face-to-face world. The grief was no less intense online.[2]

Over the years I have participated in a variety of online communities that have engaged me as much if not more than the face-to-face communities of which I have been a part. For years I was more comfortable interacting with new people online than face-to-face. People with lots of experience in online communication get very good at communicating their emotions through text. The famous smiley faces or "emoticons" made up of ASCII characters such as :-) have become shorthand for communicating emotions online. Abbreviations have become a common method for online communicators to telegraph their emotional reactions, or the tone of their comments. Some common abbreviations include IMHO (for "in my humble opinion," a good way to soft pedal a statement that sounds very aggressive), or LOL (for "laugh out loud," a way to communicate happiness or humor). I have even received communication from people in which emotions are coded into the message like HTML code, such as "I got your letter this morning. <SARCASM> Boy, you really are one classy guy. </SARCASM>."

When I was barely a teenager I participated in an online bulletin board called "Eclectic," which eventually grew into "Eclectic I" and "Eclectic II." Though modems at the time had a maximum speed of 300 bps (about as fast as the average person can read) I spent up to ten hours a day trading messages with the other members of the Eclectic community. We had a book club, where we discussed science fiction novels, a public affairs board, where we would debate the hot issues of the day, and a general discussion board where we would pontificate about whatever was on our minds.

One week I asked my mom if I could host a party for some of my Eclectic friends, and she said yes, assuming that all of the other users were nerdy boys between ten and fourteen, just like me. The first guest who arrived was a grizzled, overweight Vietnam vet who showed up on his Harley Davidson motorcycle. The next was a thirty-five-year-old nurse. Then a variety of engineers showed up from Texas Instruments (a local high-tech company), as well as a good collection of young nerdy boys. We all sat down and chatted for a bit, but soon the kids were running around and swimming in the pool and my mother was chatting with the nurse and the biker. We couldn't get past our differences in person, so we retreated to our more familiar groups. Once we all got home, however, we were back into our stride; we talked about that party for the next year, and eventually convened some others.

The friends I made through the Eclectic bulletin board back in the early 1980s were very important to me, and in some respects we became more connected to each other because of the lack of face-to-face contact. The superficial differences that would have separated us if our only interactions had been face-to-face were removed, and we were allowed to interact intellect-to-intellect, which removed the burdens of preconceived notions we might have formulated about each other. Most engineers at Texas Instruments wouldn't have taken the time to join a book club with a twelve-year-old, much less assume that he had anything interesting to say. Once we did join this community, however, those connections did have a chance to be made.

Those were the early days of computer networking, and with the Internet and the massive spike in Web users, many online communities are moving in the direction of homogenization. However, subject-area-focused communities are again matching up wildly different personalities, but usually the communications stay focused on the particular subject area. In the early days of bulletin boards the communities were diverse because there weren't too many people that went through the trouble of figuring out how to log on to online services. Many people wouldn't tolerate the primitive interfaces and green-on-black screens that scrolled information slowly across the screen left to right. (When I first saw the throughput of a 1,200-baud modem, the next step in the technological evolution, I wondered what I was ever going to do with all that speed.)

It was certain, however, that we had disputes on Eclectic, even at 300 baud in all uppercase. People would be in bad moods and make snippy comments and go after each other. People would hurl insults and later apologize, and cliques would form between different people on the board. There were some members of the online community that I would be friendly with, and then we would have arguments. Even though we never spoke in real time, we still had full relationships that were as complex as face-to-face relationships. The complexity in interpersonal relations comes from the complexity of the people making up each side of the relationship, not the bandwidth or sophistication of the communication method they use.

Networks that have been created to connect terminally ill children, for example, have shown the power of online interaction in combatting loss. One of the fastest-growing demographic groups on the Web has been senior citizens, who gravitate to the Web in spite of their lack of experience with technology because it is a good way to connect with others and to experience a broader community.

All of this harkens back to periods when letters were the only way for separated loved ones and family members to communicate. Online dispute resolution once again demonstrates the power of the written word. Some observers have suggested that the Web has revitalized the lost art of letter writing. Many members of the younger generation write dozens of emails a day, and they can be very communicative in their language, even if many of the sentiments communicated are passed along in abbreviations or code. Often students and young professionals can pick up on the usefulness of an online dispute resolution platform long before someone from the older generation can come around to acknowledging its utility. Much of this comes from the development of an online eloquence that the younger generation has created out of necessity. American youth has adapted quickly to the new communication options found on the Web. I got my first computer when I was eleven, but many kids today have a computer that they work with before they can even talk. I am certain that soon they will pity my lack of online eloquence just like I pitied the older generation before me.

As one of the participants in the ODR focus groups at Royal Roads put it, "Take Shakespeare and tell me if his characters are devoid of emotion. I don't need to see someone rocking in his chair to know if he is nervous, provided of course, that he knows how to write."

HOW CAN NEUTRALS BE CONVINCED OF THE UTILITY OF ODR?

Many of the dispute resolution professionals I speak with are profoundly skeptical about ODR. Several ADR professionals with years of experience have approached me at various conferences and meetings, patted me on the shoulder, and informed me that online dispute resolution won't work. One person even told me that "online dispute resolution" is an oxymoron, because dispute resolution, by definition, must be face-to-face.

Most ADR professionals are comfortable with ODR in online-only contexts, if only because face-to-face mediation is virtually impossible. But if face-to-face interaction is possible, many neutrals presume it is preferable.

Once neutrals become experienced with ODR platforms, however, they come to understand the unique capacities of online interaction. They also come to see how online interaction can be a powerful complement to face-to-face interaction. Building online dispute resolution environments in such a way that they can easily be integrated into and complement face-to-face ADR will make dispute resolution professionals more comfortable with ODR over time.

Based on my conversations around the country, most ADR professionals can easily envision how audio- and videoconferencing will allow for the delivery of effective dispute resolution services over the Internet, mostly by replicating face-to-face ADR processes. However, there are advantages to online dispute resolution service delivery and computer-mediated communication that cannot be integrated into purely synchronous, face-to-face ADR service delivery. We are just beginning to use these techniques, but mediators should seek training in the new tools available online and try them out to see what benefits they can offer. When high-quality audio- and videoconferencing do become available, practitioners will be able to bring their experience with text-based ODR platforms to the task of designing hybrid ODR processes.

WHEN SHOULD A DISPUTE GO TO ODR?

Many businesses are reluctant to turn their customers over to an ODR service provider. Some businesses think that their customer service departments are doing dispute resolution. On one level, customer service departments are in the dispute resolution business, but they are not responsible for building a fair, impartial dispute resolution system to handle consumer complaints.

As a general rule, ODR should be called in after the customer service staff has done all they can. A dispute should only go to ODR if the customer service staff is unable to resolve the matter after repeated interactions with the complainant. Disputes should not be sent to a third-party ODR service provider until the business has put a good-faith effort into resolving the matter. This ensures that the business has done all it can, and it stops the matter from escalating the last step into court.

All of that said, one truism of dispute resolution practice is that the best place to resolve any dispute is as early in the life of the dispute as possible. Most dispute resolution systems are designed like locks in a canal, in which a matter advances to a more formal process only after a simpler process was unsuccessful in helping to resolve that dispute. For example, if an employee in a corporation is beginning to feel that her workplace is uncomfortable, it does not make sense for that employee immediately to jump into formal labor arbitration. Initially the employee may discuss the situation with her supervisor and ask for certain changes to be made in the working environment. If that strategy is not successful in resolving the matter, she may contact the human resources department. Should internal mechanisms prove inadequate for resolving the concerns of the employee, the employee might ask that an outside mediator be brought in to attempt to resolve the situation. If that is not successful, the matter may escalate to arbitration and/or a court proceeding. The next step is only commenced once the prior option was not able to generate a resolution.

The corollary of this argument is also true: the longer a dispute goes on, the harder that it is to resolve. Often the initiating event in a dispute becomes less of the focus over time and the actions taken by the parties during the dispute become the focus (much like Nixon facing impeachment not for the Watergate break-in, but for his lies attempting to cover up the break-in.) The longer a dispute goes on the more issues that need to be resolved in order for the parties to feel the matter has been dealt with.

One of the strengths of online dispute resolution is that complaints can be addressed much earlier than they might otherwise be addressed if the only redress option available was a face-to-face interaction. If the employee who is beginning to feel uncomfortable in her workplace is given access to an online dispute resolution mechanism that she can use anonymously, she may be much more willing to do something about her concerns before they escalate than if her only option was to confront the matter face-to-face.

Time can also become an escalating factor in a dispute. A complainant can raise a concern with the best intentions only to be confronted by silence or inaction from the other side. As this waiting continues, the complainant's frustration level may rise, and a relatively minor issue in the complainant's eyes can escalate into a much more serious issue.

HOW SHOULD COMPANIES ADVERTISE THE AVAILABILITY OF ODR SERVICES?

Companies are frequently reluctant to advertise the availability of dispute resolution services. They think that it will lead consumers to conclude that their site generates a lot of disputes. In fact, the opposite is true. When presented with a fair, neutral, and well-thought-out complaint-handling process, most consumers feel that the business offering those services wants to do right by its customers. Increasingly customers are coming to look for adequate redress options when they decide to engage in a transaction with a company or website.

Dispute resolution is a lot like going to the dentist's office. Most people don't think about how great the dentist's office is, and how they'd like to spend more time in the dentist's office. In fact, most people don't think about the dentist's office at all on a day-to-day basis, unless they're dentists. However, if your filling comes loose, you can't help but think about the dentist's office. In fact, the dentist's office may be your favorite place, and you will not want to go anywhere but the dentist's office until the problem is fixed. Dispute resolution is the same way. Most people do not think about how much fun dispute resolution is on a daily basis. However, when confronted with an unpleasant dispute, it is difficult to think about anything other than resolving that dispute.

Online dispute resolution services do not have to appear at the top of every page of a website. It may be, like eBay, that the availability of dispute resolution services is only made clear at one point in the initial transaction process, and is only advertised on a page two or three levels down in the website under customer service. The availability of the service needs to be clear to anyone looking for the service, but it does not have to detract from the marketing messages the business is attempting to communicate to its customers.

WON'T NEW TECHNOLOGY ELIMINATE ONLINE DISPUTES?

I was at a conference where a presenter asserted that new e-commerce technologies meant the end of disputing. Because everything was going to be double- and triple-checked by advanced computer algorithms (EDI and XML), he argued, there would never be any disputes. This is a common sentiment in some technology and engineering circles. Disputes are an operational error, they reason, and over time operations will become more efficient, removing the operational errors. The argument concludes that online dispute resolution mechanisms will eventually be put out of business by technological efficiency.

Dispute resolution professionals know that this is nonsense. There will always be disputes. Humans will make mistakes, or new transaction problems will arise that were not considered when the technology was designed. The Internet allows transactions to reach around the world. The power of online technology to prevent disputes is dwarfed by the potential for online technology to create conflict. The challenge is to supplement the growth of new international commercial networks with the infrastructure required to maintain confidence in them.

HOW CAN ONLINE RESOLUTIONS BE ENFORCED?

One of the biggest challenges of ODR is its enforceability. Sometimes enforceability in ODR is readily achievable. ICANN is an excellent example of this. When a panelist in a UDRP process transfers a domain name, ICANN can easily enforce that decision because they have absolute control over the database that assigns domain names to their owners. In B2C e-commerce disputes, this type of absolute enforceability is not possible. If a product is shipped to a purchaser and the wrong amount of money is charged, the shipper cannot compel the purchaser to return the item or to pay more money. It is possible to initiate legal actions or some other form of penalty, but absolute enforceability along the ICANN model is not an option.

Complaint sites like PlanetFeedback.com or TheComplaint-Station.com can serve as potential negative consequences to a company or individuals that refuse to participate in a dispute resolution process. The business ratings services (BizRate.com, Open-Ratings.com, and so on) can also play an important enforcement role. Online credit rating companies and trust infrastructure companies like eCredit and GeoTrust can also factor into the unwillingness of certain companies to participate in dispute resolution processes, providing an additional incentive for them to cooperate.

These services play an important role in making e-commerce more robust and trustworthy. For instance, complaint sites can frequently drive unresolved disputes in to online dispute resolution, giving the company an opportunity to address the concerns of the complainant so as not to generate negative feedback. Also, online dispute resolution services can refer complainants who are faced with companies who refuse to participate in a dispute resolution process, giving the complainant an opportunity to express their frustration and warn others away from doing business with that particular transaction partner.

It is important to note that most companies and individuals will not participate in an online dispute resolution process if they feel that there are no negative consequences to their refusing to participate. The potential positives that can come from a dispute resolution process are frequently not enough to compel participation. In other words, there needs to be both a carrot and a stick to get companies and individuals to participate in dispute resolution.

One of the key concepts of dispute resolution is BATNA, or the best alternative to a negotiated agreement. Parties to a negotiation will constantly evaluate their BATNA in deciding what outcome they will find desirable or acceptable. If they feel that their alternative to an agreement is tolerable, if not desirable, then they will be less inclined to work toward an acceptable resolution with the other party. Collaboration between online dispute resolution services and feedback and ratings services can help to make the alternative to agreement look less desirable, and therefore encourage parties to work harder for a mutually acceptable resolution.

Face-to-face dispute resolution services often operate the same way. In small claims court mediation the neutrals often spend a lot of time describing how inadequate the court hearing will be. Instead of having unlimited time to make your case, as most people reared on *Perry Mason* and *Ally McBeal* may assume, the judge will more likely ask two or three questions and render a decision. Courts have no incentive to make people enjoy the process. On the contrary, most courts are overburdened and want to keep people out of court. As a result, the formal legal option is not usually very desirable. Small claims mediators often communicate this fact in great detail to the disputants they work with, because it serves to weaken their BATNA, giving them a stronger incentive to reach agreement in mediation.

HOW MUCH SHOULD ODR SERVICES COST?

Online dispute resolution is still a very new phenomenon, so there is a lot of confusion about how ODR services should be priced. Much of this confusion comes from the uncertainty of ODR consumers about how much the services should be worth.

While pricing models vary between ODR providers, there are some common trends. In auction or e-commerce disputes there is usually a one-time filing fee paid by the initiator of the case. This filing fee is usually between $15 and $25, depending on which site the case came from and the value under dispute. This low filing fee is often not enough to even pay the mediator for the services rendered.

If the rates are too high for these low-end services then parties will never elect to use them. B2C e-commerce disputes are frequently worth less than $500, and many of them are between $50 and $75. If the mediator charges $50 for the first hour of service no party will ever elect to utilize ODR. Pricing for ODR must be cognizant of the fact that there is a clear incentive for parties to offer a full money-back guarantee for any disputed transaction worth less than the cost of the dispute resolution procedure. Parties will inevitably do this calculation in their heads at the time of the transaction if they are required to pay for the ODR process. Many parties will balk at the use of ODR if the cost of the process is more than a quarter of the transaction value. The transaction-based pricing models raise a variety of issues because of this dynamic.

The argument has been made that there is an economic benefit to the overall marketplace when dispute resolution services are available, and that benefit should be calculated into the cost. Customers are more likely to buy something if they know there is redress available to them should anything go wrong. For instance, no one argues in a courthouse that the cost of a court proceeding is more than the cost of a small claims case. There is a network value to having the court there to resolve the dispute, even if the cost of the court process exceeds the value of the dispute. The county might save money by calling off the court hearing and just paying the cost to the parties, but that would disrupt the larger system, which benefits the community. ODR resources work similarly. If the value of a particular dispute is less than the cost of the ODR mechanism, that doesn't mean that ODR is not useful in resolving that dispute.

SquareTrade and eBay are a good example of this. Users of eBay need to pay a small filing fee when a mediator is brought into their case, but eBay pays SquareTrade for its services as well. There is an acknowledgement that eBay is getting value from the presence of SquareTrade in their trading environment, and eBay is helping to cover the cost of SquareTrade's services by pitching in on paying the cost of the neutral.

The result of this observation is that transaction-based pricing is not necessarily the best fit for all ODR implementations. It might make more sense in the long run to require the website to pay up front for dispute resolution services.

In the face-to-face dispute resolution world this pricing controversy is even more protracted. The roots of the dispute resolution movement in the United States lie in the community mediation movement, which attempted to integrate free dispute resolution into communities and courthouses across the country. In these models, free or on-staff mediators are made available to disputants to help them work out their differences as an alternative to going before a judge. Many of these programs were designed to be funded by state legislatures or local courthouses, and they were intended to be provided as an extension of the local legal infrastructure. This part of the dispute resolution field grows out of a social justice background, in which dispute resolution is free from the pressures of the market and becomes an accepted and important part of the community's way of doing business.

Local independent mediators frequently resent the presence of community mediation programs, as they set an unrealistic price expectation for dispute resolution services. If mediation is being given away for free at the local courthouse, some argue, it is harder for independent mediators to prove that their services are worth paying for. As a result, independent mediators have had a hard time charging reasonable rates for their services. This is a difficult paradox for many mediators, as community mediation usually provides the first cases that professional mediators cut their teeth on, giving them an opportunity to obtain real experience in advance of putting up their shingle as a private practitioner.

This dispute between free dispute resolution services and fee-based dispute resolution services will likely transfer into the world of ODR as well. Some government agencies are already beginning to offer free ODR services that compete with the for-profit services currently available. Some low-end ODR providers are also entering the marketplace, determined to compete on price with the established companies by offering less-expensive technology. These developments ensure that the confusion over how best to price ODR services will likely continue for some time.

CHAPTER SEVENTEEN

Conclusion

—◦◦◦—

S oon after my wife and I joined the Peace Corps in 1995, I was dismayed to read that *Newsweek* (received two months late in the rural Horn of Africa) had declared it the "Year of the Internet." Here I was in a country that had fewer than a thousand computers, 90 percent of which were concentrated in the capital city, and the rest of the world was logging on to the new industrial revolution. It was difficult for a computer geek like me, who had never been away from email for more than a week since 1983, to go cold turkey off of technology for two years. I got through it, but it wasn't easy.

When we returned to the United States at the end of our service we were shocked at the changes that had taken place. Every magazine advertisement had a Web address at the bottom for customers to visit. Every business card had an email address below the phone number. Because we had been outside of the country for a couple of years we could see how significant the changes had been. In contrast, our friends who had remained in the States were pretty blasé about the whole thing. Yeah, they seemed to say, this is how things work now. If anything, they seemed a little frustrated that things weren't moving faster.

THE INTERNET'S IMPACT:
HYPE VERSUS SUBSTANCE

In the wild roller-coaster ride that has been the Internet boom, it is easy to forget that all of this has happened in only seven or eight years. We are at the beginning, not the end, of the changes global networks will bring to the planet. Social change often happens in exactly this way. There is hype about a coming development and expectations are inflated. Then when the change comes there is a period of excitement, but it is quickly followed by a backlash when the reality doesn't live up to the hype. People move on to the next thing, not really understanding how the new technology has fundamentally changed the way things are done. It is the central reason for humanity's success in the evolutionary process: the ability for people and societies to adapt to new developments and then to move on to the next challenge. It works great for evolution, but not so great for dot-com stock prices.

People have said that the Internet is only going to have the same impact as the telephone or television. That is a revolutionary statement. Think of the magnitude of the impact television has had on humanity. For better or for worse, the television has played a central role in the creation of a global society. It has shaped law, politics, war, culture, and education. It has brought images from the other side of the world into our living rooms. Some analysts have argued that it was really the VCR that brought down the Iron Curtain, as the proliferation of videotapes made it impossible for centralized propaganda to control the images of life on the other side of the divide. If the Internet is to have a similar impact it will truly be revolutionary. In all probability, based on what we've seen so far, the impact of the Internet will probably be greater.

In the course of the rise and fall of the dot-coms it is unquestionable that a major societal change has taken place. More than half of all Americans now have daily access to the Internet. Instead of a medium dominated by white, male computer nerds, the majority of Internet users are now women. The 'Net is becoming more diverse, as non-English-language websites are starting to outnumber English sites. The consulting firm Accenture predicts that by 2007 the most common language on the Internet will be Chinese.[1]

Businesses are finding that it is impossible to return to the ways things were done before the Internet's expansion. Customers now insist on twenty-four-hour Web-based support. Employees expect to be able to work from anywhere inside or outside the enterprise, getting instant access to the information they need to do their jobs. These expectations are now reaching into government, media, and the nonprofit sector. Customers have gotten used to the always-on, always-responsive nature of the Internet, and even though many dot-coms have died, the vision that created them remains.

The personal computer-focused vision of the late 1990s has also given way to a new vision for the global network that goes beyond the desktop. The Internet is now available on wristwatches and cellphones. Instead of fancy websites requiring fiber optic cables and fast processors, much of the new content being deployed on the Internet is intended to be viewed on a monochrome cell-phone screen, or even read over the phone by a computerized voice. The Internet is changing and adapting into something that is not a flashy add-on, but a reliable, ever-present part of the infrastructure. Soon our access to the public network will be one of the utilities we rely on in our daily life, like electricity. We won't be able to comprehend how we'd go about getting things done without it.

The Internet is not a panacea. The Internet is not going to cure world hunger, and it's not going to narrow the gap between rich and poor. No matter how good a programmer you are, you can't use the Internet to download a loaf of bread if your family is hungry. The Internet is merely a tool that can be used in creative ways to address new challenges. It gives people capabilities that they didn't have before. Anyone on the planet can now put up a Web page that can instantly be seen anywhere else on the planet. Communication can be sent around the world for free. Regardless of how hyped the Internet was, and how harsh the backlash has been, this is still an important new capability for humanity.

THE FUTURE OF ONLINE DISPUTE RESOLUTION

Online dispute resolution is intimately tied to the expansion and development of the Internet. The rapid rise in the growth of the 'Net fueled the growth in ODR, and the backlash and slowdown in the 'Net has temporarily slowed the growth of ODR. But like the Internet, the expansion and refinement of ODR is inevitable, and it goes beyond the flavor-of-the-month attention spans of the media and the stock market.

One fellow ODR entrepreneur has observed repeatedly that we are in the "scratches on cave walls" stage in developing the ODR field. New technologies, processes, and strategies are constantly appearing and disappearing, and ADR practitioners are only beginning to get their hands on ODR tools. Many of the existing ODR experiments have been implemented in a haphazard way and given spotty support. This is how early-stage technology works: you throw lots of spaghetti strands on the wall to see which ones stick.

What we do know is that some implementations of ODR have been successful, and that they will continue to grow. Many global institutions have examined the landscape for online redress and concluded that online dispute resolution is the best (and only) way to go. The decisions have been made that will result in the development of robust, reliable, and efficient global ODR networks, even if the first line of code that will support these networks has not yet been programmed.

The story of ODR so far has been written by a handful of academics and some individual entrepreneurs. Now the larger ADR institutions are coming into the picture, learning from the experiences of the academics and the start-ups. Soon ODR will be taken to the next level, with governments, courthouses, and international organizations integrating ODR into the way they do business. Eventually ODR may move from the private sector to the public sector, as government agencies and international institutions come to realize its benefits.

ODR will also be shaped by the future of technology. If broadband Web access becomes widely available, supporting seamless and effective videoconferencing, the practice of ODR will quickly shift from text-based processes (like the ones discussed in this book) to video-based interactions. More likely, text and video will be used in the same processes, with the neutral utilizing each option based on the needs of the disputants. If wireless access becomes the norm, people may have the ability to engage in dispute resolution procedures on their handheld devices or cellular phones. If artificial intelligence advances rapidly, we may witness a growth in the use of non-human mediators and arbitrators. Translation technology may eventually allow for seamless interactions between people who do not speak the same language. All of these what-ifs may sound like science fiction, but their development will play a crucial role in determining the future of ODR. The only sure thing is that technology will continue to evolve, and in a few years our current tools and techniques will look primitive.

At the time of this writing there is only one book about ODR. At the end of this year there will be several, and then several more the year after. In a few years there will be dozens of books about ODR, each helping to refine the practice of ODR and to make it more effective. The theory and practice of ODR will grow alongside each other, each helping to advance the field and to improve the overall effectiveness of the dispute resolution services provided online.

One likely development is that in the future the distinction between "ADR" and "ODR" will become blurry. Jim Melamed has observed that if you squint a little bit and look into the future, all ADR starts to look like ODR. The use of technology in dispute resolution procedures is already commonplace, and as the tools are refined and practitioners become more aware of ODR techniques it will probably become even more integrated. The observations in this book and books like it may eventually be built into all dispute resolution training programs, because it will be understood that anyone who provides dispute resolution services will eventually be expected to work in an online context.

Businesses will come to use online dispute resolution as a matter of course. ODR will be integrated into contracts, built into online marketplaces, and accepted as the default means of redress in a wide variety of industries. Instead of a single provider emerging to service all potential application areas, dozens of different projects and providers will emerge, each customizing ODR technology to fit the needs of their particular niche. Small applications of ODR built to handle B2C transactions on a vendor's site will exist alongside ODR mechanisms built to handle multimillion-dollar B2B disputes in private exchanges. Industry standard ODR mechanisms, such as the application of XML to insurance subrogation disputes, will lead to new efficiencies in business that generate millions in savings for those that participate. Employees and employers will come to rely on ODR to resolve workplace matters before they escalate, and government will use ODR tools and techniques to keep constituents happy and garner public input on regulations before they become law. Each category will experience fits and starts, with some successes and some failures, but over time the experiments will become commonplace, and the tools of ODR will be integrated into the status quo.

This is the ultimate aspiration for ODR: no hype, no bombast, simply to become the way things are done. If online dispute resolution services can live up to their promise as effective, efficient, and fair mechanisms for helping disputants resolve their problems, then it is very likely that we will see this aspiration become a reality.

—ᨓ— **Appendix**

For the latest headlines in ODR, and a comprehensive library of ODR links and documents, visit www.odrnews.com.

Selected List of ODR Providers

www.allsettle.com
www.arbitrators.org
www.bbbonline.org
www.clicknsettle.com
www.cybersettle.com
www.eneutral.com
www.icourthouse.com
www.ecodir.org
www.internetneutral.com
www.iris.sgdg.org/mediation
www.resolvemydispute.com
www.novaforum.com
www.onlineresolution.com
www.ombuds.org
www.resolutionforum.org
www.resolveitnow.com
www.settleonline.com
www.settlesmart.com
www.smartsettle.com
www.squaretrade.com
www.theclaimroom.com
www.vmag.org
www.ussettle.com
www.webmediate.com

—ᨇ— Notes

Preface

1. I am the first to admit that the acronym chosen for this field, ODR, is an unfortunate one. It makes one think first of unfortunate smells. Upon its introduction, sometime around the end of 1999, there was a healthy discussion of alternatives, but over the last two years they have all gone by the wayside. I have belatedly resigned myself to the term and use it throughout this book, which undoubtedly will help to further cement its position.

Chapter One

1. I am indebted to Henry Perritt, Jr., the current Dean of the Chicago-Kent School of Law, for making the connection between the current challenges faced on the Internet and the institution of fair courts. His observations on this topic in the keynote paper for the first National Center for Automated Information Research (NCAIR) conference on online dispute resolution are largely reproduced here, as they are an excellent historical background to the field of ODR.

2. Mnookin, R., and Kornhauser, L. "Bargaining in the Shadow of the Law: The Case of Divorce." *Yale Law Journal,* 1979, *88*, 950–968.

3. Martin, P. W. "Digital Technology, Access to Legal Information, and Dispute Resolution—Viewed from a Developing Country, NCAIR Conference," May 22, 1996. www.law.cornell.edu/papers/ncr96pwm.htm
Last visited October 28, 2001.

4. Link, A. S., ed. *The Papers of Woodrow Wilson (1966–1993).* Princeton: Princeton University Press, 1992, *30*, pp. 248–55.

5. Sander, F. Presentation at the 1976 American Bar Association Pound Conference. www.asl.edu/miscinfo/adr.htm
Last visited June 14, 2002.

6. Bickerman, J., and Smoyer, D. *Legal Times,* December 5, 1997.
www.bickerman.com/corporations.shtml
Last visited March 1, 2002.

7. Ibid.

8. Ibid.

9. Ibid.

10. Department of Justice, Report of the Interagency ADR Working Group to the President on Alternative Dispute Resolution (January 2001).
mediate.com/articles/president.cfm
Last visited June 14, 2002.

11. Ibid.

12. In the United States, "local" phone calls, meaning the majority of calls within a particular area code, are paid for monthly on a flat-fee basis, so there is no additional cost for length of call. I know that this is different in Europe. This has led to a very different landscape for telecommunications in Europe, as users have had to pay for their local phone calls. This has hampered the expansion of the Internet as well, as most people still access their Internet service over the phone. As a consequence, many of the largest European ISPs are free or very low cost to users, because users are unwilling to pay for Internet access on top of the cost of their phone call.

13. Katsh, E., and Rifkin, J. *Online Dispute Resolution.* San Francisco: Jossey-Bass, 2001.

14. Perera, R. "Internet Shopping Heading for the Trillions; Online Buyers Rang Up $354 Billion Last Year, and We're Just Getting Started." IDG News Service, May 29, 2001.
www.pcworld.com/news/article/0,aid,51084,00.asp
Last visited October 28, 2001.

15. Katsh & Rifkin.

16. Any ADR practitioner interested in becoming involved with ODR should become a member of ACR's online section, and any business interested in staying on top of the major developments in the ODR field should join as well. The online section of ACR is the sole ODR professional organization in the world at the time of this writing.

17. Gibs, J. "Conflict Resolution: Rising Above the Oncoming Flood." B-to-B Commerce, Marketing and Selling to Businesses, Conflict Resolution, BBC00-C05, Jupiter Research, November 1, 2000.

Chapter Three

1. Melamed, J. Divorce Mediation and the Internet. January 2002.
www.mediate.com/articles/melamed9.cfm
Last visited June 2, 2002.

2. Steiner, P. *The New Yorker, 69,* 20, July 5, 1993, p. 61.

3. "Consumer Complaint Handling in America," from a study conducted by TARP/eSatisfy for the White House Office of Consumer Affairs, 1979 and 1985, and cited by the Better Business Bureau.

Chapter Four

1. Fiorina, C. Comments presented at the meeting of the Global Business Dialogue on e-Commerce (GBDe), Hotel InterContinental, Miami, Florida, September 26, 2000.
2. Dembeck, C. "U.S. B2B to Reach $6 Trillion by 2005." *E-Commerce Times,* June 27, 2000. www.ecommercetimes.com/perl/story/3653.html
Last visited June 14, 2002.
3. "A Dot-Calm Falls Over the Office: Burned-out Workers are Bucked Up by the Slowdown." *Businessweek Online,* January 29, 2001.
www.businessweek.com/2001/01_05/b3717099.htm
Last visited June 14, 2002.
4. Rose, F. "The Father of Creative Destruction—Why Joseph Schumpeter is Suddenly All the Rage in Washington," *Wired.* March 2002.
www.wired.com/wired/archive/10.03/schumpeter.html
Last visited June 14, 2002.
5. Posted by JHELMICK, in an emailed response to John Dvorak's article on web entropy, December 22, 2001.
discuss.pcmag.com/n/main.asp?webtag=pcmag&nav=messages&msg=2931.2
Last visited June 14, 2002.
6. Fukiyama, F. "The Virtual Handshake: e-Commerce and the Challenge of Trust." From the Merrill Lynch Forum, 2001.
www.ml.com/woml/forum/ecommerce1.htm
Last visited June 14, 2002.

Chapter Five

1. "FTC to Host Public Workshop to Explore Online Dispute Resolution. Alternative Dispute Resolution for Consumer Transactions in the Borderless Online Marketplace to be Explored." Press release, February 9, 2000.
www./mediate.com/adrnews/adrnews1.cfm
Last visited June 14, 2002.
2. "Alternative Dispute Resolution for Consumer Transactions in the Borderless Online Marketplace." Testimony of Roger Cochetti on Behalf of the Electronic Commerce and Consumer Protection Group, before the Federal Trade Commission, Washington, D.C., June 6, 2000.

web.archive.org/web/20001211163400/www.ecommercegroup.org/
testimony.htm
Last visited June 14, 2002.

3. *OECD Guidelines for Consumer Protection in the Context of Electronic
Commerce, 12/9/1999.* These guidelines, approved on December 9, 1999, by
the OECD Council, are designed to help ensure that consumers are no less
protected when shopping online.
www.oecd.org/pdf/M00000000/M00000363.pdf
Last visited June 14, 2002.

4. Rabinovich-Einy, O. "Going Public: Diminishing Privacy in Dispute Resolution in the Internet Age." August 2001. Unpublished report on file with author.

5. Nader, L. "Styles of Court Procedure: To Make the Balance." In *Law in Culture and Society.* Berkeley: University of California Press, 1969, p. 69.

6. Phillips, P. Comments presented at the ABA Task Force on E-Commerce &
ADR Meeting, June 22, 2001, Washington, D.C.

7. Rabinovich-Einy, O. "Going Public: Diminishing Privacy in Dispute
Resolution in the Internet Age." August 2001. Unpublished report on file
with author.

Chapter Six

1. Monty, Jean. Comments presented at the meeting of the Global Business
Dialogue on e-Commerce (GBDe), Hotel InterContinental, Miami, Florida,
September 26, 2000.

Chapter Seven

1. Barsamian, A. Filing from Cybersettle.com for the FTC/DOC Conference
on Alternative Dispute Resolution in E-Commerce, June 6, 2000.
www.ftc.gov/bcp/altdisresolution/comments/barsamian.htm
Last visited June 14, 2002.

2. National Association of Insurance Commissioners. 1999 Summary Report.
www.naic.org/1research/Research_Division/Reports/life_and_health_
summary.htm and
www.naic.org/1research/Research_Division/Reports/pc_summary.htm
Last visited June 14, 2002.

3. Current Trends in Product Liability II. Excerpt found at
web.archive.org/web/20011109054901/http://www.cybersettle.com/
press/Background/#industryfacts
Last visited June 14, 2002.

4. Ibid.

5. Ibid.
6. Dowell, T. W. "Surety Bonds: Sure Way to Build Business." *Amarillo Business Journal,* June 7, 1999.
   businessjournal.net/stories/060799/ABJ_administration.html
   Last visited June 14, 2002.

Chapter Eight

1. Report of the Interagency ADR Working Group to the President, 2001.
   www.mediate.com/articles/president.cfm
   Last visited June 14, 2002.
2. Ibid.
3. Ibid.
4. For more information, see Kathlyn Noecker's article, "Arbitration Agreements. Don't Block EEOC Enforcement," Faegre & Benson LLP, 2002.
   www. Faegre.com/articles/article_print.asp?id=643
   Last visited June 14, 2002.

Chapter Nine

1. Beierle, T. "Innovative EPA On-Line Dialogue Shows Internet Aids Public Participation in Environmental Decisionmaking." *Resources for the Future,* February 6, 2002.
   www.rff.org/reports/PDF_files/democracyonline.pdf
2. Nuclear Regulatory Commission, *Policy Issue* (Information). SECY-96-188, August 29, 1996, p. 15.

Chapter Eleven

1. Lessig, L. *Code and Other Laws of Cyberspace.* New York: Basic Books, 1999.
   Taken from Chapter 1: Code is Law.
2. Hoffman, I. "Julia, Jimi and Cybersquatting: An Update." 2000.
   www.ivanhoffman.com/julia.html
   Last visited June 14, 2002.
3. Mueller, M. "Rough Justice: An Analysis of ICANN's Uniform Dispute Resolution Policy." From the Convergence Center website.
   dcc.syr.edu/roughjustice.htm
4. Geist, M. "Fair.com?: An Examination of the Allegations of Systemic Unfairness in the ICANN UDRP," August 2001.
   aix1.uottawa.ca/~geist/geistudrp.pdf
   Last visited June 14, 2002.

Chapter Twelve

1. Warters, W. C. *Mediation in the Campus Community: Designing and Managing Effective Programs.* San Francisco: Jossey-Bass, 1999.

Chapter Fifteen

1. Rabinovich-Einy, O. "Going Public: Diminishing Privacy in Dispute Resolution in the Internet Age." August 2001. Unpublished report on file with author.
2. Mayer, C. E. "Arbitration Clauses Block Consumers from Taking Companies to Court." *Washington Post,* May 22, 1999, p. A1.
3. Galanter, M. "Reading the Landscape of Disputes: What We Know and Don't Know (and Think We Know) About Our Alledgedly Contentious and Litigious Society." *UCLA L. Rev.,* 1983, *31,* 61.

Chapter Sixteen

1. Eisen, J. B. "Are We Ready for Mediation in Cyberspace?" *B.Y.U. L. Rev.,* 1998, *4,* 1305, 1354.
   www.innovationlaw.org/pages/probing_mediation.htm
   Last visited October 28, 2001.
2. Rheingold, H. *The Virtual Community.* Boston: MIT Press, 2000. Excerpt taken from Chapter 1.
   www.well.com/user/hlr/vcbook/vcbook1.html

Chapter Seventeen

1. b.twext.cc/plan
   Last visited June 14, 2002.

—⁓— Suggested Reading

Almaguer, A., and Baggott III, R. W. "Shaping New Legal Frontiers: Dispute Resolution for the Internet," *Ohio St. J. on Disp. Resol.,* 1998, *3,* 711, 726.

Alternative Dispute Resolution for Consumer Transactions in the Borderless Online Marketplace, Comments to the Federal Trade Commission from the National Consumers League, the Electronic Privacy Center, and Consumer Federation of America.
www.ftc.gov/bcp/altdisresolution/comments/ncl.htm
Last visited October 28, 2001.

American Bar Association Annual Meeting, August 1, 1997, San Francisco, California. "Using the Internet to Settle Disputes."
www.mediate.com/aba/abaout.cfm
Last visited October 28, 2001.

American Bar Association Task Force on E-Commerce and Alternative Dispute Resolution: Draft Preliminary Report and Concept Paper, May 2001.
www.law.washington.edu/aba-eadr

Anderson, J. F., and Bingham, L. "Upstream Effects From Mediation of Workplace Disputes: Some Preliminary Evidence from the USPS." *Lab. L. J.,* 1997, *48,* 601.

Attisani, D. "Reinsurance Coverage for Declaratory Judgement Expenses." *Journal of Reinsurance,* Summer 2001, *8* (3), 1–27.

Barsamian, A. Filing from Cybersettle.com for the FTC/DOC Conference on Alternative Dispute Resolution for E-Commerce, June 6, 2000.
www.ftc.gov/bcp/altdisresolution/comments/barsamian.htm
Last visited June 14, 2002.

Beierle, T. "Democracy On-Line: An Evaluation of the National Dialogue on Public Involvement in EPA Decisions." Resources for the Future, February 2002.
www.rff.org/reports/PDF_files/democracyonline.pdf
Last visited March 3, 2002.

Bickerman, J., and Smoyer, D. *Legal Times,* December 5, 1997.
www.bickerman.com/corporations.shtml
Last visited March 1, 2002.

Bordone, R. C. "Electronic Online Dispute Resolution: A Systems
Approach—Potential, Problems, and a Proposal." *1998 Harvard
Negotiation Law Review.*
eon.law.harvard.edu/property00/jurisdiction/bordoneedit.html
Last visited October 28, 2001.

Brett, J. M., Goldberg, S. B., and Ury, W. L. *Getting Disputes Resolved:
Designing Systems to Cut the Costs of Conflict.* San Francisco: Jossey
Bass, 1993.

Bronfman, C. Cybersettle.com panel discussion: "Online Mediation: Why
It Works and What Is the Future." Association of the Bar of the City
of New York, April 2, 2001.

Brownlee, K. "Embrace—Don't Fear—New Claims Technology." *Claims
Magazine.* February 1999.
www.claimsmag.com/Issues/October99/embrace.asp

Budnitz, M. E. "Arbitration of Disputes Between Consumers and Financial
Institutions: A Serious Threat to Consumer Protection," *Ohio St. J.
on Disp. Resol.,* 1995, *10,* 267.

Cobb, S., and Rifkin, J. "Practice and Paradox: Deconstructing Neutrality in
Mediation." *Law and Social Inquiry,* 1991, *16,* 25–63.

Cona, F. A. "Application of Online Systems in Alternative Dispute
Resolution." *Buff. L. Rev.,* 1997, *45,* 975.

Coulton, G. G. *Medieval Village, Manor, and Monastery.* New York:
Cambridge University Press, 1925. New York: Harper & Row, 1960.

Current Trends in Product Liability II. Excerpt available at
www.cybersettle.com/press/Background/#industryfacts

Dawson, J. P. *A History of Lay Judges.* Cambridge: Harvard University Press,
1960. Reprinted by The Lawbook Exchange, Ltd., 1999.

DeStephen, D., and Helie, J. "Online Dispute Resolution: Implications for
the ADR Profession."
www.mediate.com/articles/helie1.cfm
Last visited October 28, 2001.

Donahey, M. S. "Current Developments in Online Dispute Resolution."
J. Int'l. Arb., December 1999, 115–130.

Eisen, J. B. "Are We Ready for Mediation in Cyberspace?" *B.Y.U. L. Rev.,*
1998, *4,* 1305, 1354.
www.innovationlaw.org/pages/probing_mediation.htm
Last visited October 28, 2001.

eSatisfy/TARP. "Consumer Complaint Handling in America," from a study conducted by TARP/eSatisfy for the White House Office of Consumer Affairs, 1979 and 1985, and cited by the Better Business Bureau.
www.e-satisfy.com/research.asp

Felstiner, W., and others. "The Emergence and Transformation of Disputes: Naming, Blaming and Claiming." *L. & Soc. Rev.,* 1980, *15,* 631.

Frezza, B. "How the Internet Will Change the Rule of Law." *Internet Week,* September 22, 1997.
www.internetweek.com/columns/frezz0922.htm
Last visited October 28, 2001.

Friedman, G. H. "Alternative Dispute Resolution and Emerging Online Technologies: Challenges and Opportunities." *Hastings Comm. & Ent. L. J.,* 1997, *19,* 695.

Galanter, M. "Reading the Landscape of Disputes: What We Know and Don't Know (and Think We Know) About Our Allegedly Contentious and Litigious Society. *UCLA L. Rev.,* 1983, *31,* 61.

Galanter, M., and Cahill, M. "Most Cases Settle: Judicial Promotion and Regulation of Settlements." *Stan. L. Rev.,* 1994, *46,* 1339, 1377, n. 167.

Garavaglia, M. "In Search of the Proper Law in Trans National Commercial Disputes." *N.Y.L.S. Ch. J. Int'l. & Comp. L.,* 1991, *12,* nn. 31–35.

Gellman, R. "A Brief History of the Virtual Magistrate Project: The Early Months."
mantle.sbs.umass.edu/vmag/gellman.htm
Last visited October 28, 2001.

Gibs, J. "Conflict Resolution: Rising Above the Oncoming Flood." Jupiter Research, B-to-B Commerce, Jupiter Concept Report BBC-00C05. November 2000.

Gibson, K., Thompson, L., and Bazerman, M. "Shortcomings of Neutrality in Mediation." *Negotiation Journal,* January 1996, 69–79.

Global Business Dialogue on E-Commerce, Position Paper on Alternative Dispute Resolution. September 26, 2001.
www.gbde.org
Last visited October 28, 2001.

Goldsmith, J., and Lessig, L. "Grounding the Virtual Magistrate," May 1996.
mantle.sbs.umass.edu/vmag/groundvm.htm
Last visited October 28, 2001.

Hardy, T. "The Proper Legal Regime for 'Cyberspace'," *U. Pitt. L. Rev.,* 1994, *55,* 993, 994.

Hill, R. *Arbitration International,* April 1999.
www.umass.edu/dispute/hill.htm
Last visited October 28, 2001.

Hobson, C. "E-Negotiations: Creating a Framework for Online Commercial Negotiations." *Negotiation Journal,* July 1999, *15* (3), 201–218.

Hoegle, R. L., and Boam, C. P. "The Internet and Jurisdiction-International Principles Emerge but Confrontation Looms." *J. World Intell. Prop.,* 2000, *3,* 31, 45–46.

Insurance Information Institute's Fact Book, 1999, excerpt available at www.cybersettle.com/press/Background/#industryfacts

Insurance Networking Magazine, August 20, 2001.
www.insurancenetworking.com/

Internet Corporation for Assigned Names and Numbers (ICANN), Uniform Domain Name Dispute Resolution Policy.
www.icann.org/udrp/udrp.htm
Last visited October 28, 2001.

Johnson, D. R. "Dispute Resolution in Cyberspace."
www.eff.org/pub/Legal/Arbitration/online_dispute_resolution_johnson.article
Last visited October 28, 2001.

Johnson, D. R., and Post, D. "Law and Borders—The Rise of Law in Cyberspace." *Stan. L. Rev.,* 1996, *48,* 1367.

Kahnin, B., and Nesson, C. (eds.) *Borders in Cyberspace: Information Policy and Global Information Infrastructure.* Boston: MIT Press, 1997.

Kang, J. "Cyber-Race." *Harv. L. Rev.,* 2000, *113,* 1131, 1133.

Karamon, M. C. "ADR on the Internet." *Ohio St. J. on Disp. Resol.,* 1996, *11,* 537.

Katsh, E. *The Electronic Media and the Transformation of Law.* New York: Oxford University Press, 1989.

Katsh, E. "Dispute Resolution in Cyberspace." *Conn. L. Rev.,* 1996, *28,* 953.

Katsh, E. "The New Frontier: Online ADR Becoming a Global Priority." *Disp. Resol. Mag.,* Winter 2000, 14–17.

Katsh, E. "Online Dispute Resolution," in J. Aresty and J. Silkenat (eds.), *Guide to International Business Negotiations.* Chicago: American Bar Association, 2000.
www.umass.edu/cyber/aresty.htm
Last visited October 28, 2001.

Katsh, E. "The Online Ombuds Office: Adapting Dispute Resolution to Cyberspace."
mantle.sbs.umass.edu/vmag/katsh.htm
Last visited October 28, 2001.

Katsh, E., and Rifkin, J. *Online Dispute Resolution.* San Francisco: Jossey-Bass, 2001.

Katsh, E., Rifkin, J., and Gaitenby, A. "E-Commerce, E-Disputes, and E-Dispute Resolution: In the Shadow of "eBay Law." *Ohio St. J. of Disp. Resol.,* 2000, *15,* 705.
www.umass.edu/cyber/katsh.pdf
Last visited October 28, 2001.

Kaufman-Kohler, G. "Choice of Court and Choice of Law in Electronic Contracts." Part of Seminaire de l'Association genevoice de Droit des Affaires, Aspect Juridiques Decommerce Electronique, Schulthess, Zurich, 2001. pp. 12–62.

Kaufman-Kohler, G., and Harms, J. "Online Dispute Resolution: State of the Art, Issues, and Perspectives: Where Are We? And Where Are We Going?" Convening paper for the E-Law Colloquium, Geneva, November 16, 2001.

Lessig, L. *Code and Other Laws of Cyberspace.* New York: Basic Books, 1999.

Lessig, L. "The Law of the Horse: What Cyberlaw Might Teach." *Harv. L. Rev.,* 1999, *113,* 501, 531.

Lide, E. C. "ADR and Cyberspace: The Role of Alternative Dispute Resolution in Online Commerce, Intellectual Property and Defamation." *Ohio St. J. on Disp. Resol.,* 1996, *12,* 193, 218.

Macduff, I. "Flames on the Wires: Mediating from an Electronic Cottage." *Negotiation Journal,* 1994, *10,* 5, 10–11.

Martin, P. W. "Digital Technology, Access to Legal Information, and Dispute Resolution—Viewed from a Developing Country, NCAIR Conference." May 22, 1996.
www.law.cornell.edu/papers/ncr96pwm.htm
Last visited October 28, 2001.

Maryland's On-Line Mediation Service
www.mediate-net.org/
Last visited October 28, 2001.

Mnookin, R., and Kornhauser, L. "Bargaining in the Shadow of the Law: The Case of Divorce." *Yale L. J.,* 1979, *88,* 950, 968.

Mueller, M. "Rough Justice: An Analysis of ICANN's Uniform Dispute Resolution Policy." From the Convergence Center website.
dcc.syr.edu/roughjustice.htm

Nader, L. "Styles of Court Procedure: To Make the Balance." In *Law in Culture and Society.* Berkeley: University of California Press, 1969, p. 69.

National Association of Insurance Commissioners. 1999 Summary Report. www.naic.org/1research/Research_Division/Reports/life_and_health_summary.htm and www.naic.org/1research/Research_Division/Reports/pc_summary.htm Last visited June 14, 2002.

NUA Internet Statistics. "How Many Online?" www.nua.ie/surveys/how_many_online/index.html Last visited October 28, 2001.

Nuclear Regulatory Commission, *Policy Issue* (Information), SECY-96-188, August 29, 1996, p. 15.

Olmstead, W. "Electronic Dispute Resolution at the NRC." May 1996. mantle.sbs.umass.edu/vmag/olmst.htm Last visited October 28, 2001.

Ozawa, C. "Making the Best Use of Technology." In L. Susskind, S. McKearnan, and J. Thomas-Larmer (eds). *The Consensus Building Handbook: A Comprehensive Guide to Reaching Agreement.* Thousand Oaks, CA: Sage Publications, 1999, pp. 401–428.

Perera, R. "Internet Shopping Heading for the Trillions; Online Buyers Rang Up $354 Billion Last Year, and We're Just Getting Started." IDG News Service, May 29, 2001. www.pcworld.com/news/article/0,aid,51084,00.asp Last visited October 28, 2001.

Perritt, Jr., H. H. "Dispute Resolution in Electronic Network Communities." *Vill. L. Rev.,* 1993, *38,* 349.

Perritt, Jr., H. H. "President Clinton's National Information Infrastructure Initiative: Community Regained?" *Chi.-Kent L. Rev.,* 1994, *69,* 991.

Perritt, Jr., H. H. "Electronic Dispute Resolution: An NCAIR Conference." May 1996. mantle.sbs.umass.edu/vmag/perritt.htm Last visited October 28, 2001.

Plucknett, T. *A Concise History of the Common Law.* Union, NJ: The Lawbook Exchange, 1956, pp. 205–206.

Ponte, L., and Cavenaugh, T. *Alternative Dispute Resolution in Business.* Cincinnati: West Education Publishing, 1999.

Quinley, K. "Embrace—Don't Fear—New Claim's Technology." *Claims Magazine.* February 1999. www.claimsmag.com/Issues/October99/embrace.asp

Rabinovich-Einy, O. "Going Public: Diminishing Privacy in Dispute Resolution in the Internet Age." August 2001. Unpublished report on file with author.

RAND report on Cybersettle, available at www.rand.org. Excerpt available at www.cybersettle.com/press/Background/#industryfacts

Rheingold, H. *The Virtual Community: Homesteading on the Electronic Frontier.* New York: HarperPerennial Library, 1994, p. 3. www.virtualcommunity.net Last visited October 28, 2001.

Rogers, J. "Insurance Moves to 'B2B' Over the Net." The California Conduit. port4.com/feature-auisa000205.html Last visited June 14, 2002.

Rohde, L. "Internet Access Is Almost Everywhere; Children, Women, and Minorities are Going Online More, Study Finds." IDG News Service, February 20, 2001. www.pcworld.com/news/article/0,aid,42063,00.asp Last visited October 28, 2001.

Rule, C. "New Mediator Capabilities in Online Dispute Resolution." www.mediate.com/articles/rule.cfm Last visited October 28, 2001.

Sander, F .E. A., and Goldberg, S. B. "Fitting the Forum to the Fuss: A User-Friendly Guide to Selecting an ADR Procedure." *Negotiation J.,* 1994, *10,* 49, 56.

Scherk v. Alberto-Culver Co., 417 U.S. 506, 520 (1974).

Schneider, M. E., and Kuner, C. "Dispute Resolution in International Electronic Commerce." *J. Int'l. Arb.,* September 1997, *5,* 10–11.

Segaller, S. *Nerds 2.0.1: A Brief History of the Internet.* New York: TV Books, 1998, pp. 29–52.

Settlement Online Systems (SOS) website, New South Wales, Australia. www.settlementonlinesystems.com.au/

Sharma, N. "Asia—An Insurer/Reinsurer Perspective." *Journal of Reinsurance,* Summer 2001, *8* (3), 29–41.

Shell, G. R. "Computer-Assisted Negotiation and Mediation: Where We Are and Where We Are Going." *Negotiation J.,* 1995, *11,* 117, 121.

Simpson, D. "ODR and Insurance." May 18, 2001. port4.com/cgi-local/dcforum/dcboard.cgi?az=read_count&om=2&forum=DCForumID6

Sternlight, J. R. "Panacea or Corporate Tool?: Debunking the Supreme Court's Preference for Binding Arbitration." *Wash. U. L. Q.,* 1996, *74,* 637.

Sternlight, J. R. "As Mandatory Binding Arbitration Meets the Class Action, Will the Class Action Survive?" *Wm. & Mary L. Rev.,* 2000, *42,* 1.

Talbot, M. "Girls Just Want to Be Mean." *The New York Times Magazine,* February 24, 2002. Late Edition, sec. 6, p. 24, col. 1.

Thiessen, E. "Beyond Win-Win in Cyberspace." *Ohio State J. of Dispute Resolution,* 2000, *15* (3), 643.
www.smartsettle.com/more/beyondbeyondwinwin.html
Last visited October 28, 2001.

Thornburg, E. G. "Going Private: Technology, Due Process and Internet Dispute Resolution." *U.C. Davis L. Rev.,* 2000, *34,* 151.

Underhill, C. "Dispute Resolution at the Earliest Stages: Internal Complaint Handling and Customer Refunds." Paper presented at the OECD/ICC/HCOPIL conference on B2C ADR, December 11–12, 2000.

Valley, K. "The Electronic Negotiator." *Harv. Bus. Rev.,* January/February 2000, 16–17.
www.mediate.com/articles/valley.cfm

Virtual Magistrate. "Virtual Magistrate—Its First Decision"
lists.elistx.com/archives/interesting-people/199605/msg00054.html
Last visited October 28, 2001.

Walther, P. "Are the Parties Really Better Off in Arbitration?" Comtex News Network.
newsre.com/index.asp?layout=story&doc_id=3029

Weiner, A. "Regulations and Standards for Online Dispute Resolution: A Primer for Policymakers and Stakeholders." February 15, 2001.
www.odrnews.com

Wheeler, M. "Computers and Negotiation: Backing into the Future." *Negotiation J.,* 1995, *11,* 169, 170.

White, R. "Reinsurance of Declaratory Judgement Expenses." January 1992. Cited in Attisani, D. "Reinsurance Coverage for Declaratory Judgement Expenses." *Journal of Reinsurance,* Summer 2001, *8* (3), 1–27.

Winston, G. "Virtual Settlement Online." *Canadian Underwriter,* January 2000.

Wittenberg, C. A., and others. "Why Employment Disputes Mediation Is on the Rise." *PLI/Lit.,* 1998, *578,* 747, 750.

⎯⎯ Index

~~~ About the Author

Colin Rule is a senior associate at Raab Associates and director of its Online Public Disputes project (www.publicdisputes.org). He has worked in the dispute resolution field for more than a decade as a mediator, trainer, and consultant. He is currently the co-chair of the Online Section of the Association for Conflict Resolution (ACR), a fellow at the Center for Information Technology and Dispute Resolution at the University of Massachusetts–Amherst, and a board member of the New England ACR.

In 1999, Rule co-founded Online Resolution, an online dispute resolution service provider, and served as its CEO (2000) and president (2001). Previously, Rule was general manager of Mediate.com, the largest online resource for the dispute resolution field. Rule also worked for several years with the National Institute for Dispute Resolution in Washington, D.C., and the Consensus Building Institute in Cambridge, Massachusetts.

Rule has presented and trained throughout Europe and North America for organizations including the Federal Mediation and Conciliation Service, the U.S. Department of State, the International Chamber of Commerce, and the Center for Public Resources. He has also taught and lectured at the University of Massachusetts–Amherst, Bentley College, the Massachusetts Institute of Technology, Southern Methodist University, the University of Ottawa, Lasell College, and Brandeis University.

He has authored more than twenty articles in prestigious ADR publications such as *Consensus*, *The Fourth R*, *ACR News*, and *Peace Review*. He writes the online conflict resolution column in *ACResolution Magazine* and serves as editor of ODRNews.com, a daily news resource chronicling developments in the ODR field. He holds a master's degree from Harvard University's Kennedy School of Government in conflict resolution and technology, a bachelor's degree in peace studies from Haverford College, and has completed advanced coursework in dispute resolution at the University of Massachusetts–Boston.